MONTGO
ROCKVIL
ROCKW
WITHDRAWN

W9-DHG-519

uptospeed

Photoshop CS2

| The only book focused exclusively on the new features in Photoshop CS2.

Ben Willmore

DEC 12 2005   315886

The Experts Agree...

"Hands-down, this is simply the best book for 'getting up to speed' with Photoshop CS2. Adobe should include it with every copy of Photoshop."

–*Chris Murphy* Co-Author: Real World Color Management (www.ColorRemedies.com)

"I've been using Photoshop for over a decade, so when I wanted to get up to speed on just the new stuff in CS2, I turned to Ben's Up to Speed book"

–*David Blatner* Co-Author: Real World Photoshop (www.moo.com)

"Ben has a real gift for teaching Photoshop, and the uncanny ability to make difficult concepts seems absolutely simple. I have every book Ben's ever written, and when he comes out with a new one, I buy it! Ben has a way of cutting to the chase and explaining things in a way that just make sense. His approach to training has won him legions of fans, and this book continues his tradition of making Photoshop easy and understandable. If you want to really dig under the skin of Photoshop CS2's amazing new features, this is the book to buy! Highly recommended!"

–*Scott Kelby* President, National Association of Photoshop Professionals (www.PhotoshopUser.com)

"Learn what's new, and discover what you need to know without all the fluff. Yet another book from Ben that proves he's a true master."

–*Russell Brown* Senior Creative Director: Adobe Systems Incorporated (www.RussellBrown.com)

"At a recent meeting of the BetterPhoto.com instructors, I offered them all a free book. All 17 instructors unanimously requested a copy of Ben's book. He's that good!"

–*Jim Miotke* Founder: www.BetterPhoto.com

"This book is a must have! Whether you're new to Photoshop or a seasoned pro, it will help you get up to speed on the latest features in no time flat. Ben's conversational writing style makes for an enjoyable read, and the excellent organization of the book helps you learn everything you need to transition seamlessly into Photoshop CS2."

–*Tim Grey* Co/Author: Color Confidence, Real World Digital Photography (www.TimGrey.com)

"Ben's book gets to the heart of Photoshop CS2 - what has changed, what is new, and how you can get the most out of the features as quickly as possible. With 'Up to Speed', you will be taking advantage of Photoshop CS2 in no time at all."

–*Katrin Eismann* Author: Photoshop Retouching & Restoration (www.PhotoshopDiva.com)

ii

"Ben's sessions at PhotoshopWorld are always standing-room only. His latest book provides ample reason as to why he's so popular. He breaks down the complex and arcane side of Photoshop into something that is understandable. And few things are more fun than becoming better at Photoshop. It's a great book."

–Jim Workman Publisher: Photoshop User Magazine (www.PhotoshopUser.com)

"Almost every page gave me at least one useful tip... but that was no real surprise. What I liked most, aside from the clean layout, was the way big changes were differentiated from "tiny tweaks". Obviously, Ben Willmore knows exactly which topics Photoshoppers want to learn about, from handling Raw images to understanding HDR, and from working with the new Adobe Bridge to building variable data pages. This is a must-read for anyone moving up to CS2."

–Dan Brill Publisher: Graphic Exchange Magazine (www.gxo.com)

"Ben Willmore's Up to Speed with CS2 is a must read for every digital photographer who is concerned with speeding up workflow, quickly getting a handle on the new photographic gems and generally wrapping their brains around the great new features like Bridge, the new Camera Raw, Lens Correction and my personal favorite, Vanishing Point."

–Kevin Ames Author: Photoshop CS: The Art of Photographing Women (www.AmesPhoto.com)

"Ben Willmore is the world's foremost expert on the in's and out's of Photoshop, especially when it comes to the where's and what-for's of all the awesome new features in Photoshop CS2. If you use Photoshop, buy this book. Period. It will save you time, money and (if you are a middle-aged male), hair."

–Jack Davis Co-Author: How to Wow: Photoshop for Photography, Photoshop Hall of Fame inductee

"Ben is a teacher's teacher. He's someone I steal from, uh, rather appropriate from freely. When I need to learn a new technique, Ben's easy-going explanations are just fantastic. His new book hits all the right notes with Photoshop CS2. Rather than rehash a lot of old stuff, he cuts right to the chase, and in that easy-going writing and teaching style of his. Ben has a knack for explaining the complex in plain English. That is the mark of a great teacher and this book just reinforces again that Ben is a great teacher."

–Jack Reznicki Author: Studio & Commercial Photography (www.Reznicki.com)

The Experts Agree...

"Learning a new version of Photoshop is always a challenge. Ben's "Up to Speed" is the most efficient way to move forward from Photoshop CS to CS2. All is written in Ben's unique and easy to follow style. Highly recommended!"
—**Uwe Steinmueller** Founder: www.OutbackPhoto.com

"Up to Speed: Photoshop CS2' is exactly the book you want to have next to you when moving up from Photoshop CS. Organized into logical, digestible chapters, every change and addition is clearly and patiently explained by one of the most respected Photoshop authors and instructors today: Ben Willmore."
—**Jay Nelson** Editor: Design Tools Monthly (www.Design-Tools.com)

"Ben's books are like getting all the answers before you even know what the questions are. I tested this software, and I spent most of my time as I was reading saying to myself 'I didn't know CS2 did that.' This book is nicely done."
—**Vincent Versace** Photographer Extraordinare (www.VersacePhotography.com)

"If you want a comprehensive and easy to read update on the latest version of Photoshop, then Ben's book is the one for you. Ben's writing is clear, concise and packed with all the latest info, and his valuable personal insights. Ben is no shill, he doesn't just tell you what's new and great... if he sees a weakness he's quick to point that out as well. I've already made room on my must read-it-all list for the latest of Ben's beautifully designed, and info-packed books.
—**Taz Tally** Author: Avoiding the Output Blues (www.TazSeminars.com)

"Up to Speed saved me hours of time acclimating to the new version of Photoshop. Having all this information in one convenient, easy to understand format, eliminated hours of trial and error, reading articles, searching books, and searching the Internet for information. Making the transition from CS to CS2 was a snap thanks to this book."
—**Lewis Kemper** Columnist: PC Photo Magazine (www.LewisKemper.com)

"Up to Speed is the quickest way to learn how to take advantage of all the powerful new features in Photoshop CS2. Ben does an excellent job at distilling technical information into a book that is highly informative, easy to follow, and easy to read."
—**Jay Kinghorn** Co-Author: Perfect Digital Photography (www.ProRGB.com)

WITHDRAWN

"Attention all Photoshop users! Before you launch Photoshop CS2, read Ben Willmore's latest book – Photoshop CS2: Up to Speed. The book, crisply written in Ben's easy-to-understand style, not only gets you up to speed, but it takes you to Mach I when it comes to learning and implementing all the totally cool features in CS2, which leaves all other image-editing programs in the dust."

—*Rick Sammon* Author of 25 Photography Books (www.RickSammon.com)

"When it comes to taking complex Photoshop procedures and making them easy to understand, Ben is the master. His book is where I turn for answers to my Photoshop projects."

—*Jim DiVitale* Member: PhotoshopWorld Dream Team (www.DiVitalePhoto.com)

"If you already work efficiently with Photoshop, this is the book for you. Ben presents Photoshop CS2's new features – and only the new stuff – so that you read what you need to learn, not what you already know."

—*Peter Bauer* Author: Photoshop CS2 for Dummies

"Ben Willmore is the clearest and most concise Photoshop teacher I know. His book is on the top ten list of Photoshop books I recommend to every beginning Photoshop student."

—*George DeWolfe* Senior Editor: View Camera and Camera Arts Magazines (www.GeorgeDeWolfe.com)

"This book gives an in-depth, direct, and thorough account of how to use CS2's new features, written in Ben's signature friendly and approachable style. I highly recommend this well thought out piece to anyone wanting to get up to speed with CS2."

—*Dave Montizambert* Author: Creative Lighting Techniques for Studio Photographers (www.Montizambert.com)

"Thanks to Ben Willmore's Up to Speed, the journey from one Photoshop version to another has never been faster or easier."

—*George Lepp* Columnist: Outdoor Photographer (www.LeppPhoto.com)

"What a relief! Thanks to Ben, I can get down to work with CS2 instead of plowing through other manuals that make my head spin. Call it speed-learning or call it common sense. Just make it part of your learning curve for Photoshop CS2!"

—*Dan Burkholder* Author: Making Digital Negatives for Contact Printing (www.DanBurkholder.com)

Adobe Photoshop CS2: Up to Speed

Ben Willmore

Peachpit Press
1249 Eighth Street
Berkeley, CA 94710
(510) 524-2178
(510) 524-2221 (fax)
Find us on the World Wide Web at: http://www.peachpit.com
Peachpit Press is a division of Pearson Education

Copyright © 2005 by Ben Willmore
Cover design: Chris Klimek, Ben Willmore
Book design: Ben Willmore
Project Editor: Wendy Sharp
Contributing Editor: Regina Cleveland
Production & Prepress: Ben Willmore, Hilal Sala
Direct-to-plate printing: Courier Printing

Notice of rights:

All rights reserved. No part of this book may be reproduced or transmitted in any form or by any means, electronic, mechanical, photocopying, recording, or otherwise, without the prior written permission of the publisher. For information, contact Peachpit Press at permissions@peachpit.com

Notice of Liability:

The information in this book is distributed on an "As is" basis, without warranty. While every precaution has been taken in the preparation of this book, neither the author nor Peachpit Press shall have any liability to any person or entity with respect to any liability, loss, or damage caused or alleged to be caused directly or indirectly by the instructions contained in this book or by the computer software and hardware products described herein.

Trademarks

Adobe, the Adobe logo, and Photoshop are registered trademarks of Adobe Systems, Incorporated. Many of the designations used by manufacturers and sellers to distinguish their products are claimed as trademarks. Where those designations appear in this book, and Peachpit was aware of a trademark claim, the designations appear as requested by the owner of the trademark. All other product names and services identified throughout this book are used in an editorial fashion only and for the benefit of such companies with no intention of infringement of the trademark. No such use, or the use of any trade name, is intended to convey endorsement or other affiliation with this book.

ISBN 0-321-33050-1

9 8 7 6 5 4 3 2

Printed and bound in the United States of America.

Photo Credits

All of the images in this book are copyrighted by Ben Willmore, with the following exceptions:

Cover Image

Cheetah image:
©2005 Corel
Design:
Chris Klimek
Ben Willmore

Section I, Page 2

Dancer Image:
©2005
iStockphoto/
ruisergio
Design:
Regina Cleveland

Chapter 1, Page 4

Head Image: ©2005
www.stockbyte.com
Design:
Ben Willmore

Chapter 2, Page 22

Surgeon Image:
©2005 Photospin
Design:
Regina Cleveland

Chapter 2, Page 25

Cup image:
©2005 iStockphoto/
prhanna

Section II, Page 42

Girl/Bubbles Images:
©2005 iStockphoto/
bradleym and
mammamaart
Design:
Regina Cleveland

Chapter 3, Page 44

Egg Image: ©2005
iStockphoto/mevans
Design:
Regina Cleveland

Chapter 4, Page 54

Dragonfly Image:
©2005
www.stockbyte.com
Design:
Regina Cleveland

Chapter 5, Page 66

Swan Image: ©2005
iStockphoto/Joss
Design:
Regina Cleveland,
Ben Willmore

Chapter 6, Page 78

Woman image:
©2005 iStockphoto/
lovleah
Design:
Regina Cleveland

Section III, Page 90

Primate images:
©2005 iStockphoto
Banana Image:
©2005 PhotoSpin
Design:
Regina Cleveland

Chapter 7, Page 92

Sleeping Woman
Image: ©2005
iStockphoto/
lisegagne
Design:
Regina Cleveland

Chapter 8, Page 110

Arches Image:
©2005
iStockphoto/
Haban
Design:
Regina Cleveland

Chapter 9, Page 132

Images: ©2005
iStockphoto/
Marje & Urban
Cow
Design:
Regina Cleveland

Chapter 10, Page 152

Leaf Image:
©2005
iStockPhoto/
BritishBeefUK
Design:
Regina Cleveland

Dedication:

To my mom, Dode.

A nurturing soul who,
against her better judgment,
purchased my first Apple][
in the late 70's and sent me to
CompuCamp in the early 80's.

Had she not overcome
her doubts, my career
would have taken a
different turn and this
book would not exist.

Dode passed away on
Valentine's Day, 1984.

Acknowledgements

I remember writing my very first seminar handbook. My editing team consisted of me, myself and the geek in the mirror. That was over a decade ago. Since then my adventures with Photoshop have put me in the path of some incredibly talented and gifted individuals, some of whom I wrangled into being a part of this book. They are:

The Queen—Regina Cleveland might as well be my outer cortex for she makes it possible for my gray matter to function properly. Had she not been a part of this project, it would have been like piloting a ship across the ocean with part of its hull missing. Regina makes it possible for me to concentrate on what's important because I know she'll handle all the details. She went way beyond the call of duty (as usual) tackling the chapter opener images as well as her usual role, which is to proof and edit every word I write.

The Peachpitters—Nancy Ruenzel, for enthusiastically supporting my idea for this book. When it comes to publishers, she's a swan in a sea of pigeons. Wendy Sharp, for her unwavering dedication to excellence and for mothering this project to its conclusion. Thanks also to Hilal Sala, our production coordinator and Julie Bess, our indexer.

The Brain Posse— Dan Burkholder and Jeff Tranberry (My Secret Weapon at Adobe) kindly took time out of their busy lives to review chapters and technical issues with a fine-tooth comb. They didn't just provide tech editing, they challenged me to write a better book.

The Safety Net—Richard Harrington, Jay Kinghorn, Kevin Ames, George Lepp, Jeff Gamet, and the great color master Chris Murphy, all generously lent an opinion when I needed it the most.

The Artiste—Chris Klimek for his awesome cover design.

The Stock Brokers—Patrick Lor at iStockphoto.com, Stephanie Robey at PhotoSpin.com, and Jerry Kennelly at stockbyte.com, for kindly letting Regina and I run loose in their wonderful image collections.

The Mother Ship—John Nack and the folks at Adobe who pump out exciting new versions of Photoshop about every 18 months. I want to especially thank Chris Cox, Mark Pawliger, Jeff Tranberry and Tom Attix.

And finally, to Bruce Fraser for helping with CMYK conversions and pdf file creation.

About The Author

A senior engineer from NASA once said that this man gave the best technical seminar he ever attended. That same year a computer-phobic who had been struggling with Photoshop for years proclaimed that "He takes the Boogie Man out of Photoshop!" This seems to be Ben Willmore's special gift; he has an uncanny ability to connect with users of every level and mind-set; whether it's first-timers taking their first sniff of Photoshop, or razor-sharp nerds and nerdettes who are on the fast track to technical enlightenment. The common echo that Ben leaves in his wake seems to be "Aha! I finally GET Photoshop!"

Considered to be one of the all-time great Photoshop gurus, Ben is one of those guys who zooms around the country standing in front of sellout crowds while he spreads his particular brand of illumination. To date, he has personally taught over 45,000 Photoshop users on three continents. His descriptions of Curves and Channels are thought to be the best in the industry and his breakthrough teaching style of "not-just-how-but-why," has made him the in-house instructor of choice for companies such as Mercedes Benz, Adobe Systems, America Online, the U.S. Airforce, Lexis Nexis and Fisher-Price Toys. His award-winning, best-selling book, *Photoshop Studio Techniques* is said to be "Arguably, one of the best Photoshop books ever written." by Photoshop User's publisher, Jim Workman. He is co-author (with Jack Davis) of the best-seller, "*How to Wow: Photoshop for Photography*," as well as a contributing author to the *Photoshop World Dream Team* book.

He continues to be a featured speaker at photography and publishing conferences and events worldwide, including Photoshop World, American Society of Media Photographers (ASMP), Professional Photographers Association (PPA) and the Royal Photographic Society of England. He's a member of the PhotoshopWorld Dream Team, is a PEI Photoshop All-Star, and writes for numerous digital imaging and photography publications, including a monthly column for *Photoshop User* magazine. In 2004 he was inducted into the Photoshop Hall of Fame. His reputation as the "expert's expert" prompted NAPP's president, Scott Kelby, to say, "When we get stuck, we call Ben!"

In late 2005, Ben will be taking his Photoshop adventures on the open road where he will live and work in a touring bus while he pursues his passion for photography and teaching. To keep track of Ben while he is exploring America, visit: www.whereisben.com.

Table of Contents

Section I: *Foundations*

Section II: Design

Section III: Photography

Introduction

Whenever Adobe churns out a new version of Photoshop, we find ourselves scrambling to learn the latest features. Each upgrade becomes more robust than the last, making the task of learning a daunting one. You can turn to books for help, but if it's just the new features you want, the books can be more intimidating than Photoshop because they're not designed to focus on the upgrade alone. Until now, Photoshop books could be grouped into one of three categories:

1) All encompassing 'bibles' that try to cover everything.

2) Cookbooks that present the reader with brief "recipe" techniques and no in-depth coverage.

3) Books that specialize in a particular area and are very in-depth (retouching, channels, color management, etc.).

So, what's missing? There isn't one book out there that caters to the user who just wants in-depth coverage of the newest features of Photoshop. If you buy the bible type book, you'll likely waste a weekend with an often frustrating and time-consuming search through hundreds of pages. Ferreting out the new stuff with the specialist books is just as maddening because they only cover a fraction of the new features, and the recipe books just skim the surface, leaving you without any true understanding of the finer points that make Photoshop's features so powerful.

Up to Speed is the first book that cuts away the fat of what you already know about Photoshop and goes right to the new features. To make your knowledge upgrade as quick and effortless as possible, I include just enough information about older features so the new ones will make sense. And unlike the sales presentations or generic overviews that come out with every new release, this book presents all the features in my signature style: intuitive, crystal clear and in-depth; everything that you need to truly get "up to speed" with the new features of Photoshop.

Who Should Read This Book

You don't have to be an expert to benefit from this book. *Up to Speed* is for all users who have a working knowledge of Photoshop CS. However, if you're not already comfortable with the CS version of Photoshop, this book might not be appropriate for you. If that's the case, I recommend you read my other book, *Photoshop Studio Techniques*, which covers the majority of features in Photoshop, both old and new.

How It's Organized

This book is divided into three sections: Foundations, Design and Photography. I organized it this way so you can quickly get right to the features that will be the most useful to your line of work. However, if you're a designer, I urge you to read through the Photography section, and if you're a photographer, visa-versa. There are some features that are likely to hold little or no appeal for designers (like HDR imaging), just as there will be some that might not be interesting to photographers (like the Variables feature), but overall, most features in Photoshop have multiple uses for all types of users.

Each chapter is organized so that you can quickly glance at the first page to get a good sense of what the chapter will cover. If the chapter deals with preexisting features that have either been changed, moved or eliminated, you'll see a section on that first page called "Where's My Stuff?" When Adobe moves things around, it can mess with your head, so this section tells you what to need to know to avoid getting upgrade vertigo when you start using CS2.

Keyboard commands are displayed for both Mac and Windows operating systems. Screen shots are from a Mac OS X system, but if you're a Windows user, don't worry, because even though they are cosmetically different, all the tools, palettes, menus, and dialog boxes are functionally identical. Photoshop CS2 did bring a few changes that are specific to just Windows, and those are covered as well.

What's Missing

There are two Photoshop related applications that are not covered in this book: ImageReady (the web graphics application that comes bundled with Photoshop) is not covered because there have been essentially no changes, and Version Cue (the version management software that comes with the entire Creative Suite) because it is beyond the objective of this book, which is to get you up to speed with Photoshop's newest features and quickly and smoothly as possible.

The Lowdown on CS2

While not the biggest upgrade in Photoshop's history, CS2 packs a serious punch. Is it worth the price? Absolutely. In the short time I've used CS2, there are already a load of new features (such as Bridge, Smart Objects, HDR imaging and Warping) that I can't imagine doing without.

Adobe served up generous helpings for every type of Photoshop user, so whether you're in photography, design, production or beyond, you should find plenty of new features and enhancements that will get you fired up. I won't list everything here—you can go to the Table of Contents for that—but there are some scene stealers worth mentioning.

Everybody should get something worthwhile from Bridge, which replaces CS's File Browser. It operates as a separate application and supports your work in Photoshop in ways that are far more powerful than its predecessor. Another crowd pleaser is that we can now edit menus to suit our needs, which means you can get rid of those menu items you never use. The new image warping feature is mesmerizing and so much fun, it's hard to leave alone. Worth chuckling about is Adobe's noticeable fondness for the word, "Smart." They've given us Smart Objects, Smart Guides, and Smart Sharpen, and it's almost as if they're trying to convince us that there are miniature brains implanted in these features. Another feature, which every type of user should fall in love with, is the Vanishing Point filter, which lets you edit and retouch your images in near-3D perspective (I think this one deserved to be called "Smart" too!). The Layers palette got an extreme makeover, and there will surely be dissenting points of view on whether this is a good thing or not. Personally, I'm still trying to get my rhythm back. I wish you luck with it.

If you're a digital photographer you can start licking your chops because Adobe went to town with CS2. Camera Raw has matured in truly substantive ways that should make a big difference to you, especially if you regularly work with large numbers of images. You now have full-blown HDR imaging support, improved 16-bit support, an awesome new Image Processor, and better retouching tools and filters that make it easier than ever to retouch your photos.

I imagine you're eager to move ahead and dive into the universe of CS2. There's a lot to digest, so take your time and enjoy discovering the new toys that await you.

—Ben Willmore

uptospeed

Section I
Foundations

Chapter 1
Bridge

JUST WHEN YOU THOUGHT IT was safe to settle in and get comfortable with the File Browser, Adobe pulled a fast one and replaced it with a completely new application called Bridge. This newcomer is a stand-alone application, which means that it works not only with Photoshop, but with all of the Creative Suite applications.

There are similarities between the old and the new; the things you liked to do in the File Browser, you can still do in Bridge, but Bridge goes far beyond the File Browser's capabilities. I particularly like Bridge's ability to process files in the background while you work in Photoshop.

Below is an overview of what we'll be covering in this chapter:

- **Introducing Bridge:** A quick tour so you know the territory before you begin exploring.
- **Navigating Folders:** Navigating and finding files and folders on your hard drive using the new features in Bridge.
- **Thumbnails & Previews:** A myriad of ways to view your images, from adjusting thumbnail sizes to watching slide shows.
- **The Tools Menu:** Allows you to perform commands that are usually found in other Creative Suite applications.
- **Labeling & Rating:** Lets you quickly rate images on a five star scale or apply color labels to them.
- **Tiny Tweaks:** Lots of other little stuff hiding in the nooks and crannies of CS2.

Where's My Stuff?

When a major feature is replaced with an entirely new application, there is bound to be some initial discomfort. Hopefully, this chapter will ease the transition. Here's what you need to know:

- **Flag Icon Missing:** Flagging has been replaced with a five star rating system. You can rate an image using the **Label** menu. Images that were flagged in earlier versions of Photoshop will appear with a one star rating.
- **Binoculars Icon Missing:** This icon was a shortcut for the **File>Search** command, which has been replaced with the **Edit>Find** command in Bridge. There is no longer an icon associated with that feature, so type **Command-F** (Mac) or **Ctrl-F** (Win) as a shortcut.
- **Favorites & Search Results In Folders Tab:** Favorites has now been given its own tab that is grouped in the same pane as the Folders tab. To return to a previous search result after viewing another folder, click the new Back button.
- **Raw Format Images Look Different:** See *Chapter 7: Camera Raw 3.0* for more details.

- **Desktop Choice in Folder List:** This option has been replaced with the 'Computer' choice which makes it much less convenient to quickly navigate to your desktop. The fastest way to get to your desktop is to click on the Favorites tab and then click on Desktop.
- **Thumbnail Size Options in the View Menu:** These options have been replaced with the Thumbnail Size slider that appears in the lower right of the Bridge window.
- **Automate Menu Options:** These options are now found under various submenus of the new **Tools** menu.
- **Sort Menu Missing:** The **Sort** menu has been moved and can now found by choosing **View>Sort** in Bridge.
- **Edit>Append Metadata and Replace Metadata:** These commands have been moved to the side menu of the Metadata pane that's found in the lower left corner of the Bridge window.
- **Edit>Apply Rotation:** This feature is not available in Bridge.
- **Cache Choices in the File Menu:** These choices have been moved to the **Tools>Cache** menu.
- **Edit>Rank:** Ranking has been replaced with the options found under the **Label** menu in Bridge. Unfortunately, images that were ranked in previous versions of Photoshop show no visual indication of being labeled.

Introducing Bridge

When Adobe took the File Browser out of Photoshop and built a stand-alone application, they ended up creating the equivalent of a Grand Central Station for file management and processing. It turns out that there are significant advantages to divorcing Photoshop from the File Browser and creating the newly independent Bridge:

1) As an independent application, it can be used by other applications that make up the Adobe Creative Suite. (As of this writing, Acrobat is the only application in the Suite that doesn't support Bridge.)

2) More than one window can be opened, which allows you to browse the contents of more than one folder.

3) It can be used when Photoshop is busy running actions, batch processing files, or when Photoshop is not running at all.

4) The Bridge window can be left open on a second monitor while you work with Photoshop on your primary monitor.

Now that you know why Bridge evolved the way it did, let's take a brief tour of its interface so you can take full advantage of its features.

Launching Bridge

Before you start using Bridge, you'll need to figure out how to launch it. Sure, you can access it like any other program by double-clicking on its icon in the Finder (Mac) or Program Manager (Win), but that's the less elegant method. There were three ways to access

NOTE

Auto Launch Bridge
If you'd like Bridge to launch each time you launch Photoshop, then choose **Preferences >General** from the **Photoshop** menu (Mac), or **Edit** menu (Win) and turn on the Automatically Launch Bridge checkbox.

the old File Browser, all of which still work to access Bridge, and now there are two more ways:

1) Choose **Image>Browse** from Photoshop.
2) Type **Shift-Command-O** (Mac) or **Shift-Ctrl-O** (Win) in Photoshop (does not work in other Creative Suite applications). By the way, those are Oh's, not zeros.
3) Type **Option-Command-O** (Mac) or **Alt-Ctrl-O** (Win). This is the standard keyboard shortcut that is used across all the Adobe Creative Suite applications that support Bridge.
4) Click the Browse icon (folder with magnifying glass icon in Photoshop) in the Options bar that extends across the top of your screen.
5) Choose *Reveal in Bridge* from the pop-up menu that appears near the lower left of each Photoshop document window.

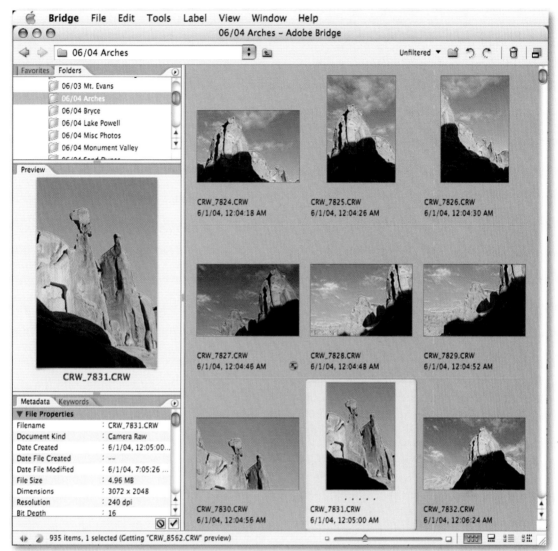

Bridge is an independent application designed to work with all the applications in the Adobe Creative Suite. Compared to Photoshop CS's File Browser, Bridge is beefed up, sporting its own menu bar and an expanded feature set.

Working with Panes

With default settings, the main Bridge window is divided into four panes. Along the left side are the Favorites/Folders pane, the Preview pane and the Metadata/Keywords pane, while the right side contains the Thumbnails pane. You have many choices for adjusting the size of each pane and controlling which panes are visible:

■ To resize a pane, drag the divider bars that separate one pane from another.

■ To change which tabs are grouped into each pane, drag a name tab onto another pane.

■ To create an additional pane that contains a single tab, drag from a name tab of a pane to the divider bar that separates two panes.

■ Toggle the visibility of individual tabs by choosing their names from the **View** menu.

- Toggle the visibility of all the panes that appear on the left side of the window by clicking the left/right arrow icon found near the lower left corner of the window.
- Double-click any name tab to collapse that pane making only the name tab visible (double-click again to expand the tab back to its former size).

Now that you know how to launch Bridge and navigate its panes, let's start exploring what you can do with this new program.

Navigating Folders

There are a multitude of ways you can navigate to a particular folder in Bridge. Many will be familiar to users of the File Browser, but some are entirely new.

The Folders Tab

This is command central when it comes to navigating a hard drive. Let's take a look at your options for traversing the depths of your computer.

Computer View Versus Desktop View

At the base level of the folder list is a choice called Computer, which is where all your hard drives appear. This is a change from the File Browser, which listed your Desktop as the base level. I much preferred the old setup because it made it easy to quickly access files on your desktop. In the new setup, you have to navigate your way through the following path (obstacle course!) to get to the desktop on a Mac: **Hard Drive/Users/ User Name/Desktop**. I'll show you a much faster method for accessing your desktop when we talk about the Favorites tab.

The Folders view now uses Computer as the base of the folder structure.

Navigating The Folder List

Click on the triangle next to any drive or folder (or double-click the drive/folder icon) to reveal the subfolders contained in that drive or folder. I prefer to navigate the folder list using the following keyboard shortcuts: up and down arrow keys to move up or down in the folder list, and the right and left arrow keys to expand or collapse the selected folder.

Navigating Via Menu and Thumbnails

If you decide to hide the left side of the Bridge window (by clicking on the double arrow icon near the bottom left corner of the window), you'll have to navigate your drive using the pop-up menu that appears above the thumbnail pane of the main Bridge window. Clicking on that menu will list the path that was used to get to the currently viewed folder. If you choose Computer from this list, you'll be starting at the base level of your computer and all your hard drives will appear as large folders in the thumbnail area. You can double-click on drives and folders within the thumbnail area to navigate to a specific location on your drive. If you need to move up one level from your current position, then click the Go Up icon that appears to the right of the pop-up menu. You can also click the Go Forward and Go Back icons that appear to the left of the pop-up menu to go to previously viewed folders. These choices are much more useful after using the Favorites feature, which we'll talk about next.

The pop-up menu above the Thumbnails pane displays the path used to navigate to the currently active folder.

The Favorites Tab

You'll find the Favorites tab grouped into the same pane as the Folders tab in the upper left of the Bridge window. The Favorites tab is where you can store frequently used folders and where you'll find a few special choices that are new to this version of Photoshop.

Default Favorites

The Favorites pane contains a few special entries by default:

Computer: Brings you to the base level of your computer where you will find all your hard drives. This is useful when you need to switch the drive you are navigating.

Adobe Stock Photos: Allows you to search and purchase stock photography from on-line vendors. This feature is covered in detail in *Chapter 6: Small Gems for Design*.

Version Cue: Displays features related to Version Cue. Version Cue will not be included unless you purchased the entire Creative Suite.

Collections: Lists search presets that you've saved after using the **Edit>Find** command.

Desktop: Navigates to the desktop of the current user (in Mac OSX and Microsoft Windows XP, multiple users can be set up on one machine and files are only visible for the user who is currently logged in).

Choose File>Add To Favorites or drag a folder from the thumbnails to add it to the list of Favorites.

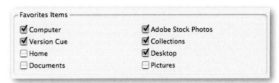

The Favorite Items choice is available in the General pane of the Bridge Preferences dialog box.

Adding & Removing Favorites

You can add any file or folder to the Favorites list by first selecting the file/folder and then either dragging it to the bottom of the Favorites list or choosing **File>Add to Favorites**. I usually add project folders to the list (like the ones used to create this book) along with the folders that contain my personal photography, stock photography and other frequently used folders.

To remove a Favorite, **Control-click** (Mac) or **Right-click** (Win) on a Favorite and choose *Remove from Favorites* from the pop-up menu that appears.

If you accidently remove one of the default folders, just choose *Preferences* from the **Bridge** menu (Mac) or **Edit** menu (Win) and turn on the appropriate checkbox in the Favorites Items area near the bottom of the dialog box.

Accessing Saved Favorites

Once you have your Favorites list populated with a bunch of files and folders, you can do the following to quickly navigate your hard drive:

Click a folder name to instantly navigate to that location on your hard drive. You can then deviate from that location by navigating the folder list or double-clicking on folders that appear in the Thumbnail pane of the Bridge window.

Click a file name to open the file with a single click. This can be useful for files like your company logo or template files that you use over and over.

Click the pop-up menu that appears above the Thumbnail pane to access Favorites when the left side of the Bridge window is hidden.

Choosing Edit>Find will bring up the Find dialog box.

The Find Command

If navigating to a particular folder is not enough to display the images you're looking for, you might want to try the *Find* command.

The **Edit>Find** command is almost identical to the *Search* command that was available in the File Browser. Since this functionality is not really new, let's concentrate on the features that were not available in the File Browser's *Search* command.

Find All Files

This choice simply grays out the search criteria fields and causes Bridge to display all the files that are in a particular folder. This might sound like it would produce the same results as simply clicking on the folder within the Folders pane of Bridge, but there is one important difference: using this checkbox, along with the *Include all Subfolders* checkbox, will cause Bridge to display the contents of multiple folders, which is not possible using the Folders pane.

Search Past Versions of Version Cue Files

If you've purchased the Adobe Creative Suite, this choice allows you to search the Description and Commands fields from Version Cue enabled documents (Version Cue is not included with the stand-alone version of Photoshop.)

Match

This new pop-up menu allows you to modify your search results to include 'any' or 'all' of the search criteria you've specified. I use *If all criteria are met* for the vast majority of searches I perform. I mainly use the *If any criteria are met*

when I'm searching with keywords and I'm not sure which keyword I should use (house, home, cabin or building, for example).

Show Find Results In A New Browser Window

This choice will prompt Bridge to create a new window for your search results, leaving the previously viewed window open in the background. This is useful when you plan to perform multiple searches and want to view the results of all the searches when finished.

Save As Collection

You can save a set of search criteria as a preset that Adobe calls a *Collection*. After you finish performing a search, the *Save As Collection* button will appear in the upper right of the Thumbnails pane. Clicking this button will cause Bridge to prompt you to name your search preset and ask if you always want to start the search from the current folder, which will cause the preset to use the folder that was specified in the search dialog box at the time the preset was created.

Once you've saved a search as a *Collection*, you can perform the search at any time in the future by clicking on Collections in the Favorites pane and then clicking on the name of any preset search from the thumbnail pane of Bridge.

I use collections to quickly search for images that I've tagged with certain keywords (like Hero and Superhero, which are the keywords I assign to my best photography examples).

Now that you know how to navigate folders and search for images, let's take a look at how you can preview those images within Bridge.

Clicking the Save as Collection button will cause this dialog box to appear.

Thumbnails & Previews

Once you've navigated to a folder, thumbnail images that reflect the contents of the folder will start appearing in the large thumbnail pane of the Bridge window.

View Options

Once thumbnail images are generated, you can choose how to view them by clicking on one of the icons that appear in the lower right corner of the Bridge window. The choices from left to right are Thumbnails, Filmstrip, Details, and Versions and Alternatives. Let's look at how each of those views works and explore the new Slide Show view that can be accessed from the **View** menu.

Thumbnails View

This is the default view in Bridge and is similar to what was available in the File Browser. This view displays thumbnail images that appear similar to how 35mm slides would look when viewed on a light table.

Thumbnail Size: You can control the size of the thumbnail images by adjusting the slider that appears at the bottom of the Bridge window. This feature replaces the options that were found

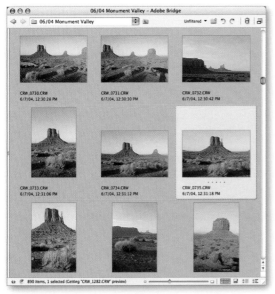

Viewing the contents of a folder in Thumbnails view.

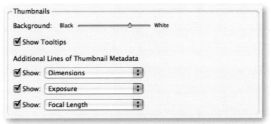

The Thumbnails area of the Preferences dialog box.

under the **View** menu in Photoshop CS's File Browser and resembles the similar feature which is found in Apple's iPhoto application. The slider lets you make the thumbnails as tiny as 18x18 pixels, or as large as 514x514 pixels.

Thumbnail Background: You can change the color that is used as a backdrop for the thumbnails by choosing *Preferences* from the **Bridge** menu (Mac) or **Edit** menu (Win) and adjusting the Thumbnails Background slider. Moving the slider toward the left will darken the background, while moving the slider toward the right will brighten the background.

Additional Metadata: With default settings, a document's file name is the only information displayed below each thumbnail image. To add up to three additional lines of information below each thumbnail image, you can choose from the *Show* pop-up menus that appear in the Thumbnails area of the Preferences dialog box .

This feature has all sorts of uses, from determin-

This menu shows the metadata choices that can be viewed below each thumbnail image.

ing if a series of images are appropriate for HDR imaging (by having a consistent aperture setting—HDR techniques are covered in *Chapter 8: HDR Imaging*), to viewing the copyright info for each image so proper credits can be added to an InDesign layout.

Displaying extra metadata. In this case, Dimensions, Exposure, and Lens.

Viewing the contents of a folder in Filmstrip view.

Show/Hide Document Names: Choosing **View> Show Thumbnail Only** or typing **Command-T** (Mac) or **Ctrl-T** (Win) will toggle the visibility of the document name that usually appears below each thumbnail image. This feature is useful when you want to view as many thumbnails as possible within a given amount of space.

Now that you've seen what's new in Thumbnail view, let's start exploring the views that are new to Bridge.

Viewing thumbnails with the document names hidden.

Filmstrip View

This view offers a large central preview image with thumbnail images below (much like the Simple layout that's available in Web Photo Gallery). Clicking on a thumbnail will cause that photo to appear as a large preview. To cycle through the images in the current folder, click the left and right arrow icons that appear above and to the right of the thumbnail images. If you'd prefer to have the thumbnails run across the right side of the window, then click the icon that appears to the right of the two arrow icons I just mentioned.

I always type **Command-T** (Mac) or **Ctrl-T** (Win) to hide the document names before using this mode, otherwise the thumbnail area tends to look rather busy. Also, note that the thumbnail size slider is still available in this view, which can be useful if you want to control how many thumbnails fit across the bottom of the window.

Details View

This view displays the contents of a folder in a vertical list with a thumbnail for each image on the left and document metadata to the right.

I use this view to quickly check the mode and size of images that I'm about to send to a printing company. I usually move the thumbnail size slider all the way to the left so I can fit as many files as possible in the limited space available on-screen. That way I can quickly tell if any of the images still need to be converted to CMYK mode

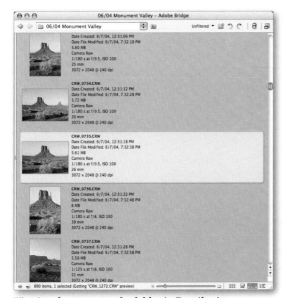

Viewing the contents of a folder in Details view.

Viewing the contents of a folder in Versions and Alternatives view.

and check to make sure that no low resolution images slipped in.

Versions & Alternatives View

This special view allows you to view different versions of a document that have been saved into a Version Cue project. Version Cue is part of the Adobe Creative Suite but is not included when you buy Photoshop as a stand-alone product. To create a project (assuming you have Version Cue properly configured), choose **File>Save As** from Photoshop, click on the *Use Adobe Dialog* button and choose *New Project* from the *Project Tools* pop-up menu (which looks like a toolbox). Then, to save your Photoshop document into the newly created project, double-click on the project's name so you're viewing its content and click the Save button. Once you've done that, you can choose **File>Save A Version** to save the current state of your document as a new version.

All the views we've looked at so far can be found as both icons in the lower right of the Bridge window and choices that appear under the View menu. You can press **Command-** (Mac) or **Ctrl-** (Win) to cycle though the view modes (that's a \, not a /). Now let's explore the one viewing mode that is found only under the **View** menu.

Slide Show View

Choosing **View>Slide Show** or typing **Command-L** (Mac) or **Ctrl-L** (Win) will invoke Slide Show mode. In this mode, the contents of a folder will be displayed as large, individual preview images on a gray background.

The background color might look the same as that which is used behind the thumbnail images, but the settings that control the thumbnail background do not affect the slide show. You're pretty much stuck with the default color.

You can control the slide show presentation using keyboard commands. To see a list of available commands, type **H** while in Slide Show view. The most commonly used keyboard shortcuts are those for advancing the slide show (**right** and **left arrow** keys), for pausing/playing the show (**spacebar**) and for exiting the show (**esc**).

> **NOTE**
>
> **Navigating PDF Files**
> *If a slide show includes PDF files, use the **Right** and **Left Arrow** keys to flip through the pages of a PDF. When you reach the last page of the file, pressing the right arrow key will switch to the next PDF file. Add the **Command** key (Mac), or **Ctrl key** (Win) when using the arrow keys to switch between individual PDF files.*

SLIDE SHOW KEYBOARD COMMANDS	
Keyboard	**Shortcut Result**
H	Toggle Keyboard Command List
Esc.	Exit Slide Show Mode
L	Toggle Looping
C	Cycle Through Caption Modes:
	Full, Compact, Page Number, Off
S	Increase Slide Duration 1 Second
	(60 seconds = max duration)
Shift-S	Decrease Slide Duration 1 Second
Space	Pause or Plan Slide Show
W	Toggle Full Screen/Window Mode
D	Cycle through Display Modes:
	Centered, Scale to Fit, Fill Window
Left Arrow	Previous Document
Right Arrow	Next Document
Cmd/Ctrl-Arrows	Next/Previous Page in a PDF file
[	Rotate Counterclockwise
]	Rotate Clockwise
1-5	Set Rating
6-9	Set Label
Comma (,)	Decrease Rating
Zero (0)	Clear Rating
Period (.)	Increase Rating
Apostrophe (')	Toggle Rating

The slide show is based on the previews that Bridge generates for each image. These preview images are no larger than 1024x1024 pixels. If you have a screen that can display more than that, the default size of the preview images will not fill your screen. Typing **D** multiple times will toggle between different display modes (Unscaled, Scale to Fit and Fill Window). Some of these views might look a little blurry since Bridge is just scaling up the low resolution preview image, but that's a limitation you'll have to live with.

Compact & Ultra-Compact Modes

Now that you've seen the viewing choices, let's take a look at two special modes that make it easier to view multiple folders and place images into Adobe Creative Suite applications.

Compact view shown with document names hidden.

Compact Mode

This mode presents you with a small Bridge window, hides the left panes (Folders, Preview, etc.), and hides many of the icons that usually appear at the top of a Bridge window. There are three methods to access this special mode: **1)** Click the Compact Mode icon (the right-most of the five icons that appear near the upper right corner of a Bridge window), **2)** Choose **View>Compact Mode**, **3)** Type **Command-Return** (Mac) or **Ctrl-Enter** (Win).

Placing multiple Compact mode windows side by side allows you to view the contents of multiple folders without having to juggle a bunch of full-screen windows.

This mode has some special features that make it especially useful when working with Adobe Illustrator and Adobe InDesign. With default settings, this window floats above all other document windows, allowing you to view the contents of a folder while working in other Creative Suite applications. This also allows you to drag an image directly from a Bridge window into an Illustrator or InDesign document for placement on a layout page.

If you'd rather that these Compact Mode windows didn't float above other application windows, just turn off the *Compact Window Always On Top* option that's found in the side menu that appears in the upper right of each Compact Mode window.

 *Ultra-Compact view*

Ultra-Compact Mode

This mode presents you with a collapsed version of a Bridge window where the only thing that is visible is the folder name.

I often set up several of these Ultra-Compact mode windows, each one pointing to a folder that I'm using for a particular project (such as the folders that contain the images used in each chapter of this book). I line them up at the bottom of my screen so I can view the contents of any one of the folders with a simple click of the Compact or Full Mode icons that appear just to the right of the folder name.

This can also be useful when working in Adobe InDesign. Just resize the document window to make space for the Ultra-Compact windows at the bottom of your screen. Once your document is setup that way, you can click on the Compact Mode icon to expand the window, drag an image onto an InDesign layout, and then click the Ultra-Compact Mode icon again to collapse the folder back down to the bottom of your screen and continue working in InDesign. Unfortunately, you cannot drag from a Bridge window to place an image into a Photoshop document, so this drag-and-drop functionality is limited to InDesign and Illustrator users.

Previewing PDF Files

Bridge includes the ability to preview multi-page PDF files. When in Thumbnail view, clicking on a PDF file will cause Bridge to display Previous Page arrow icons below the preview image that appears in the Preview pane on the left side of the window. You'll also find similar icons when viewing a PDF file in Filmstrip view. We discussed navigating PDF files in Slide Show mode earlier in this chapter.

Double-clicking on a PDF file will cause Bridge to launch Adobe Reader (formerly known as Acrobat Reader). If you'd rather open one of the pages of the PDF file in Photoshop, then **Control-click** (Mac) or **Right-click** (Win) on the thumbnail for

When previewing a PDF file, icons will appear below the preview image allowing you to navigate through the pages of the document.

the PDF file, and choose **Open With>Adobe Photoshop CS2** from the menu that appears. That will cause Photoshop to prompt you to select the page you'd like to open and specify the resolution setting to be used.

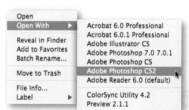

The Open With menu will appear when Control-clicking (Mac), or Right-clicking (Win) on a PDF thumbnail.

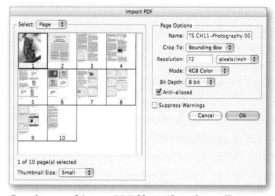

Opening a multi-page PDF file in Photoshop will cause the Import PDF dialog box to appear.

The Tools Menu

The File Browser's Automate menu has been replaced with the **Tools** menu in Bridge. Many of these features are covered in other chapters where we could devote more space for in-depth coverage. My approach here is to look at how this menu differs from what is found in Photoshop CS's File Browser.

The Tools menu in Bridge replaces the Automate menu from Photoshop CS's File Browser.

Batch Rename

Adobe has made slight modifications to the *Batch Rename* command. The menus used to specify the appearance of file names might look half as long as the ones that are available in Photoshop's File Browser, but in reality, these new menu choices offer sub options that allow you to replicate the file naming that was possible in the File Browser. You can even include camera related settings (like the exposure or lens used) by choosing from the options available under

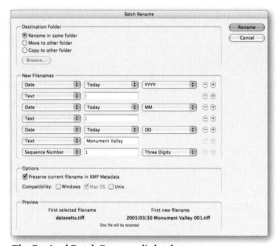

The Revised Batch Rename dialog box.

the *EXIF Metadata* choice. You can also attach the old file name to an image using metadata by turning on the *Preserve current file name in XMP metadata* checkbox. That can be useful if you want to retain the original file name that was assigned by your digital camera. If you preserve the current file name, you can in effect undo a batch rename by using the *Preserved Filename* option from the file name pop-up menus.

Version Cue

This menu offers choices related to Version Cue. This program allows you to keep track of multiple versions of the same file and makes it easy share files with others. Version Cue is beyond the scope of this book, so I won't be providing more than a cusory overview of this feature.

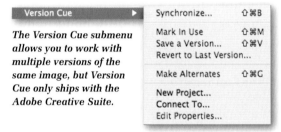

The Version Cue submenu allows you to work with multiple versions of the same image, but Version Cue only ships with the Adobe Creative Suite.

Photoshop Services

The choices found under this side menu allow you to share photographs on-line and order prints to be delivered to your door. These options are covered in-depth in *Chapter 10: Small Gems for Photography*. The only thing that isn't covered in that chapter is the *Choose Location* option, which simply allows you to specify the country in which you reside so that the proper pricing and shipping information will be displayed when ordering prints using the *Photo Prints* choice.

The Photoshop Services submenu allows you to share and print your images on-line.

Photoshop

The vast majority of the choices in this submenu were transplanted from the File Browser. The new Image Processor feature (along with the new Web Photo Gallery templates) is covered in *Chapter 10: Small Gems for Photography* and the Merge to HDR feature is covered in Chapter 8: HDR Imaging. Let's take a look at what's not covered in those chapters.

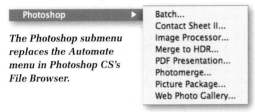

The Photoshop submenu replaces the Automate menu in Photoshop CS's File Browser.

PDF Presentation

You'll be presented with the *Save Adobe PDF* dialog box after you choose *PDF Presentation* from the *Photoshop* submenu and specify a name for the file. Adobe has completely revised the *Save* dialog box associated with PDF files (both in PDF Presentation and when using the *Save As* dialog box to save a file). The new dialog box offers an *Adobe Presets* pop-up menu that allows you to quickly load settings. The main area of the dialog box is divided into five sections:

General: This section allows you to include page thumbnails and optimize the PDF for fast loading on a web page.

The General pane of the Save Adobe PDF dialog box.

Compression: This section allows you to scale down images to achieve a smaller file size and to choose the type of compression you'd like to have applied to the file.

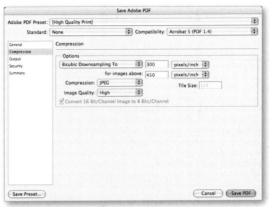

The Compression pane of the Save Adobe PDF dialog.

Output: This section allows you to automatically convert images to CMYK mode (via the *Color Conversion* and *Destination* pop-up menus) and to set the document to conform to different PDF-X specifications. The PDF-X format is briefly discussed in *Chapter 6: Small Gems for Design.*

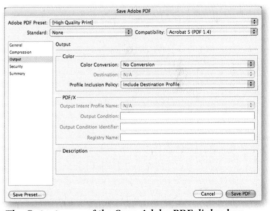

The Output pane of the Save Adobe PDF dialog box.

Security: This section allows you to assign a password that would be required to open or print the image. These settings will be grayed out if you choose one of the PDF-X presets (because that standard does not allow for password protection).

The Security pane of the Save Adobe PDF dialog box.

Summary: This section summarizes the settings that have been specified in the entire dialog box and warns you of any potential problems that might occur when using those settings.

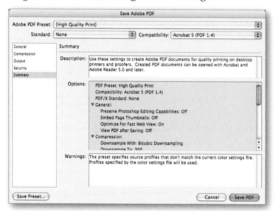

The Summary pane of the Save Adobe PDF dialog box.

Cache

The choices found under this submenu were moved from the **File** menu in Photoshop's File Browser. The only thing Adobe changed was the wording of the menu: *Purge Cache* became *Purge Cache for This Folder*, and *Purge Entire Cache* became *Purge Central Cache.*

Adobe also added a section on the cache to the Preferences dialog box. To access the Cache settings, choose *Preferences* from the **Bridge** menu (Mac) or **Edit** menu (Win) and then click on the *Advanced* choice on the left side of the dialog box.

The Cache submenu allows you to save or purge the cache that contains image thumbnails and previews.

These new *Preferences* settings allow you to determine how Bridge stores the thumbnail and previews that it generates for each image (that's what's contained in the cache). Using the centralized cache will store all these mini-images in a folder on your hard drive, just like the File Browser used to do. The main difference here is that you can choose the location for the cache file. This can be useful if you like to store your photographs on an external drive and want to store the cache files in the same location. That way they won't cause your internal drive to slowly fill to capacity.

The *Use Distributed Cache Files When Possible* setting will save the cache files directly into each folder that you browse. The cache consists of two files. Both are called Adobe Bridge Cache and only differ in the file extension used (.bct and .bc). The advantage of saving cache files into each folder is that those files will be used when the folder is viewed from a different copy of Bridge, while using the centralized cache will cause each copy of Bridge to generate its own thumbnails. I love the idea of automatically saving the cache files, but I find it annoying that they are saved for every folder I ever point to in Bridge. That means that my desktop, the documents folder, the Photoshop folder and many others have these pesky little files showing up all the time, even though I don't store photographs in those locations. I simply wish there was a setting that would allow me to set a minimum number of image files necessary before Bridge would save the cache files (maybe we'll get that in CS3).

The Cache settings are found in the Advanced section of the Bridge Preferences dialog box.

Append/Replace Metadata

These two choices used to appear under the **Edit** menu in the File Browser and have been moved to Bridge's **Tools** menu.

The Append Metadata command will add metadata while preserving any existing metadata already embedded in the file.

The Replace Metadata command will add metadata after deleting any existing metadata embedded in the file.

If you find that these choices are grayed out it simply means that you don't have any Metadata presets saved. To save a preset, click on any image within Bridge, choose **File>File Info**, enter the metadata you'd like to save and then choose *Save Metadata Template* from the side menu of the dialog box.

These options are great for quickly applying metadata (copyright notices, keywords, etc.) to a large number of images. The only difference between *Append* and *Replace* is that *Append* will add the template data to any existing metadata, while *Replace* will wipe out any existing metadata when applying the template data.

Labeling & Rating

In Photoshop CS's File Browser, you had the option of Flagging an image or assigning it a Rank. Both of those options have been replaced with the new rating and label system.

5-Star Rating System

This new system allows you to apply a star rating to each image, between one and five. The rating you apply will appear below each of the thumbnail images and can be used for sorting and filtering which thumbnails are displayed. There are numerous methods for applying a rating:

Label Menu: This is probably the slowest method available, but is good for those who are not good at remembering keyboard shortcuts.

The Label menu allows you to apply a rating or label to the currently selected thumbnail images.

Keyboard Shortcuts: Holding **Command** (Mac) or **Ctrl** (Win) and typing a number between Zero and 5 will apply a rating to the currently selected thumbnails.

Star Icons: Clicking on a thumbnail within Bridge will cause five small dots to appear below the image. Clicking any of those dots will add a corresponding number of stars to the currently selected thumbnails.

Flag In File Browser: Any images that were flagged in Photoshop CS's File Browser will appear with a single star rating in Bridge.

The images above have been rated (two also have a color label applied) and the results are filtered to only view files that have been assigned 3 or more stars.

Applying Color Labels

You can also label your images using one of five colors (red, yellow, green, blue or purple). This can be done by either choosing from the **Label** menu or by holding **Command** (Mac) or **Ctrl** (Win) and typing a number from 6 through 9 (there is no keyboard shortcut for the purple label).

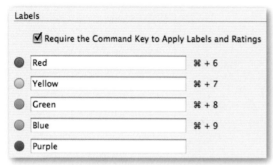

The choices available under the Label menu will reflect the names that you've assigned to each color.

You can assign names to each of the five colors by choosing *Preferences* from the **Bridge** menu (Mac) or **Edit** menu (Win) and clicking on the *Labels* choice on the left side of the dialog box. The names you enter in the *Preferences* dialog box will be reflected in the **Label** menu in Bridge. Turning off the *Require the Command Key to Apply Labels and Ratings* checkbox will allow you to apply ratings and labels using the number keys on your keyboard (without having to hold the **Command** or **Control** key).

You're not allowed to rate or label an image that is currently open in Photoshop. A small document icon will appear below the thumbnail image for any files that are open.

Filtering & Sorting Based on Labels

Once you've applied a label or rating, you can filter and sort your images based on that information.

Filtering Which Images Are Visible

You can limit which files are visible by choosing from the Filtered/Unfiltered menu in the upper right of the Bridge window. This menu will reflect any names that you've assigned to the label

The Filter pop-up menu is found in the upper right of the Bridge window. It allows you to limit the files that are visible based on their rating or label.

colors. I like to select the *Show Unrated Items Only* choice before I start rating images. That causes images to disappear as I rate them so I don't have to scroll through a long list of images to find the ones that are left unrated.

Sorting Images

The choices found under the **View>Sort** menu allow you to sort your images based on the rating or label that has been applied.

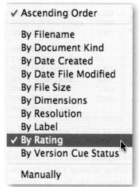

The By Label and By Rating choices in the View>Sort menu allow you to sort the currently visible thumbnails based on the rating or labels applied to the images.

The rating, labeling, filtering and sorting capabilities available in Bridge make it easy to single out the few dozen great images you might have out of the thousands of shots taken for a particular project.

Tiny Tweaks

Now that we've covered most of the major changes that happened when Photoshop's File Browser was morphed into Bridge, let's take a look at the small tweaks that are lurking in the lesser known corners of the program.

- **View Illustrator & InDesign Fonts:** Illustrator CS2 and InDesign CS2 include a list of fonts and swatches used in each document. This metadata can be read in Bridge. This (along with the new *Save Swatches for Exchange* command) makes it much easier to incorporate the same fonts and colors in a Photoshop image.

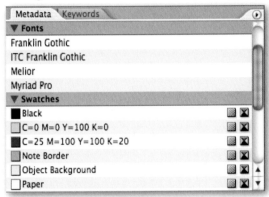

- **Copy/Paste Files:** If dragging thumbnails onto a folder in the Folder list is impractical, then do the following: Select multiple images, choose **Edit>Copy**, navigate to another folder, and choose **Edit>Paste** to place duplicates of the files in the second location.
- **Keyword Sets Stay Put:** In Photoshop CS's File Browser, trashing your Preferences would also trash any keyword sets you had created in the Keywords pane of the File Browser. In contrast, Keyword sets are maintained when resetting Bridge's Preferences.
- **Improved File Info Dialog Box:** You can now apply the settings found in the **File>File Info** dialog box to more than one file. You'll also find a few new IPTC fields in *File Info* dialog box and custom file info panels will now show up in the Metadata pane in Bridge.

- **Choose File Associations:** You can set which application will be used to open documents that are in different file formats (causing QuickTime to display .mpg files for instance) by choosing *Preferences* from the **Bridge** menu (Mac) or **Edit** menu (Win) and clicking on the *File Type Associations* choice on the left side of the *Preferences* dialog box.

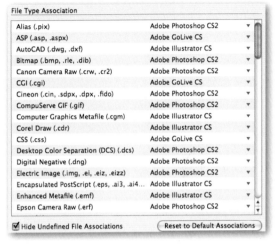

- **Return to Photoshop:** Since Bridge is a separate application from Photoshop, you can't simply close its window to return to Photoshop. Typing **Command-Option-O** (Mac) or **Ctrl-Option-O** (Win) from Photoshop will switch you to Bridge. Typing the same keyboard shortcut in Bridge will switch you to Photoshop without opening any images.
- **Open and Hide Bridge:** You can type **Command-Option-Shift-O** (Mac) or **Ctrl-Alt-Shift-O** (Win) or hold **Option** (Mac) or **Alt** (Win) when double-clicking on an image to open an image in Photoshop and simultaneously hide Bridge.

As you can see, the transition from the File Browser to Bridge doesn't have to be a difficult one. It just takes a little time to get familiar with the new territory, locate your old friends and discover the new features that will hopefully make an enormous difference to your workflow.

Welcome Screen

Adobe®Photoshop® CS2

What's New in Photoshop
New Features At A Glance
New Feature Highlights
See It In Action (video clips)

Tutorials
Learn the Basics
Advanced Techniques (Channel)
Working with What's New

Chapter 2
General Tweaks

IF YOU'RE WONDERING WHETHER YOU should read this chapter, throw your hesitation out the window. These pages cover such an abundance of refinements and new features that I consider them essential reading for anyone upgrading to CS2. There are gems to be found for all walks of Photoshop users, photographers and designers alike.

Some of the changes, like the new Warp feature, are noticeably spectacular, but many of the smaller features (like better cursor visibility) can be just as valuable. Here's a quick glance at what you'll find in this chapter:

- **Warping:** A dynamite feature that allows you to bend and distort a layer in interesting ways.
- **Editing Menus:** Learn to hide and color code the menu commands to streamline Photoshop's interface.
- **Color Management:** They just can't leave well enough alone. There is no new functionality, but to keep you on your toes they moved and renamed many color management features.
- **New Preferences:** There are quite a few new Preference choices and knowing when to take advantage of them can make your life easier.
- **Tiny Tweaks:** There are a huge number of small changes quietly flying under the radar. As a whole, they really are the core of this chapter.

Where's My Stuff?

To avoid shock the first time you use CS2, make sure to read through this list:

- **Assign & Convert to Profile:** These commands have been moved from the **Image>Mode** menu to the **Edit** menu to be more consistent with other Adobe products.
- **Type Related Preferences:** These preferences have been moved to their own pane.
- **Can't Paste from Clipboard:** If Photoshop doesn't see something you've copied from another program, try running the *AlwaysImportClipboard.reg* file that is found on the Photoshop install CD.
- **Less Memory Left Over:** They upped the Memory & Image Cache Preferences (from 50 to 70%) so Photoshop uses more memory.
- **Pasted Graphics Are Small:** You must have the new *Resize Image During Paste/Place* preference turned on.
- **Actions Missing:** Adobe changed the default actions. To get back the old ones, choose **Sample Actions** from the side menu of the Actions palette.
- **Can't Install on All My Macs:** Adobe now requires activation on the Mac, so you'll have to purchase separate license agreements to use Photoshop on more than two Mac machines.

Warping

The new Warp feature in Photoshop CS2 allows you to bend and distort images almost as if they were printed on Silly Putty. Choosing **Edit>Transform>Warp** will cause a variety of warping options to appear in the Options bar at the top of your screen. You can use Photoshop's preset Warp shapes, or create your own custom Warp, or use a combination of both.

The Options bar settings found when Warping a layer.

Preset Warp Shapes

The Warp pop-up menu in the Options bar allows you to choose between one of fifteen preset Warp shapes. After choosing a shape, you can adjust the Bend setting to control the severity of the warp that's being applied.

There are three ways to change the Bend setting: enter a number in the Bend text field, click on the name of the setting and drag left or right, drag the hollow square that appears on the Warp grid that appears on the image.

The Warp Presets menu.

You can also adjust the Horizontal and Vertical distortion settings (simply marked H and D in the Options bar) to determine if the distortion will be applied symmetrically or not.

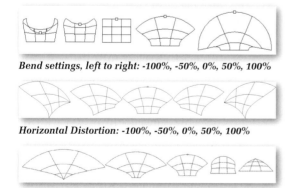

Bend settings, left to right: -100%, -50%, 0%, 50%, 100%

Horizontal Distortion: -100%, -50%, 0%, 50%, 100%

Vertical Distortion: -100%, -50%, 0%, 50%, 100%

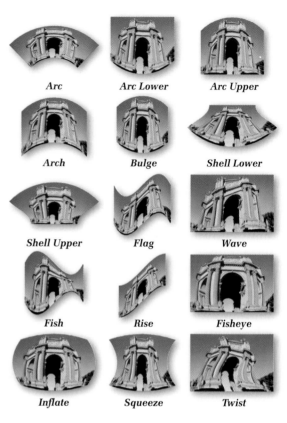

Arc   Arc Lower   Arc Upper

Arch   Bulge   Shell Lower

Shell Upper   Flag   Wave

Fish   Rise   Fisheye

Inflate   Squeeze   Twist

Below are a few tips to keep in mind when applying a warp to a layer:

- Type **Command-H** (Mac) or **Ctrl-H** (Win) to toggle the visibility of the Warp grid.
- Click and drag within the Warp grid (but not near the hollow square on the grid) to reposition the layer.
- Click the Warp icon in the Options bar to toggle between warping and standard transformations (like scale, rotate and distort). You can also choose from the **Edit>Transform** menu to access transformations. You can freely switch back and forth between these two methods of transforming a layer.
- Choose **Transform Selection** from the Select menu (or when **Control-clicking** (Mac) or **Right-clicking** (Win) on a layer within the image) to warp the shape of the selection instead of the image that is inside the selection.

Custom Warp Shapes

You can make some amazing Warp shapes by using a combination of Warp presets, standard transform commands and the Horizontal and Vertical Distortion settings. If you want to take your warping skills to the next level, you'll want to learn how to take advantage of the Custom Warp setting (the default setting when starting a warp).

Modifying a Custom Warp

In this mode, you'll be presented with a grid that features hollow squares at each corner (known as corner points) and eight handles that have solid circles at on their ends (two of these handles stick out of each corner point).

Original images with unmodified Custom Warp.

Corner points placed in position.

Corner handles adjusted to match shape of cup.

Handles and points fine-tuned to better match cup.

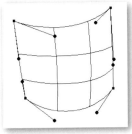

Final warp grid used to match photo to cup.

Result of using Multiply mode to combine layers.

Adjusting the corner points and handles will determine the outer shape of the warp. The handles control the direction in which the edge of the warp will travel as it moves away from each corner point (these handles work just like the ones used with Photoshop's Pen tool).

Clicking and dragging within the center grid section will distort the image without modifying the outer shape of the warp. It takes quite a bit of practice before you'll be able to get precise control over the warping grid.

If you're having trouble getting the shape you desire, then consider starting with one of the Warp shape presets that are found in the **Warp** pop-up menu (that appears in the Options bar) and then switch to the Custom choice where you can modify the preset by dragging the points and handles that make up the grid.

To reposition the layer, hold **Command** (Mac) or **Ctrl** (Win) and press the mouse button within the central grid (keep away from the points and handles). If you need to scale or rotate the layer, click the Warp icon in the Options bar to toggle to Photoshop's **Free Transform** command (as mentioned on the previous page). Once you're done transforming the layer, click the Warp icon in the Options bar to toggle back to Warp mode so you can further adjust the warp that's being applied to the layer.

Pressing **Enter/Return** after warping a layer will cause the warp to become permanent. Choosing **Edit>Transform>Warp** a second time will place another undistorted warp grid over the previously warped layer.

Warping Smart Objects

If you'd like to maintain the ability to modify a warp after it's been applied, then consider applying it to a layer that has been converted into a Smart Object. That way you'll be able to re-edit the warp by choosing **Edit->Transform->Warp**, and you'll be able to edit the contents of the layer by double-clicking on the layer's thumbnail image. Smart Objects are covered in-depth in Chapter 4: Smart Objects.

Editing Menus

In Photoshop CS, you were able to change the keyboard shortcuts associated with menus. With CS2, Adobe has gone a step further and made it possible for you to assign colors to each menu item, as well as specify which items should appear in the menus. This allows you to significantly simplify the menu structure, making it much easier to find the commands you use the most. To change the color or visibility of menu commands, choose **Edit>Menus**.

Working with Presets

At the top of the dialog box, you'll find a list of presets (known as Sets). There are nine presets that come pre-installed with Photoshop CS2. Most of these defaults simply add color to certain menu commands (the *Basic* and *Printing & Proofing* Sets hide com-

NOTE

Deleting Sets

If you find any of the default Sets to be less than useful, you can remove them. To remove the currently selected set, click the Trash can icon that appears to the right of the Set pop-up menu.

mands). The *What's New - CS2* Set can be especially useful when you're new to this version of Photoshop because it highlights all the new commands that were added in CS2 (but does not highlight existing commands that contain new features). I find that the default Sets leave too many menu commands visible, which makes the color coding less effective because I still have to hunt and peck to find menu commands.

Editing Menu Commands

To create your own menu command Set, choose the type of menu you'd like to work with (application or palette), navigate to a particular menu command and click on the eyeball icon to the right of the command to toggle its visibility, or click in the color column to assign one of seven colors.

The color menu.

When editing the color and visibility of menu commands, you'll find the following limitations:

- Certain menu commands cannot be hidden because their absence could potentially cause problems when working with images.
- You cannot change the order of the commands or move a command from one menu to another.
- Hiding all the commands in a menu will not hide the menu itself (since it will always have the *Show All Menu Items* choice available).

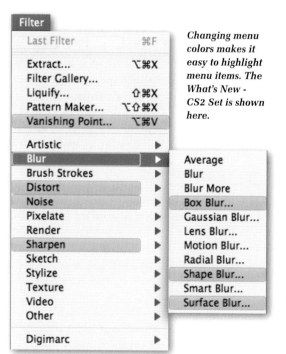

Changing menu colors makes it easy to highlight menu items. The What's New - CS2 Set is shown here.

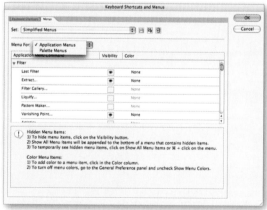

Choose Edit>Menus to access this dialog box.

MENU ITEMS THAT CANNOT BE HIDDEN
File>Close
File>Save
File>Save As
Edit>Menus
Workspace>Reset Menus
Help>Photoshop Help

Once you're finished editing the color and visibility of menu commands, you can click OK to see the changes reflected in Photoshop. If you'd like to be able to quickly switch between different sets of menu commands (via the Set pop-up menu), then click the New Set icon (floppy disk with down-pointing arrow icon) to assign a name to the currently active set of menu commands.

Suggested Uses

Now let's look at how we might put these modified menu command sets to good use:

- To make it much faster and easier to find the commands that you use frequently, hide all the menu commands that you rarely use.
- To make commands easier to see within the menus, apply color to the ones you use the most.
- In a classroom environment, hide most of the commands so beginners are not overwhelmed at the number of commands available. Then, as the class progresses, make more commands visible and apply color to the commands that will be featured in each lesson.

Left: The Filter menu displayed using default settings.
Right: The same menu showing commonly used filters.

Working with Modified Menus

Now that you know how to create, edit and save sets of menu commands, let's see how we might make them more useful.

Viewing All Menu Commands

If you need to use a menu command that has been hidden, choose **Show All Menu Items** from the bottom of the menu that would usually contain the hidden command. That will cause all the items in that menu to become visible for the length of time you are viewing the menu. You can also hold **Command** (Mac) or **Ctrl** (Win) and click on a menu to

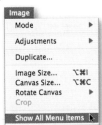

The Show All Menu Items command will appear in all menus that contain hidden commands.

display all the commands. I find that to be more useful since I can click on multiple menus instead of having to choose **Show All Menu Items** from each menu I want to view.

Save as a Workspace

If you'd like to be able to quickly switch between different menu sets, then consider saving the menu edits you've made as part of a workspace. A workspace is a preset that can include not only menu commands, but keyboard shortcuts and palette locations. Choosing **Window>Workspace>Save Workspace** will allow you to specify what you'd like to save in the workspace. Once you've saved a few workspaces, you can quickly switch between them by choosing from the **Window>Workspace** menu.

If you want to get really fancy, you can also assign keyboard shortcuts to the workspaces you've saved by choosing **Edit>Keyboard Shortcuts**.

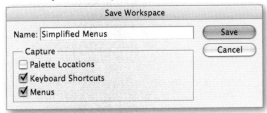

Edited menus can be saved as part of a workspace.

These saved workspaces are ideal if you wear many hats at work and need to quickly switch between using creative and production oriented commands. It can also be excellent for classroom environments where you want to quickly switch which commands are visible for different classes that are being taught.

Color Preferences

If you're forced to work with menu commands that have been edited by others and find the colors chosen to be more distracting than useful, you can hide the color by doing the following: Choose **Preferences>General** from the **Photoshop** menu (Mac) or **Edit** menu (Win) and turn off the *Show Menu Colors* checkbox. That will cause Photoshop to ignore any colors assigned to menus, while still honoring the visibility settings for each menu command.

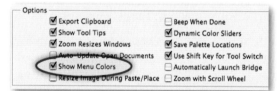

You can turn off the display of menu colors in the General section of Photoshop's Preferences dialog box.

Color Management

Forgive me for venting, but color management is confusing enough on its own without the seemingly unnecessary tampering that took place with CS2. Adobe really didn't add any new functionality, but in their infinite wisdom they saw fit to mess around with the features that many of us were just getting used to. So, enough whining, let's grin and bear it, shall we?

They Moved Stuff

The **Color Settings**, **Assign Profile** and **Convert to Profile** dialog boxes have all been moved to the **Edit** menu because that's where they can be found in other Adobe applications.

The **Assign Profile** and **Convert to Profile** dialog boxes are unchanged, but slight tweaks were made to the **Color Settings** dialog box:

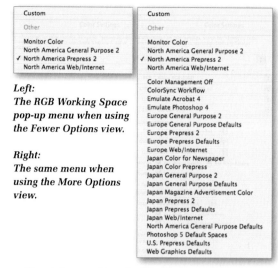

Left:
The RGB Working Space pop-up menu when using the Fewer Options view.

Right:
The same menu when using the More Options view.

- The *Advanced Mode* checkbox has been replaced with a button that toggles between *More Options* and *Fewer Options*.
- The number of choices found by default in the **RGB Working Space** pop-up menu have been reduced. To see the full list, click the *More Options* button.
- They changed the order of the choices found in the **Settings** pop-up menu. All the choices that were available in CS are still available.
- The **Simulate Paper White** and **Simulate Ink Black** choices have been removed from the **View>Proof Setup** menu. They now must be chosen in the **View>Proof Setup>Custom** area.

Proof Setup

The **View>Proof Setup** menu is where you can tell Photoshop to simulate what an image would look like when printed on a particular device (such as an ink jet printer) or viewed in a different color mode (like CMYK mode). Choosing **View>Proof Colors** will simulate what an image will look like on-screen (also known as soft proofing), while the choices in the **File>Print With Preview** dialog box allow you to simulate the same device or mode on your desktop printer. The only changes that were made to this dialog box are the renaming of a few checkboxes. The *Paper White* and *Ink Black* settings are now called *Simulate Paper Color* and *Simulate Black Ink*.

Choose View>Proof Setup>Custom to access this dialog.

Sync Settings Between Applications

You can now quickly sync the color management settings used in all the Adobe Creative Suite applications (Photoshop, InDesign, etc.).

To apply consistent settings in all the Creative Suite applications, choose **Edit>Creative Suite Color Setting** from Bridge (this commmand is only available if you've installed the full Adobe Creative Suite and does not appear in the stand alone version of Photoshop). When you first open the dialog box, you'll find the same four presets that are shown in Photoshop's **Color Settings** dialog box, along with any settings that you've saved from one of the Creative Suite applications. To see the full list of settings available, turn on the *Show Expanded List of Color Settings Files* checkbox. Choosing one of the settings from the list and then clicking the Apply button will transfer those settings to each of the Creative Suite applications.

The Suite Color Settings dialog box.

Print With Preview

Quite a few changes have been made to the color management section of the **File>Print with Preview** dialog box. That area is only visible when the *More Options* button has been clicked (known as the *Show More Options* checkbox in CS). The changes in this area were primarily designed to make the settings more straightforward for beginning and intermediate Photoshop users (essentially making it more difficult to screw things up), which has the unfortunate side effect of making the settings more difficult to understand for advanced users. Let's take a look at each change and see how it will affect your workflow.

NOTE

Color Resource
To learn more about color management, visit Chris Murphy's web site at www.colorremedies. com. He's the person I call on when I have questions about color management. He's also the co-author of the book: Real World Color Management.

Choose What to Reproduce

At the top of the color management section you have two ways to reproduce your image: choosing the *Document* option will simply print your image without any special processing, while choosing the *Proof* option will cause Photoshop to simulate what the image would look like if it was converted to a different color mode (such as CMYK mode) or printed to a different device (such as a particular printing press).

The vast majority of Photoshop users just want their images to look right when they are printed. If that describes you, then always choose the *Document* option in the **Print with Preview** dialog box. If you go with that option, you can skip over the next section, which covers proof settings.

Accurately reproducing color on a Phaser 6200 printer.

Simulating CMYK mode on a Phaser 6200 printer.

Left: Document setting used, Right: Proofing newsprint

Choosing Proof Settings: When the *Proof* setting is used, the **Proof Setup Preset** pop-up menu at the bottom of the dialog box will become available. This is where you choose the mode or device you'd like to simulate. With default settings, you'll find only one choice available (**Working CMYK**). To add additional choices to the menu, click *Cancel* in the **Print with Preview** dialog box, choose **View>Proof Setup>Custom**, enter the settings you'd like to use, then click the *Save* button and save them to the Proofing folder (the default location). In previous versions of Photoshop, you were limited to using the choice that was currently active in the **View>Proof Setup** menu.

When simulating an output device (via the *Proof* setting), you'll find checkboxes for *Simulate Paper Color* and *Simulate Black Ink*. When both of those checkboxes are turned off, white areas in the image will be reproduced as white, and black areas will appear black in the printed result. That can cause your printed results to simulate the color but not the contrast of the device you are intending to simulate. To understand what turning on the checkboxes will do, just imagine that you're trying to simulate what an image would look like when printed in the newspaper.

Newsprint (the paper used for newspapers) is nowhere near as bright as the paper used in most laser or ink jet printers, and the blackest black that can be reproduced on the newsprint is a lot less dark than that which you can get out of most printers. Turning on the *Simulate Black Ink* checkbox and *Simulate Paper Color* checkboxes will cause Photoshop to print the image as it would really appear in the newspaper. It does this by adding ink to the white areas of the image

(effectively simulating the relative dullness of newspaper whites), and by using less ink in black areas (simulating the lackluster black that you get when printing on newsprint). It's really a personal choice; some people only want to see an approximation of what the colors will look like (without the contrast change that the checkboxes produce), while others want the more accurate version that simulates both the color and the contrast you'll achieve when printing in the newspaper (or any other device).

Choose How The Colors Will Be Handled
Once you've made the choice between simply printing your image or simulating a color mode or device, you have another critical decision to make. You have to decide if you want Photoshop or your printer driver to take on the job of making the colors look right. This is an either/or situation. If they are both allowed to jump in and try to make color decisions, then you're guaranteed to get bad color. That's known as double color management, which is just like hiring two companies to each create eyeglasses that perfectly match your prescription and then deciding to wear both pairs of glasses at the same time!

Avoiding Double Color Management: To accurately reproduce an image, your computer needs a description of how your printer reproduces color. This description comes in the form of a Color Profile and is often installed as part of your printer's print driver (if not, you can usually download it from the manufacturer's web site). When you print an image, this profile translates the information fed to the printer so that it gets a customized image designed specifically to look good with the printer/ink/paper combination being used. This color adjustment can be managed by either Photoshop or your printer driver, but should not be done by both—remember the eyeglass example above? The **Color Handling** pop-up menu is where you indicate how the color adjustment should be handled.

Choosing *Let Printer Determine Colors* (the equivalent of setting the **Profile** pop-up menu to **Printer Color Management** in Photoshop CS) will cause the **Printer Profile** pop-up menu to become grayed out (because you're indicating that you want the print driver to handle that setting). When using that setting, you'll need to choose the proper Color Profile. After you click OK in the **Print with Preview** dialog box, you're presented with a another dialog box that contains settings specific to your printer.

Choosing *Let Photoshop Determine Colors* (the equivalent of choosing a printer profile from the **Profile** pop-up menu in Photoshop CS) will allow you to feed Photoshop the Color Profile needed to accurately reproduce color on your printer (via the **Printer Profile** pop-up menu). The options you find below the **Printer Profile** menu depend on the choice you made at the top of the color management area (*Document* or *Proof*).

NOTE

Color Geek Translation

The simplified layout of the Print with Preview dialog box can be confusing if you're used to dealing with color management terms and settings, so here's a translation of what's going on behind the scenes:

Printing a Proof with Simulate Paper Color and Simulate Black Ink Checkboxes off: *converts the image from its source color space to the proof space using a Relative Colorimetric rendering intent with Black Point Compensation turned on.*

Printing a Proof with Simulate Black Ink Checkbox on: *converts the image from its source color space to the proof space using a Relative Colorimetric rendering intent with Black Point Compensation turned off.*

Printing a Proof with Simulate Paper Color on: *converts the image from its source color space to the proof space using Absolute Colorimetric rendering intent.*

If you used *Proof*, then you'll find the *Proof Setup Preset* settings which we talked about earlier. If you used *Document*, then you'll find a **Rendering Intent** pop-up menu and a *Black Point Compensation* checkbox. Setting the **Rendering Intent** to **Relative Colorimetric** and turning on *Black Point Compensation* will usually produce the closest match between how an image looks on-screen and when printed.

If you don't have a compelling reason to use the *Let Printer Determine Color* setting, or are just unsure as to which option to use, then stick with the *Let Photoshop Determine Colors* choice because it lets you specify all the color-related settings in a single dialog box.

Creating Custom Printer Profiles: You'll also find a choice called **No Color Management** (the equivalent of setting the **Profile** pop-up menu to **Same As Source** in Photoshop CS) in the **Color Handling** pop-up menu. That choice is primarily used when outputting targets that will be used for creating custom printer profiles. These custom profiles are used when the ones that came with your printer aren't producing satisfactory results (example: when you're using a different brand of ink or paper than the manufacturer's profile was designed for). When using this option, you'll also need to make sure that you choose *No Color Adjustment* when you click OK and get to the dialog box that contains settings specific to your printer.

The *No Color Management* setting is only needed while the profile is being created. Once you have the finished profile, you can use it to improve your results by choosing it from the **Printer Profile** pop-up menu when using the *Let Photoshop Determine Colors* option.

Now that we've made it through the technical purgatory known as color management, let's breathe a sigh of relief and move on to lighter topics.

New Preferences

Now let's take a look at what's changed in Photoshop's Preferences. You don't want to overlook Preferences because they have everything to do with how Photoshop behaves, and it's important to know what to expect so you don't get blindsided. To access the different Preference panes shown here, choose their names from the **Photoshop>Preferences** menu (Mac) or **Edit>Preferences** menu (Win). Let's look at each new or changed Preference item in the order they appear within the **Preferences** dialog box.

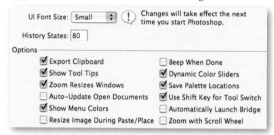

Options found in the General Preferences pane.

General

Adobe added a half dozen new Preferences to the General Preference pane. Let's start at the top and work our way to the bottom so you're fully informed about what's new.

UI Font Size

This new setting allows you to increase the size of the text that appears in palettes. It can be useful if your vision isn't as sharp as it used to be, or if you are using one of the new ultra-high resolution displays that use pixels which are much

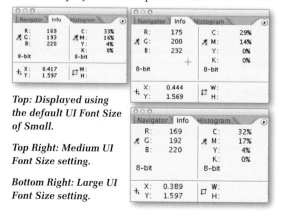

Top: Displayed using the default UI Font Size of Small.

Top Right: Medium UI Font Size setting.

Bottom Right: Large UI Font Size setting.

smaller than those used on a standard display. After changing this setting, you will have to quit and relaunch Photoshop for the new setting to take effect.

Show Menu Colors

Turning this checkbox off prevents colors that have been assigned to menus from showing up. Editing and applying color to menus was covered earlier in this chapter.

Resize Image During Paste/Place

Turning on this setting will cause Photoshop to automatically scale images that are being pasted or placed into a document that is smaller than the source image. That means you no longer have to zoom out and scale an oversized image that was pasted into a smaller document.

This feature might sound good, but there are potential problems. For instance, I commonly use the **Image>Reveal All** command to expose the areas of an image that extend beyond the document bounds. Because of that, I wish there was a simple way of toggling the *Resize Image During Paste/Place* setting on and off so that I could decide which setting to use at the time I paste or place an image. In many cases I need to keep images at their original size so I end up leaving this checkbox turned off.

Automatically Launch Bridge

This setting causes Bridge to launch each time you open Photoshop. I leave it turned on because I depend heavily on Bridge, and I don't like to wait for it to launch the first time I go to use it after opening Photoshop. If you're not familiar with Bridge, make sure to check out *Chapter 1: Adobe Bridge*.

Zoom with Scroll Wheel

Turning on this setting will allow you to quickly scroll in or out on your image by rotating the scroll wheel that is available on most two button mouses. That's nice, but I think it's even better when you hold **Shift** to limit the magnifications used to ones that make the image look its best (400%, 200%, 100%, 50%, 25%, etc.).

File Handling

Adobe changed the default setting for two of the checkboxes found in the *File Handling* pane.

Enable Large Document Format (.psb)

This setting is not new to Photoshop, but in CS2 the default setting has been changed so that this checkbox is turned on by default.

The Photoshop file format (.psd) is limited to images that are smaller than 2 Gigabytes or 30,000 pixels in any dimension (100 inches at 300PPI). The Large Document Format (.psb) was developed as an alternative to the Photoshop file format. (Adobe didn't change the Photoshop file format because that would cause it to be incompatible with older versions of Photoshop). The Large Document Format supports images that are up to 300,000 pixels in any dimension. This file format was first available in Photoshop CS, but had to be enabled by changing a Preference setting that was turned off by default.

The Large Document Format is useful when you have ultra-complex layered images that cause the file size to grow to over 2 Gigabytes, or when working with ultra-high resolution panorama images that contain more than 30,000 pixels in the width. Be aware that files saved in this format cannot be opened in Photoshop 7 or earlier versions. Having this Preference turned on makes the Large Document Format available in the Save As dialog box.

Version Cue Workgroup File Management

This is another setting that is not new to Photoshop. It's mentioned here because Adobe changed this preference so that it is turned on by default in CS2.

Options found in the File Handling Preferences pane.

Version Cue is a piece of software that is included with the Adobe Creative Suite but is not included when you purchase Photoshop as a stand-alone product (which is why you won't find extensive coverage of the feature in this book). This software allows you to store multiple versions of a file and easily switch between past and current versions without having to save multiple files. Having this setting turned on will cause the *Use Adobe Dialog* button to appear in the Open and Save dialog boxes. Clicking that button will allow you to access features that are specific to Version Cue.

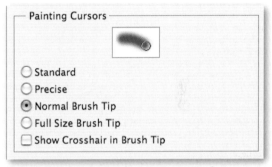

Options found in the Displays & Cursors Preferences.

Display & Cursors

Two new options are available under the *Painting Cursors* area of the *Display & Cursors* Preferences pane.

Full Size Brush Tip

The round edge of Photoshop's default brush indicates the halfway point at which the color you are painting with will fade out. Turning on the *Full Size Brush Tip* option will cause the brush cursor to indicate where the brush will stop affecting the image (the actual edge of the brush instead of the middle of the fadeout). It might take a while for you to get comfortable with this option, but once you do, I think you'll find it much easier to precisely control where your painting and retouching tools are affecting your image.

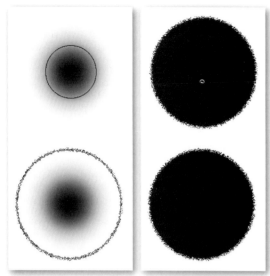

The image at the left shows the difference between using the Normal Brush Tip setting (top) and the Full Size Brush Tip setting (bottom). The left images show the on-screen view, while the right images indicate which areas of the image were affected (everything darker than white appears as black in that view).

Show Crosshair in Brush Tip

This option will cause a crosshair to appear in the middle of your brush cursor. This is especially useful when using the *Full Size Brush Tip* setting because it can be difficult to visualize exactly where the center of the brush is when looking at such a large cursor.

Result of using the Show Crosshair in Brush Tip option.

Guides, Grid & Slices

There is just one new setting in the *Guides, Grid & Slices* Preference pane: The *Smart Guides* setting allows you to change the color of the guides that appear when two layers' edges or centers align together. You'll find in-depth coverage of the Smart Guides feature in *Chapter 6: Small Gems for Design*.

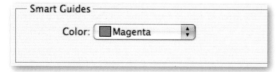

Options found in the Guides, Grid & Slices Preferences.

Memory & Image Cache

There is no new functionality in this Preference pane, but some of the default settings have been changed and one option has been removed.

Options from the Memory & Image Cache Preferences.

Increased Cache Levels

When you open an image in Photoshop, multiple scaled down versions of the image are automatically created and stored in memory. These scaled down versions are known as cached images and are used to quickly update your screen when an image is being viewed at a magnification lower than 100%. That way Photoshop doesn't have to process the entire image just to preview an adjustment or create a histogram.

A *Cache Levels* setting of 1 will store just the full-sized image and would be the setting to use if you absolutely always view your image at 100% magnification. However, that setting will cause your screen to update slower when the image is viewed at less then 100% magnification (because it has to process the entire image even though you're not viewing all the detail in the file).

Using a *Cache Levels* setting of 6 will store six scaled down versions of an image in memory (50%, 25%, 12.5%, 6.25% and 3.125%). This allows for faster screen redraw when zoomed out on high resolution images. Adobe increased the default *Cache Levels* setting from 4 to 6 in CS2.

Each cache image is half the width and height of the previous cache (or 1/4 as much info).

This change has the following advantages and disadvantages: **1)** It causes images to open a little slower since it has to scale and create more cache images **2)** It increases the screen redraw speed of images viewed at magnifications below 12.5%. **3)** It requires a little more memory to store the extra scaled versions. This memory increase is not significant since the two extra cache levels add images scaled to 6.25% and 3.125%, which don't take up much memory. **4)** It causes the Histogram palette to become less accurate (but update faster) as you zoom out on your image. Clicking on the warning triangle in the upper left of the Histogram palette will display an accurate histogram based on the full size image.

Removed Cache for Histograms

The *Use Cache for Histograms* option that was available in Photoshop CS has been removed in CS2. This change causes the histogram in the Levels dialog box to always be based on a full sized image, but has no effect on the Histogram palette (which uses cached images so that it can update in real-time while you adjust an image).

Increased Memory Usage

When Photoshop is launched, it reserves a certain amount of the memory you have installed in your computer (also known as RAM). The *Memory Usage* setting determines the exact amount of memory that is reserved for Photoshop. This memory can be used by other programs as long as Photoshop is not actively using it.

Adobe changed the *Memory Usage* setting from 50% to 70% in CS2. That will cause Photoshop to use more of your installed memory and therefore run faster, but at the expense of other programs. I don't suggest that you boost this setting much higher than 70% because pushing it too high can actually slow down Photoshop's performance. If Photoshop hogs too much of the memory installed in your computer, then your operating system and Photoshop start to fight for memory as the combination of the two call for more than is installed in your computer. When that happens, everything slows down.

Type

All the Type related settings have been moved to a Preferences pane of their own. They used to be found in the *General* Preferences pane, but additional settings were added that made that pane too crowded. The only new option in this area is the *Font Preview Size* setting which allows you to view a sample of each font when choosing from the **Font** pop-up menu that's associated with the Type tool. To learn more about this new functionality, visit *Chapter 06: Small Gems for Design.*

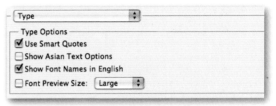

Options found in the Type Preferences pane.

Tiny Tweaks

We've made it through all the attention-grabbing features, so now let's move under the radar and explore the ones that might seem barely noticeable, but are actually quite worthwhile.

Improved Actions Palette

At first glance you might think the Actions palette is unchanged, but it only takes a few minutes of playing before you'll notice that some things are different.

Speed Improvements

Adobe has made some dramatic speed improvements to CS2's Actions palette. Most of the enhancements are due to concentrating processor use on applying the action instead of updating the screen. The following changes help to kick actions into overdrive:

- Palettes are not redrawn in Windows until the action is finished or reaches a Stop command.
- Main image windows are not redrawn until the action is finished.
- Actions are now less memory hungry since they don't use the memory needed to draw layer thumbnails after each step of the action.

This speed increase will also affect many of the choices found under the **File>Automate** menu (like **Contact Sheet** and **Web Photo Gallery**) because they use actions behind the scenes. The most dramatic speed increase can be seen with Windows operating systems. That's because a few extra tweaks were made and the previous implementation allowed for so much screen re-draw that Windows had a performance penalty over the Mac when it came to actions.

If you prefer to have Photoshop update the screen between every step of an action and effectively bring back the previous version's slow behavior, then choose **Playback Options** from the side menu of the Actions palette and turn on the *Step By Step* option.

Small Changes

The speed increase is the largest improvement to Photoshop CS2's Actions palette, but there are a few other tweaks hiding in the wings:

- Keyboard shortcuts assigned to actions now show up when viewing actions in List mode (they used to only appear when in Button mode).
- The default actions have been changed to a list of workspaces that can also be chosen from the **Window>Workspace** menu. To load the default actions that were available in Photoshop CS, choose **Sample Actions** from the side menu of the Actions palette.

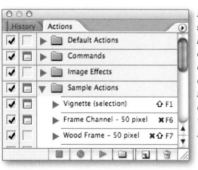

Keyboard shortcuts that have been assigned to actions now appear to the right of the action when viewed in List mode.

Improved Info Palette

The Info Palette hasn't seen many changes over the years, but with CS2 Adobe cleaned out the cobwebs, gave it a bit of a facelift and a new purpose in life, all of which has made this palette the new command central for information about your document.

Flexible Size

The Info palette always had a fixed width in previous versions of Photoshop. That caused problems if you attempted to stack multiple palettes (by dragging the name of one palette to the bottom edge of another palette) because it caused all the stacked palettes to be limited to the width of the Info palette. That's all history now because the Info palette can be resized (via its lower right corner) in Photoshop CS2. That means that you can now stack it on top of the Layers palette without limiting the width of the palette.

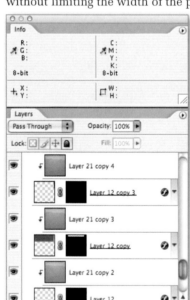

The Info palette can now be stacked on top of the Layers palette without restricting the width of the palette stack.

Status Information

Over the years, Adobe has added more and more features to the **Status** pop-up menu that appears at the bottom of most document windows. There was only enough space to display one setting at a time, so although the information was useful,

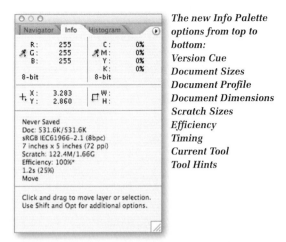

The new Info Palette options from top to bottom:
Version Cue
Document Sizes
Document Profile
Document Dimensions
Scratch Sizes
Efficiency
Timing
Current Tool
Tool Hints

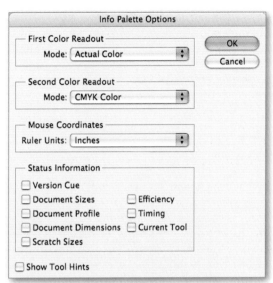

The Info Palette Options dialog box.

viewing it was annoying because most of us want to see more than one setting in a single glance. CS2 brings good news. Most of the information that is found in that special menu can now be added to the redesigned Info palette by choosing **Palette Options** from the side menu of the palette. Let's take a look at each of the new settings.

Version Cue: Indicates the Version Cue work-group status of a document (open, unmanaged, unsaved, etc). Version Cue does not ship with the stand-alone version of Photoshop and is beyond the scope of this book.

Document Sizes: The left side of this readout indicates the document's size when it contains just what's needed to print the document (a flattened version of the image with no layers, extra channels, etc.). The right side indicates the document's size when it includes all the layers, channels and other extras. This gives you a good idea of how bloated your file might be becoming and how small it will be when you're finished and want to flatten the image and save it for printing. These numbers are a good indication, but do not reflect the actual file size of the document because it does not take into account the final file format that will be used.

Document Profile: Indicates the ICC Color Profile that is being used to determine how to accurately display an image. This is useful for color geeks who want to see if an image contains the proper profile. If it indicates that an image is Untagged,

then you can choose **Edit>Assign Profile** to add a profile.

Document Dimensions: Indicates the width, height and resolution of the document based on the measurement system currently being used to display rulers on-screen (via the *Units & Rulers* Preference pane). This can be useful when determining if an image has sufficient resolution to be used for different methods of printing.

Scratch Sizes: The right side of the readout indicates how much total memory (RAM) is available to work with images. The left side of the readout indicates how much of that memory is being used for all the images that are currently open. When the number on the left becomes larger than the one on the right, then Photoshop is being forced to use your hard drive (known as the scratch disk) as a substitute for memory. Since hard drives are much slower than memory, having the number on the left constantly higher than the one on the right is a good indication that installing more memory would speed things up.

Efficiency: Indicates the percentage of time when Photoshop was able to process an image completely in memory. If the efficiency is ever below 100%, the processing of the image has been slowed down because Photoshop had to read and write data to the scratch disk (which is much slower than memory). If this number is consistently below 100%, then installing more memory could help Photoshop speed things up.

Timing: Indicates how many seconds it took to complete the last operation (filter, adjustment, etc.). This can be useful when comparing different computer setups (such as figuring out whether certain filters run faster or slower when different amounts of memory are installed).

Current Tool: For those people who are too lazy to glance at the Tool palette, this readout indicates which tool is currently active.

Show Tool Hints: Gives you quick and dirty instructions on how to use the currently selected tool. This is especially useful when you're either new to Photoshop or when a new feature is introduced. It will often indicate keyboard commands that can be used with a tool that are not immediately obvious.

Video Features

If you use Photoshop to create graphics that will be broadcast on television or reproduced on video tape or DVDs, then you'll be happy to hear about the following new features in CS2.

New Document Presets

When creating a new document via the **File>New** menu, you'll find six new preset sizes from which to choose: five different motion picture formats and one additional preset for high definition television.

| NTSC DV 720 x 480 (with guides) |
| NTSC DV Widescreen, 720 x 480 (with guides) |
| NTSC D1 720 x 486 (with guides) |
| NTSC D1 Square Pix, 720 x 540 (with guides) |
| PAL D1/DV, 720 x 576 (with guides) |
| PAL D1/DV Widescreen, 720 x 576 (with guides) |
| PAL D1/DV Square Pix, 768 x 576 (with guides) |
| HDV, 1280 x 720 (with guides) |
| HDV, 1440 x 1080 anamorphic (with guides) |
| HDV, 1920 x 1080 (with guides) |
| D4 |
| Cineon Half |
| Film (2K) |
| D16 |
| Cineon Full |

New film and video presets are available in the File>New dialog box.

Actions

Adobe partnered with two video production experts to create a new set of video related actions. You can load the actions by choosing **Video Actions** from the side menu of the Actions palette. Here's a brief rundown of what each of these actions will do for you:

Alpha Channel from Visible Layers: These actions produce an alpha channel that can be used to make transparent areas (which look like a checkerboard in Photoshop) appear transparent when overlaid on video. An inverted version of the same action is necessary when outputting to an Avid system.

Broadcast Safe Luminance: When images are used for broadcast television, the audio and video are combined into one signal. This is done by limiting the brightness range of the video and utilizing the leftover range for the audio signal (they are separate, but can bleed together). Pure white should not be used in an image destined for broadcast television as it causes an audible buzz (because it is intruding into the range usually reserved for audio), and pure black is reserved for other purposes. The Broadcast Safe Luminance action will limit the brightness range of an image so that it does not intrude into the range reserved to carry the audio signal. This will make the image look somewhat dull in Photoshop, but it will not look that way when viewed on broadcast television.

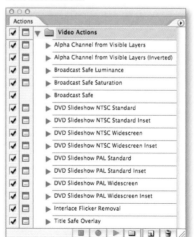

To access the video related actions, choose Video Actions from the side menu of the Actions palette.

Broadcast Safe Saturation: Overly saturated colors tend to bleed when displayed on broadcast television. This action is designed to limit the saturation of the colors that make up an image, which will prevent problems when output to video. This action should only be used when an image has overly saturated colors. The Broadcast Safe action will apply both the Luminance and Saturation actions mentioned above.

DVD Slideshow: Images that come from digital cameras and flatbed scanners use square pixels. When they are displayed on a video device they can become distorted. That's because the pixels used to display most video images are rectangular (except High Definition, which often uses square pixels). The DVD slideshow actions are designed to resize and properly distort those square pixel images so that they will look normal on video. The actions that end in "Inset" should be used when an image will be displayed on a television set (which crops the image a small amount), while the others are designed for digital projectors and other devices (that do not crop the image).

Interlace Flicker Removal: Single pixel-tall horizontal lines will flicker when viewed on a television set. To prevent this type of problem, try applying the Interlace Flicker Removal action which will blur those lines ever so slightly in an attempt to prevent flickering.

Title Safe Overlay: When you use one of the new document presets that are designed for video, you'll be presented with guides that represent the Action Safe and Title Safe areas of the image. If you prefer to use guides for other purposes, you can apply the Broadcast Safe action, which will create a layer that contains two red rectangles that indicate those safe regions (just be sure to hide that layer before sending the graphics out to a video device).

NOTE

Video Resource
If you need to learn how to integrate Photoshop into a video production workflow, then visit Richard Harrington's awesome web site at www.photoshopforvideo.com. He's the guy who created most of the new video actions in CS2.

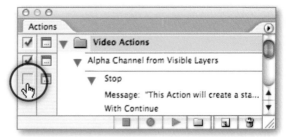

Turn off the eyeball icon next to the initial stop to prevent a descriptive message from displaying each time you run one of the video related actions.

Each of these actions displays an introduction message at the beginning of the action. If you plan to use the actions frequently, you'll probably want to disable the introduction message in each action. To do that, click on the arrow next to the action's name (to see the steps that make up the action) and then turn off the checkbox that appears to the left of the first step in the action.

Video Preview

If you have a video device hooked to your computer via a FireWire cable (such as a camcorder), then you can set up how video should be sent to the device and preview the results by choosing **File>Export>Video Preview**. Then, anytime you need to output images to video, choose **File>Export>Send Video Preview to Device** which will use the settings you previously set up to send video to a device. If you plan to use these commands on a regular basis, then consider assigning a keyboard shortcut to the menu items by choosing **Edit>Keyboard Shortcuts**.

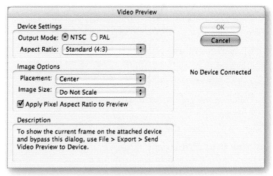

The File>Export>Video Preview dialog box.

NOTE

Power Up Devices First

Before launching Photoshop, be sure to power up the video device to which you plan to output graphics. It only looks for devices during launch and will not be able to output to devices that were not found at the time of the launch.

All The Rest

The rest of the tiny tweaks are just that–tiny. Here I present a list of the truly microscopic (but not necessarily inconsequential) changes that were introduced in Photoshop CS2:

- **Activation:** Photoshop will ask you to activate the program the first time you launch the software (this process is new to the Mac). Activating sends your serial number to Adobe over the internet (or you can call them) to make sure that it hasn't been used to install Photoshop on more than two machines. If you buy a new computer, you'll need to de-activate your old machine by choosing **Help>Transfer Activation** before you'll be able to install Photoshop on the new machine.

- **Better Cursor Visibility:** In the past it was very easy to lose sight of your cursor when moving over areas that were close to 50% gray. In Photoshop CS2, you can easily see your cursor no matter where you move it in an image.

- **Shadow/Highlight in CMYK:** The **Image>Adjustments>Shadow Highlight** adjustment now works in CMYK mode (it used to be limited to RGB mode).

- **Shift-Control-Tab on Mac:** For quite some time, you've been able to type **Control-Tab** on Mac or Windows to cycle through the currently open documents. You can now type **Shift-Control-Tab** to move backwards through the documents, which was possible on Windows, but is a new capability on the Mac. These commands are useful when you want to run a simple slide show from Photoshop.

- **New Pressure Icons:** The *Pen Pressure* checkbox that was found in Options bar of the Magnetic Lasso tool has been replaced with an icon.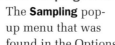

- **New Sampling Icons:** The **Sampling** pop-up menu that was  found in the Options bar for the Background Eraser and Color Replacement tool has been replaced by icons. From left to right the icons represent: Continuous, Once and Background Swatch. I don't find them to be an improvement whatsoever because the purpose of the icons are not immediately clear.

- **Floating Help:** Photoshop's Help application (**Help>Photoshop Help** from Photoshop) can now be viewed as a floating window that stays on top of all other applications (by clicking on the Compact Mode icon in the upper right of the Help window). This allows you to read the Help files while working in Photoshop.

- **Breaks The 2GB RAM Barrier:** Previous versions of Photoshop were limited to accessing 2 Gigabytes of RAM. Photoshop CS2 can access more than 2GB if your hardware and operating system allow for it. (Many older operating systems have a 2GB cap.)

- **PDF Presets:** You can setup PDF presets that can be used when saving a PDF file (via the **File>Save As** or **File>Automate>PDF Presentation** dialog boxes) by choosing **Edit>Adobe PDF Presets**.

- **Improved Scripting:** If you want to go way beyond simple actions and turn Photoshop into a robotic image processor, then you'll want to explore scripting (it's beyond the scope of this book). Photoshop's support for scripting has been expanded and the documentation has been vastly improved.

- **Dash Means Hidden:** When choosing palettes from the **Window** menu, a minus sign indicates palettes that are already open on screen, but that are partially hidden beneath other palettes. Choosing the palette name should bring it to the front.

- **Scan Money:** Photoshop CS prevented you from scanning or opening images of U.S. currency. You can now open these images and you'll be presented with a warning instead of being prevented from using the image.

> **NOTE**
>
> **Determining Screen Resolution**
>
> *To get an accurate Print Size view, create a 1 x 1 inch new document with a resolution setting of 100 Pixels Per Inch. Next, choose **Window>Navigator** and move the slider that appears at the bottom of the palette until the document width matches the one inch mark on a physical ruler that you hold up to your screen. Once the two match, choose **Preferences>Units & Rulers** from the **Photoshop** menu (Mac) or Edit menu (Win) and enter the percentage that appears in the lower left of the Navigator palette (minus any decimals) and then choose **View>Print Size** to see if the document's width matches the physical ruler.*

- **Dual Monitor Support:** Just for you Windows users. You can now have full screen documents on both monitor setups because documents are no longer confined to the application background. If you want documents and palettes to move with the application background, hold down the **Shift** key.

- **Print Size Works:** In previous versions of Photoshop, the **View>Print Size** command would rarely reflect the size a document would be when printed. In Photoshop CS2 it's possible to get the **Print Size** command to accurately reflect the printed size of a document (see note above to see how to set it up correctly).

- **Tile Horizontally or Vertically:** When choosing to tile the currently open documents (via the **Window>Arrange** menu), you now have the choice to **Tile Horizontally** or **Tile Vertically**.

The thing about Photoshop upgrades is that you can't afford to fall asleep at the wheel. If you just skim through the list of changes, you might be tempted to write some of them off as irrelevant, but inevitably there will be at least one 'tiny' change that will sneak up on you and cause you literally hours of frustration because you didn't know it could affect your work. So, while you're having fun playing with the big new toys (like warping), try to set some time aside for the less flamboyant features, because you never know which one will turn out to be your next best friend.

uptospeed

Section II
Design

Chapter 3
The New Layers Palette

THE ALMIGHTY LAYERS PALETTE HAS gone under the knife for some major surgery. Some see the changes as a vast improvement, while others view the overhaul as an unwelcome invasion into sacred territory. For better or worse, the new palette is here to stay, so let's dive in and get it working as quickly as possible so that it's not too disruptive to your workflow.

There are enough similarities between the old and the new that you won't feel completely like a duck out of water, but your brain is going to need a bit of reprogramming before you're entirely comfortable with the new design.

Below is an overview of what we'll be covering in this chapter:

- **Multi-Layer Select:** Learn to select multiple layers using a variety of techniques.
- **Manipulating Multiple Layers:** Once you have multiple layers selected, they act much like linked layers did in Photoshop CS. Learn all your options from merging to applying styles.
- **Smaller Tweaks:** Check out the smaller (but no less significant) refinements that changed the way in which the Layers palette behaves. Make sure to read this entire section, or risk great frustration because those little tweaks can sneak up on you.

Where's My Stuff?

Missing old features? Here's what happened:

- **Link Column:** The link column is gone. You can still link layers by selecting multiple layers and then clicking the Link icon at the bottom of the Layers palette.
- **Layer Mask/Layer Icon:** The icon that indicates if a layer or a mask is active is gone. To compensate, they made the border around the active item more obvious by making it show up just on the corners of the thumbnail image.
- **Layer Set Feature:** This feature (which looks like a folder) has been renamed Layer Groups and all the functionality is still available.
- **Click for Selection:** If you're used to holding **Command** (Mac) or **Ctrl** (Win) and clicking on the name of a layer to get a selection of its contents, you'll now have to be more precise and click on the layer's thumbnail image.

Subtle But Significant Changes

Below is a side-by-side comparison of the CS and CS2 Layers features. Many of the menu items that used to relate to linked layers have been replaced with choices that pertain to multiple selected layers. For instance, the Merge Linked command has become the Merge Layers command. Subtle changes have also been made to the location and style of many features. For instance, the location of the Layer Styles eyeball icons has moved slightly, and the triangle that expands or collapses the list of Layer Styles has also moved and looks a bit different.

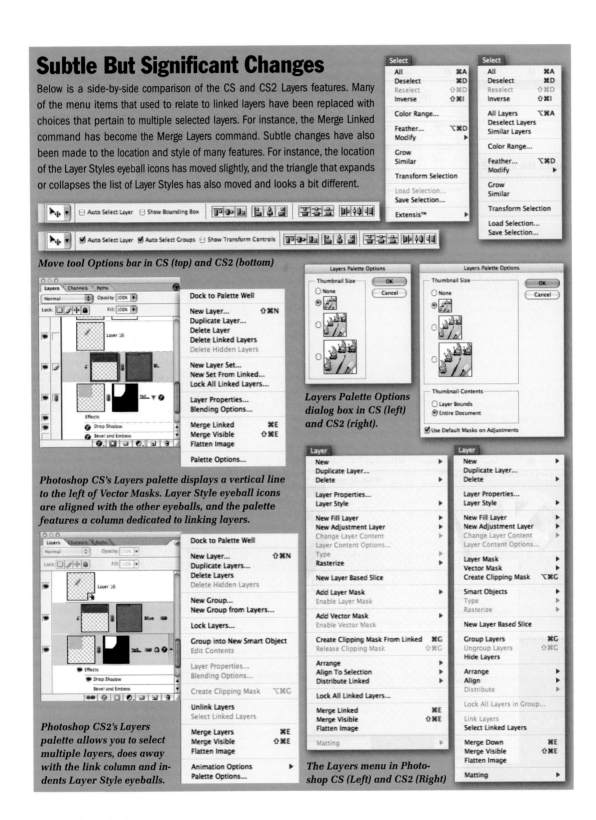

Move tool Options bar in CS (top) and CS2 (bottom)

Layers Palette Options dialog box in CS (left) and CS2 (right).

Photoshop CS's Layers palette displays a vertical line to the left of Vector Masks. Layer Style eyeball icons are aligned with the other eyeballs, and the palette features a column dedicated to linking layers.

Photoshop CS2's Layers palette allows you to select multiple layers, does away with the link column and in- dents Layer Style eyeballs.

The Layers menu in Photo- shop CS (Left) and CS2 (Right)

- **Merge Linked Command: Control-click** (Mac) or **Right-click** (Win) on a layer that is linked, choose *Select Linked Layers* and then **Control-click** (Mac) or **Right-click** (Win) again and choose *Merge Layers* from the menu that appears (or type **Command-E** (Mac) or **Ctrl-E** (Win) with the linked layers selected).

Multi-Layer Select

Photoshop CS2 brought on one of the biggest changes ever made to the Layers palette. You now have the ability to make more than one layer active by selecting multiple layers, much the same way you can select multiple files on the hard drive of your computer.

Selecting Multiple Layers

There are many ways to select multiple layers. Let's look at each approach so you can decide for yourself which one will work best for each situation you might encounter in the Layers palette.

Keyboard/Mouse Combinations

Holding **Shift** when clicking on layers (within the Layers palette) will select all the layers between the first layer and the last layer on which you clicked. Holding **Command** (Mac) or **Ctrl** (Win) when clicking on a layer will either select or de-select a layer depending on its previous state.

Auto Select Layer

When the Move tool is active, a checkbox called *Auto Select Layer* will be available in the Options bar that extends across the top of your screen. When that option is turned on, clicking within the document window will cause Photoshop to make the top-most layer (that contains pixels in that area) to become active. Holding **Shift** while clicking—with *Auto Select Layer* turned on—will add layers to the ones that are currently selected (or if the layer is already selected, it will become de-selected).

The Auto Select Layer option can be found among the Move tool's Options bar settings.

You can also click and drag while the *Auto Select Layer* checkbox is turned on to draw a selection rectangle. When you release the mouse button, Photoshop will select all the layers that contain information within the rectangle. Just make sure your initial click is over a layer that is not already selected, otherwise you'll end up moving the previously selected layers instead of doing what you intended, which is to select other layers. You can also lock the position of a layer (using the Lock icons at the top of the Layers palette) to prevent a layer from moving when multiple layers are selected.

If you're working with Groups, try out the *Auto Select Groups* checkbox in the Move tool's Options bar. When that checkbox is turned on, clicking on a layer that is inside a group (which looks like a folder) will cause the group to become selected instead of the individual layer that contains information under your cursor. Turning the checkbox off will cause Photoshop to select individual layers regardless of whether they are inside a group or not.

You can temporarily toggle the *Auto Select Layer* feature on or off by holding **Command** (Mac) or **Ctrl** (Win) while the Move tool is active. The checkbox in the Options bar will not indicate that the feature has been toggled, but for the time you hold the Command/Ctrl key, Photoshop will act as if you changed the *Auto Select Layer* checkbox. If you prefer to leave the *Auto Select Layer* checkbox turned off, then hold **Shift-Command** (Mac) or **Shift-Ctrl** (Win) and click within the document window to make another layer active. That makes it more difficult to accidently switch the layer that is active.

The *Auto Select Groups* checkbox is used when Command/Ctrl-clicking with the Move tool. The only problem is that the checkbox is grayed out when the *Auto Select Layers* checkbox is turned off. If you want to change that setting while using the Command/Ctrl-click method, turn on the *Auto Select Layers* checkbox, change the *Auto Select Groups* setting and then turn the *Auto Select Layers* checkbox back off again.

The Select Menu

There are three new options available under the Select menu that relate to selecting layers:

All Layers: This command will select all the layers in the entire document. This can be useful when you want to drag all the layers into another document or group them into a Smart Object.

Deselect Layers: This command will cause all the layers to be deselected leaving you with a Layers palette that doesn't have any layers selected. When no layers are selected, many of Photoshop's tools and menu commands will be grayed out since they need to know which layer they should affect.

Similar Layers: This command will select layers based on the contents of the currently selected layer (it's grayed out when multiple layers are selected). It can differentiate between the following types of layers: pixel-based layers, Type layers, Shape Layers, Groups, and Smart Objects. I find this to be especially useful when I want to quickly change type related settings or copy and paste Layer Styles between layers.

Select Linked Layers

If the currently selected layer is linked to other layers, you can add the linked layers to the current selection by choosing *Select Linked Layers* from either the Layer menu or the side menu of the Layers palette. I use this command a lot when I want to change the linking state of multiple layers (as I'll describe in the next section).

Select	
All	⌘A
Deselect	⌘D
Reselect	⇧⌘D
Inverse	⇧⌘I
All Layers	⌥⌘A
Deselect Layers	
Similar Layers	
Color Range...	
Feather...	⌥⌘D
Modify	▶
Grow	
Similar	
Transform Selection	
Load Selection...	
Save Selection...	

The Select menu contains some new commands that relate to layers.

Manipulating Multiple Layers

Now that you know how to select multiple layers, let's see what you can do with them. There are some limitations—for instance, you can't adjust or apply filters to multiple layers—but there are also a good number of worthwhile features that you can use when you have multiple layers selected:

- **Move:** To reposition the selected layers, use the Move tool. You can also drag them to another document.
- **Transform:** To scale or rotate the layers, choose from the **Edit>Transform** menu. (You cannot apply warping to multiple layers without first grouping them into a Smart Object.)
- **Change Stacking Order:** To move all of the selected layers to a particular position within the layers stacking order, drag one of the selected layers up or down in the layers stack (or choose from the **Layer>Arrange** menu). You can also choose **Layer>Arrange>Reverse** to reverse the stacking order of the layers.

The stacking order of the six photo layers were reversed using the Layer>Arrange>Reverse command.

- **Align/Distribute Layers:** Either choose from the options found under the **Layer>Align** and **Layer>Distribute** menus or click on the Align/Distribute icons that appear in the Options bar while the Move tool is active.

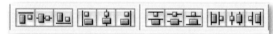

The Align and Distribute icons will appear in the Options bar when the Move tool is active and multiple layers are selected.

- **Lock Layers:** To lock the selected layers, choose **Lock Layers** from the **Layer** menu or from the side menu of the Layers palette (the Lock icons in the Layers palette are not available when multiple layers are selected).

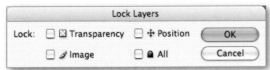

The Lock Layers dialog box.

- **Hide Layers:** Choose **Layer>Hide Layers** to turn off the eyeball icons for the selected layers and hide them in the main image window.
- **Link Layers:** Choose **Link Layers** from either the Layer menu, the side menu of the Layers palette, or click the Link icon at the bottom of the Layers palette. More later on the differences between linked layers and selected layers.
- **Delete Layers:** Choose **Delete Layers** from either the Layer menu or the side menu of the Layers palette (or click the Trash icon at the bottom of the Layers palette).
- **Duplicate Layers:** Choose **Duplicate Layers** from either the Layer menu or the side menu of the Layers palette (the As field is not available when multiple layers are selected and the Name field is only used when duplicating to a new or different document), or hold Option/Alt when dragging with the Move tool.
- **Merge Layers:** Choose **Merge Layers** from either the Layer menu or the side menu of the Layers palette (or type **Command/Ctrl-E**).
- **Apply Layer Styles:** Clicking on a Layer Style preset from within the Styles palette will apply the style to all the selected layers.
- **Create Group:** To place multiple layers into a folder (formerly known as a Layer Set, but now known as a Group), select the layers you wish to place in the folder, choose **Group Layers** from the **Layer** menu, or choose **New Group** from the side menu of the Layers palette, or **Shift-click** the Group icon at the bottom of the Layers palette (clicking the Group icon without Shift creates an empty group).

- **Create Smart Object:** To transform your selected layers into a Smart Object, choose **Group Into New Smart Object** from the **Layer>Smart Objects** menu or from the side menu of the Layers palette. Smart Objects are covered in *Chapter 4: Smart Objects*.
- **Change Text Settings:** Any text settings made while multiple layers are selected will apply to all the selected layers. This applies to changes made from the Character and Paragraphs palettes and the choices that appear in the Options bar when the Type tool is active.
- **Warp Text Layers:** Choosing **Layer>Type>Warp Text** will cause all selected layers to be warped even though the on-screen preview only shows the top selected layer as being warped. Clicking OK will warp all the selected layers.

> **NOTE**
>
> **Type Settings**
> *If the selected layers have different attributes (size, font, etc.), then the settings shown in various palettes will be those of the top selected Type layer.*
>
> **Stop Double-Clicking**
> *If you're used to double-clicking on the Type layer's thumbnail in the Layers palette, then beware, because that will deselect any previously selected layers and cause your changes to apply to a single layer.*

A single layer will reflect the changes when warping multiple Type layers, but clicking OK in the Warp Text dialog box will warp all the selected layers.

Many of the above commands can also be initiated by choosing from the menu that appears when you **Control-click** (Mac) or **Right-click** (Win) on a selected layer within the Layers palette.

If you find that any of the above commands are not available, then check to see if all the layers are visible, if there is a selection active, or if the Background is one of the layers selected. All of those instances can cause problems depending on which command you are attempting to use.

Layer Properties...
Blending Options...

Duplicate Layers...
Delete Layers

Group into New Smart Object

Rasterize Layers

Disable Layer Mask
Disable Vector Mask
Create Clipping Mask

Link Layers
Select Linked Layers

Select Similar Layers

Copy Layer Style
Paste Layer Style
Clear Layer Style

Merge Layers
Merge Visible
Flatten Image

The menu above appears when you Control-click (Mac), or Right-click (Win) on a selected layer within the Layers palette.

Linking

Linking was necessary in previous versions of Photoshop because it was the only way to align, transform or move more than one layer (that is, without putting them in a folder). But now that multiple layers can be selected, the ability to link layers is less essential. Because of that, Adobe decided to remove the link column from the Layers palette (as seen in previous versions of Photoshop). You can still link multiple layers (they just don't have a column

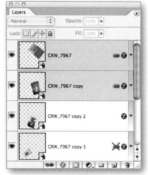

The link column from Photoshop CS is no longer available in CS2.

> ### NOTE
>
> **Linked Sets**
>
> *A linked set is a number of layers that are linked together and are independent of all other linked sets. For instance, the top three layers of a document might be linked together, which creates a linked set. Then, independent of those layers, the bottom three layers might also be linked together creating a second linked set that is not related to the first set. Selecting one or more layers from each link set would be known as having a selection that contains mixed linked sets.*

you can click on to link and unlink layers), but the process is quite different and unfortunately much more complex and bothersome than what you might be used to.

To link multiple layers, select the layers you'd like to link and then click the Link icon at the bottom of the Layers palette, or choose *Link Layers* from either the Layer menu or the side menu of the Layers palette. The results you'll get depend on which layers were selected:

- If the selected layers are not yet linked to any other layers, then they will all become linked.
- If the selection contains only linked layers, then the Link icon will unlink all the layers.
- If the selected layers are from mixed linked sets and contain only linked layers, then the layers will become unlinked.
- If the selected layers are from mixed linked sets and include at least one layer that is not yet linked, then all the selected layers will be linked and any unselected layers that were part of those link sets will be unlinked.
- If the selected layers include at least one layer from a single linked set, and one or more non-linked layers, then the linked set is extended to include the unlinked layers in the selection.
- If the selected layers include a mixture of linked and unlinked layers, holding **Command** (Mac) or **Ctrl** (Win) when clicking the Link icon will cause all the layers to be unlinked.

If you're used to linking and unlinking layers in previous versions of Photoshop, you might get frustrated because you can no longer click on the link symbol that appears on a layer to unlink that layer from the current link set. Instead, you need to select the layers you'd like to unlink from the current link set and then click the link symbol to unlink them. Clicking on one of the layers in that link set will cause the link symbols to appear (minus the layers you just unlinked).

The problem with the above technique is that it forces you to deselect the very layers you want to work with and it can be difficult to remember which layers you were originally working with.

An alternative method is to **Control-click** (Mac) or **Right-click** (Win) on one of the linked layers, and then choose **Select Linked Layers** to get all the layers in that link set selected. Now you can temporarily unlink those layers by clicking on the Link icon at the bottom of the Layers palette. Then hold **Command** (Mac) or **Ctrl** (Win), click on the layers you want to permanently unlink to remove them from the selection, and then click the Link icon one more time to re-link the layers that remain selected. It's a pain, but once you've gone through it a few times, it becomes easier.

If you don't need to permanently unlink a layer but would like to temporarily unlink it so that changes to the other linked layers will not affect it, you can temporarily disable the link. Do that by holding **Shift** and clicking on the link symbol that appears on the right side of a layer. Once you're done making changes to the linked and selected layers, then you can **Shift**-click the link symbol one more time to re-enable the link.

Shift-clicking on a link symbol will temporarily disable the link. Shift-clicking again will turn it back on.

Smaller Tweaks

Once you start to work with the revamped Layers palette and give the major new features a workout, you'll start to notice that many smaller, less noticeable features have also been tweaked. On some level they may seem less than critical, but pay attention because these changes can make a big difference to your work.

Layer Masks: A Layer Mask is a grayscale image attached to a layer where areas of black hide the contents of the layer and areas of white allow the layer to show up. The general concept of Layer Masks has not changed in CS2, but the way in which you use and view them has been altered.

Previous versions of Photoshop displayed an icon in the link column of the active layer to indicate if the layer (Paintbrush icon) or mask (Layer Mask icon) was active. That column has been removed, so you will no longer see those icons. Instead, you now have to inspect the border of the thumbnail images that appear in the Layers palette. Photoshop places L-shaped lines on the corners of the active item (layer or mask).

You can tell what is active (layer or mask) by inspecting the corners of the thumbnail images shown in the Layers palette. In this example the Layer Mask is active.

You can now drag a Layer Mask onto another layer to move it to the new location. Holding **Option** (Mac) or **Alt** (Win) will drag a copy of the Layer Mask. Adding the **Shift** key to the above technique will invert the mask when moving or copying it to another layer. Dragging a Layer Mask onto a layer that already has a Layer Mask attached will prompt Photoshop to ask you if you want to replace the mask.

Layer Sets Become Groups: In previous versions of Photoshop, you could put multiple layers into a collapsible folder that was known as a Layer Set. In Photoshop CS2, Adobe decided to rename the Layer Sets feature and call it a Group. All of the usual functionality is still available, but the menu commands used to access the feature have been reworked.

It used to be that you had to link multiple layers together if you wanted to quickly place them in a folder. Now all you have to do is select the layers and do one of the following: choose **Layer>Group Layers**, type **Command-G** (Mac) or **Ctrl-G** (Win), or hold **Shift** and click the Folder icon at the bottom of the Layers palette.

Layer Styles: As before, you can apply simple effects to a layer (drop shadows, glows, etc.) using the Layer Styles pop-up menu at the bottom of the Layers palette, but they have made a few tweaks to how they are applied.

In previous versions, if you wanted to copy the styles to another layer, you could drag the name of a Layer Style to the line that appears below each layer. In CS2, you need to drag the style to the middle of the layer instead of just below it. Also, dragging now moves the style instead of copying it. To make a copy of the style, you must now hold **Option** (Mac) or **Alt** (Win) while dragging the style. You can also drag the Layer Style icon on the right side of a layer to copy all the styles without having to view the styles as a list.

Adobe moved the eyeball icons for Layer Styles so that they are indented from the eyeball column in the Layers palette. That's not much of a change, but you might find that, as a consequence, it's much more difficult to figure out where to click to make a style visible. The eyeball column always showed a slight indent that made it easy to know where to click to toggle the visibility of a style, but the new version doesn't give any clue as to where you should click (click just to the left of the style name).

The middle three Layer Styles have been hidden. If all of them were hidden, there wouldn't be an obvious indication as to where to click to toggle them back on.

Merge A Copy: Typing **Shift-Command-Option-E** (Mac) or **Shift-Ctrl-Alt-E** (Win) will merge a copy of all the visible layers into a new layer. The new combined layer will appear above the top selected layer, or if no layers are selected it will appear at the top of the layers stack. This used to be a two step process and is useful when you need to apply a filter to a complex image (since filters only affect a single layer).

Show Layer Edges: Choosing **View>Show>Layer Edges** will cause a blue rectangle to appear around the edges of the active layers. This can

be useful when a Layer Mask is used to limit where a layer shows up (it shows you how far the image extends beyond the masked areas). It's also useful when working with layers that have a low opacity setting specified at the top of the Layers palette, which can make them difficult to see. If the content of the layer is feathered, then the box will be placed where the feathering is at least 50% opaque.

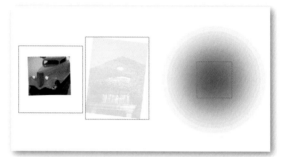

Left: This layer is masked to only reveal part of the layer's contents and the rectangle indicates how much of the image is hidden. Middle: This layer has an Opacity setting of 20% specified at the top of the Layers palette, which would make it difficult to see if placed on a complex background. Right: This layer has a feathered edge and the rectangle indicates where the layer is at least 50% opaque.

New Layers Palette Options: Choosing *Palette Options* from the side menu of the Layers palette will present you with a dialog box that contains a few new options.

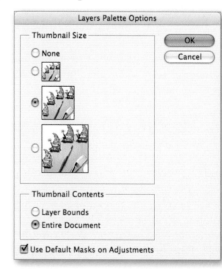

Choose Palette Options from the side menu of the Layers palette to access this dialog box.

These two Layers palettes are of identical documents. The left version is using the Layer Bounds setting, while the right one is using the Entire Document setting.

Turning off the *Use Default Masks on Adjustments* checkbox will cause Adjustment Layers to be created without the usual Layer Mask.

Setting the *Thumbnail Contents* setting to *Layer Bounds* will cause Photoshop to ignore the empty parts of a layer when creating the thumbnail images that appear in the Layers palette (instead of showing how the layer relates to the dimensions of the document). This option is useful when the layers in your document contain very small items that are almost impossible to see with the normal layers view, but it also makes it much more difficult to figure out where the contents of the layer are in relation to the rest of the document.

Adjust Opacity While Transforming: In previous versions, the Opacity and Blending Mode features in the Layers palette were grayed out when transforming a layer. In CS2, you can change both the Opacity and the Blending Mode of a layer while you are in the middle of transforming a layer. This only works when transforming individual layers; it does not work with linked layers or multiple selected layers (unless they are in a group folder, then you can change both the Blending mode and opacity of the entire group). Lowering the Opacity setting while transforming

a layer makes it much easier to figure out when the active layer aligns with the underlying layers. The Difference blending mode is especially useful when attempting to align to layers because it causes areas that align on both layers to turn solid black.

Drag a Duplicate: You can now hold **Option** (Mac) or **Alt** (Win) when dragging a layer (or layers) up or down in the layers stack to drag a copy of the original.

Most of the changes made to the Layers palette might seem to be small, but collectively they add up to be quite radical. It can take weeks or months to adjust to this new workflow depending on how often you work with layers. Reviewing this chapter a few times should help you to make the adjustments needed to get comfortable with the new Layers palette.

NEW/CHANGED KEYBOARD COMMANDS		
Feature	**Mac**	**Win**
Select layer above	Shift-Option-]	Shift-Alt-]
Select layer below	Shift-Option- [	Shift-Alt-[
Select top layer	Option-Period (.)	Alt-Period (.)
Select bottom layer	Option-Comma (,)	Alt-Comma (,)
Toggle Clipping Mask	Option-Command-G	Alt-Ctrl-G

Chapter 4
Smart Objects

S MART OBJECTS ISN'T JUST ANY new feature—it marks the dawn of an entirely different way of thinking and operating in Photoshop. Give it a test drive and you will surely marvel at its extraordinary abilities, and before you're even close to knowing all of its complexities, you will be fantasizing about how much work it's going to save you. There's no question that this feature is pure dynamite, but if you're an advanced user you might find the dynamite tends to fizzle the moment you apply a Layer Mask.

If you use a page-layout program like Adobe InDesign, you should be familiar with the concept of linked images. When you place an image on a page, you're just viewing a preview of the image that is stored on your hard drive. You're free to scale, rotate and crop the image, but you cannot edit the image directly in the page-layout program. Instead, you must open the linked image in Photoshop, resave it and then update the link to the image in the page-layout program.

Adobe took this idea and applied it to Photoshop. You can now 'place' a document into a Photoshop image as a Smart Object, which in effect embeds the layers of the placed file into the image. This Smart Object acts much like a linked file in that you are limited to scaling, transforming and masking its contents, and if you want to make edits you must do so in a separate document. What's more, you can duplicate a Smart Object layer many times over, edit the original, and all of the duplicates will automatically update to match the original.

It takes a bit of doing to get your bearings at first, but after a few tries it should be fairly straightforward. Here's what you'll learn in this chapter:

- **Introducing Smart Objects:** Learn the advantages and disadvantages of using this new technology.
- **Creating Smart Objects:** Learn to combine multiple layers into a single Smart Object.
- **Editing Smart Objects:** The fun starts when you learn to edit a Smart Object and watch your layout update to reflect the changes.
- **Transformations:** Learn to nondestructively bend and transform a Smart Object.
- **Multiple Instances:** Duplicate a Smart Object multiple times, edit the original, and see those changes cascade throughout your image.
- **Nested Smart Objects:** Placing one Smart Object inside another creates a few interesting challenges that you'll learn to overcome.
- **Smart Object Tips:** Find out what it takes to work more efficiently with Smart Objects.

Introducing Smart Objects

A Smart Object allows you to non-destructively scale and transform one or more layers while maintaining the edit-ability of those layers.

Advantages of Using Smart Objects

I'll show you how to create and manipulate these Smart Objects later in this chapter but before we get to that, let's look at what's possible when using this awesome new feature.

- You can scale, rotate or warp a Smart Object non-destructively and then edit or replace the contents of the Smart Object and Photoshop will remember all the transformations that were applied.
- You can duplicate a Smart Object multiple times, then edit the original Smart Object and the duplicates update to reflect the changes.
- You can convert a document that contains a full-color Smart Object to Grayscale mode and back again without losing color information.
- You can embed one Smart Object within another to simplify the Layers palette view of a complex document.
- You can place Adobe Illustrator files, scale them to any size while maintaining quality, and re-edit them in Illustrator.
- You can embed a Raw format image into a layered Photoshop file while retaining the ability to reinterpret the image using the Camera Raw dialog box.
- You can undo warping and other changes by exporting the contents of a Smart Object to an independent file.

Disadvantages of Using Smart Objects

Before you get into creating your own Smart Objects, you should be aware of a few disadvantages of using them.

- Smart Objects increase file size of documents because it's necessary to store both the layers that make up the Smart Object and a merged version of those layers to use as a placeholder.
- Masks attached to Smart Objects cannot be moved or transformed with the Smart Object.
- Nesting one Smart Object into another will cause the nested Smart Object to become independent of the original, so changes made to the original are not reflected in the nested one.
- Using certain features can cause the appearance of the image to change unpredictably when creating a Smart Object.

Now that you know the pros and cons of using Smart Objects, let's jump in and see what the dynamite is all about.

Creating Smart Objects

There is more than one way to create a Smart Object. You can 'place' an external file (via **File>Place**, which I'll describe later), or you can create one out of the layers that make up a Photoshop document. To go that route, select one or more layers and do the following: Choose **Group into New Smart Object** from either the side menu of the Layers palette, from the **Layer>Smart Objects** menu or by **Control-clicking** (Mac) or **Right-clicking** (Win) on a layer within the Layers palette. Before we go any further, it's important you understand that there are situations that can trip you up if you're not aware of them.

Features That Can Mess Up a Smart Object

The following features can cause an image to change appearance when grouping layers into a Smart Object:

Non Adjacent Layers: If the selected layers are not adjacent to each other in the layers stack, then the visual look of the document can change when those layers are combined into a Smart Object.

Adjustment Layers: Adjustment Layers will only affect the layers within the Smart Object.

Blending Modes: Blending Modes applied to layers will only interact with the layers found in the Smart Object and will not be able to affect the underlying layers, which may influence the document's appearance.

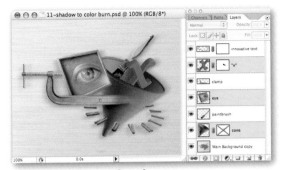

Non-adjacent layers selected.

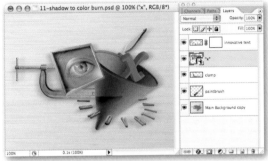

Result of grouping non-adjacent layers into a Smart Object (the layers effectively move to the same position).

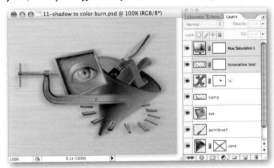

The Adjustment Layer at the top of this document is affecting all the layers.

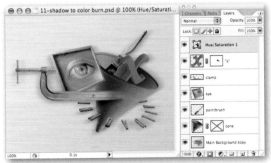

After merging into a Smart Object, the Adjustment Layer only affects the layers within the Smart Object.

The top layer is set to Multiply mode, which causes the white background on the scanned text to disappear.

After creating a Smart Object from the top three layers, the Multiply effect is no longer capable of interacting with the underlying layers, which causes the white background of the scanned text to become visible.

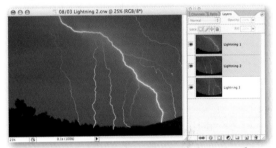

These lightning shots are combined together using the Underlying Layer Blending sliders.

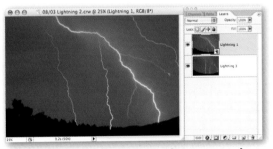

Grouping two layers into a Smart Object prevents the Blending sliders from affecting the bottom layer.

Blending Sliders: The Underlying Layer sliders in the Blending Options dialog box will only interact with the layers found in the Smart Object and will not be able to affect the underlying layers which may influence the document's appearance.

Knockout Deep: The *Knockout Deep* option in the Blending Options dialog box is limited to knocking out the layers found within the Smart Object, which will change the appearance of the document.

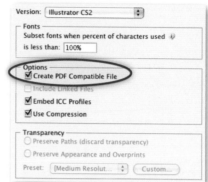

When saving an Adobe Illustrator file, be sure to turn on the Create PDF Compatible File checkbox.

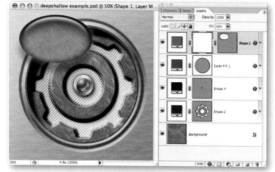

The oval in the upper left is getting its texture from the Background layer using the Knockout Deep setting.

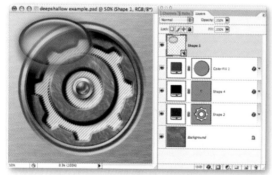

Using a Smart Object prevents the Knockout Deep setting from accessing the Background layer.

Smart Objects are not limited to containing Photoshop layers. Adobe Illustrator and Raw format images can also be turned into Smart Objects. This is done by either copying and

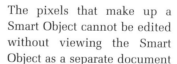

This dialog box will appear when pasting a vector-based image from Adobe Illustrator.

pasting from Illustrator, or by using the **File>Place** command. Placing a Raw file will cause the Camera Raw dialog box to appear, allowing you to specify the setting to use when opening the image. Illustrator documents can be saved in one of the following formats: Adobe Illustrator (.ai), Illustrator EPS (.eps), or Adobe PDF (.pdf). When saving in Illustrator format, be sure to turn on the *Create PDF Compatible File* checkbox, otherwise Photoshop will not be able to display the image.

Once you've created a Smart Object, it will show up as a single layer in the Layers palette. These newly created layers will feature a special icon in the lower right corner of their thumbnail image in the Layers palette, which designates them as a Smart Object.

The icon in the lower right indicates that this layer is a Smart Object.

The pixels that make up a Smart Object cannot be edited without viewing the Smart Object as a separate document (more on that later). Since the pixels are essentially locked, that means that Photoshop will not allow you to apply filters, adjust, or paint directly on the Smart Object.

However, you can effectively adjust a Smart Object by using an Adjustment Layer and clipping it to the underlying layer (via the **Layer>Create Clipping Mask** menu command). To apply a filter or paint on a Smart Object, you'll have to edit its contents or convert it into a normal layer.

Editing Smart Objects

To edit the contents of a Smart Object, either double-click on its thumbnail image in the Layers palette, or choose **Edit Contents** from the side menu of the Layers palette or from the **Layer>Smart Objects** menu.

The contents of the Smart Object will pop up in a separate document window where you can edit the layers from which it was made. Each of those layers can be modified using any of Photoshop's tools. Once changes have been made, choosing **File>Save** will update all the instances of that Smart Object within the original document.

Choosing **File>Save As** is not recommended since it will save a file on your hard drive that is independent of the Smart Object. That will prevent the changes from being reflected in the Smart Object since they were never saved back to the original document.

If you haven't made any changes to the document, then it's not necessary to save the image and you can simply close the document window to return to the original document.

Using the Layer>Smart Objects Menu

You'll find multiple editing options in the **Layer>Smart Objects** menu (these options are also available by Control-clicking (Mac) or Right-clicking (Win) on the name of a layer). Let's look at each option to see when they are useful:

Group Into New Smart Object

This option converts the currently active layers into a new Smart Object. It can also be used to nest one Smart Object into another.

New Smart Object via Copy

This option creates an independent Smart Object based on the currently active one. The resulting Smart Object might look identical to the original, but edits made to one will not affect the other.

Export Contents

This option launches a **Save** dialog box that allows you to name and save a new document that contains the layers that made up the Smart Object, leaving the parent document unchanged. This command has the added bonus of being able to extract placed Adobe Illustrator and Raw format images.

This image was created using the New Smart Object Via Copy command so that each of the images could be easily edited or replaced independent of the others.

The Replace Contents command was used on each Smart Object, which caused all transformations to be retained.

Replace Contents

This option allows you to replace the contents of a Smart Object with the contents of an external file. This is especially useful when working with Raw files as you can work with unadjusted placeholder images and replace them after finishing the layout.

Convert to Layer

This option in effect merges the layers that make up the Smart Object to create a single layer that is no longer a Smart Object. This is useful when you want to apply a filter or paint on a Smart Object. I'd suggest you apply this command to a duplicate of a Smart Object, so you still retain the edit-ability of the original Smart Object (useful if you don't like the results of applying a filter or painting on the converted layer).

Transformations

Smart Objects are unique in that you can non-destructively transform them (scale, rotate, warp, etc.). Being non-destructive means that the transformation settings are attached to the layer and while they affect its appearance, they are not permanently applied until you flatten the image or convert the Smart Object into a normal layer.

This unique quality allows you to transform the Smart Object multiple times without causing the successive transformations to damage the image. Transforming the layer a second time simply returns you to where you left off with your previ-

Left: a Raw file format image with warping applied, Right: Editing the Raw image maintains the warping.

ous transformation instead of starting fresh. That means that you can scale a Smart Object down to a fraction of its size and later scale it back to its original size without any loss of quality (you can also export a Smart Object and then use **File>Place** to place an undistorted version back into the document). Nesting one Smart Object inside another provides opportunities for even more versatility (more later in this chapter).

Multiple Instances

Duplicating a Smart Object will create an identical layer that is derived from the exact same layers that make up the original Smart Object (not a duplicate of the layers). Editing either one of the Smart Objects will cause the changes to be reflected in both Smart Objects. A duplicate is no different than the original since they both reference the exact same group of layers.

There are four methods for duplicating a Smart Object (I prefer the last one listed):

Choosing Edit>Transform>Warp on a layer that has already been warped (the mug is on a separate layer). Left: using a Smart Object allow you to re-edit a warp, Right: using a pixel-based layer causes Photoshop to treat the layer as if it hasn't been warped before.

Left: A single bolt was created and grouped into a Smart Object, which was duplicated and used throughout the document. A second Smart Object was used for each square background element. Right: Result of editing both of the Smart Objects.

1) Choose **Duplicate Layer** from the Layer menu or the side menu of the Layers palette.

2) Drag the Smart Object to the New Layer icon at the bottom of the Layers palette.

3) Hold **Option** (Mac) or **Alt** (Win) when repositioning the Smart Object with the Move tool.

4) Choose **Layer>New>Layer Via Copy**, or type **Command-J** (Mac) or **Ctrl-J** (Win).

Nested Smart Objects

You can nest one Smart Object within another by choosing **Layer>Group Into New Smart Object** while at least one Smart Object is selected. This can help to simplify overly complex images by reducing the numbers of layers that appear in the Layers palette.

To get a sense for how nesting can help when creating a complex image, go take a look at the opening image for *Chapter 5: Variables*. The spiral of business cards was created by turning each card into a separate Smart Object and then scaling and rotating each card to form a spiral. Once the spiral was created, it needed to be modified so that it matched elements in the background image and did not extend beyond the document's bounds. Warping was used to make this change, but since warping cannot usually be applied to multiple layers, the business cards were all grouped into another Smart Object, causing them to appear as a single layer which could be warped. Finally, the warped Smart Object was edited to reveal the individual business card Smart Objects from

Left: The rotated cards were grouped into a Smart Object. Right: The resulting Smart Object was warped.

The cards looked a little flat after warping the Smart Object that contained all the cards.

It was easy to warp and edit each individual card since each one was a separate Smart Object nested into a parent Smart Object that contained all the cards.

which it was made and each individual card was warped to add more dimension to the image.

There is no limit to how deeply Smart Objects can be nested. But nesting one Smart Object inside another will cause it to become independent of any other Smart Objects that are used outside the Smart Object in which it nests.

For instance, if the business card Smart Objects used in this example above appeared within the main document, and copies of them were nested into a Smart Object, then changes made to the Smart Objects used in the main document would not update those that had been nested into another Smart Object. Consequently, editing the Smart Object in which the cards were nested would not update the cards used within the main document. Nesting causes the Smart Objects to become independent of duplicates that appear outside of the Smart Object they are nested within and editing the Smart Objects will only update duplicates that appear at the same nesting level as the one that is being edited.

Smart Object Tips

Below is a collection of tips that should help you become more efficient when working with Smart Objects.

Appearance Testing: To test if the appearance of your document will change when grouping multiple layers into a Smart Object, do the following: Place the layers into a Layer Group (which looks like a folder and used to be known as a Layer Set) and change the Blending Mode of the Group (via the pop-up menu at the top of the Layers palette) from **Passthrough** to **Normal**. That will cause the appearance of the layers to reflect what would happen if they were grouped into a Smart Object.

Use a Group set to Normal mode to test what will happen when using a Smart Object.

Multi-Document Smart Objects: If you've used the same Smart Object in multiple documents (by copying and pasting or dragging between documents with the Move tool) and would like to have changes made to one Smart Object be reflected in the other documents, do the following: Make changes to one of the Smart Objects and save those changes so they appear in one document. Next, with the updated Smart Object active, choose **Layer>Smart Object>Export Contents** and save the Smart Object as an independent document. Now switch to the second document, and with the Smart Object layer active, choose **Layer>Smart Objects>Replace Contents** and point Photoshop to the file you just saved (repeat this for any other files containing the Smart Object).

Contextual Menu: Most of the Smart Object related commands can be accessed from a pop-up menu by **Control-clicking** (Mac) or **Right-clicking** (Win) on the name of a Smart Object within the Layers palette. The menu will not appear if a Layer Mask is being edited (click on that layer thumbnail to stop editing the mask).

Most of the commands found under the Layer>Smart Objects menu can also be accessed by Control/Right-clicking on the name of a Smart Object within the Layers palette.

Painting on a Smart Object: You cannot paint directly on a Smart Object layer because the pixels that make up the layer are locked (you'd have to edit the Smart Object in a separate document window to add paint to its contents). You can cheat a bit by creating a new empty layer directly above the Smart Object and then choosing **Layer>Create Clipping Mask** so that any paint added to the empty layer will only appear where the Smart Object contains information.

The down pointing arrow that appears to the left of the top layer indicates that its contents will only appear where the underlying layer is visible. That will limit the paint to showing up where the Smart Object contains information.

Applying Filters: If you'd like to apply a filter to a Smart Object without permanently altering its contents, then try the following: Duplicate the Smart Object by typing **Command-J** (Mac) or **Ctrl-J** (Win) and then turn off the eyeball icon for the original Smart Object to hide its contents. With the duplicate Smart Object active, choose **Layer>Smart Objects>Convert to Layer** and then apply the filter you desire. Finally, link the duplicate layer to the original Smart Object so that it will remain lined up with the duplicate if you reposition or transform it. If you need to later make changes to the Smart Object, edit the original, and then repeat the process described above to create a new filtered version.

Exporting Files: You can extract any placed Adobe Illustrator image or Raw format image from a Smart Object by choosing **Layer>Smart Object>Export Contents**. That makes it easy to embed the Raw data for all the photos used in a composition and then easily extract the individual Raw images at a later date.

Save to Update: Editing a Smart Object will cause a separate document window to appear that contains the layers that make up the Smart Object. Typing **Command-S** (Mac) or **Ctrl-S** (Win) is not enough to get the original document to reflect the changes made to the Smart Object, but clicking on the original document window should do the job, allowing you to switch back and forth between the documents to make additional adjustments without having to close and re-edit the Smart Object for each round of changes.

Multiple Interpretations of Raw Files: It can be useful to use different Camera Raw settings for the same Raw file, such as one to create good detail in the sky of an image and another to maintain detail in the main subject. This can be accomplished by choosing **Layer>Smart Objects>New Smart Object via Copy** and then double-clicking on the thumbnail image for the duplicate to access the Camera Raw dialog box. That will allow you to have two interpretations of the same Raw data, which you can mask together to create an idealized image.

Top: Foreground version, Middle: Sky version.

Bottom: Result of masking both versions.

Linked Layer Mask Workaround: Unlike any other type of layer, adding a Layer Mask or Vector Mask to a Smart Object will not cause the masks to be linked to the Smart Object. (Adobe just didn't have time to implement the linking feature with

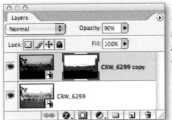

The Layers palette view of two Raw interpretations being masked to create an idealized image.

Smart Objects.) That means that moving or transforming the Smart Object will leave the masks untouched. If you absolutely must have the linking functionality, then try this somewhat awkward workaround:

1) With the masked Smart Object active, choose **Layer>Smart Objects>Group Into New Smart Object**.

2) Apply transformations when the Smart Object layer is active.

3) Choose **Layer>Smart Objects>Edit Contents** and edit the Layer Mask within the Smart Object document window and type **Command-S** (Mac) or **Ctrl-S** (Win) to update the masked document.

4) Switch back and forth between the master document and the Smart Object document to go back and forth between transforming the Smart Object layer and editing the mask.

No Illustrator Warping: Adobe Illustrator images placed as Smart Objects cannot be warped. I know of no workaround, but I thought I'd mention it so you don't rack your brain trying to figure out why it doesn't work.

Watch For Added Layers: If you add a layer to a Smart Object that was created by 'placing' an image (via **File>Place**), and the file you placed was in a file format that doesn't support layers,

This message might appear when closing a Smart Object document after adding layers.

you can run into trouble. For instance, let's say you placed a JPEG image as a Smart Object via the **File>Place** command, and then decided to edit the resulting Smart Object. If you add a layer while editing that .jpg derived Smart Object, then the image cannot be saved back into its original file format (JPEG doesn't support layers). When you attempt to save the Smart Object back into its parent document, you'll be presented with the standard Save As dialog box, and when you click Cancel and try to switch back to the original document, you'll get a warning asking if you want to rasterize the Smart Object before proceeding. (Rasterizing causes the layers that make up the Smart Object to be merged into a single layer.) There are two ways to get around this problem:

- **Discard Layers:** If you don't need to retain the layers for future editing, then choose **Layer>Flatten Image** to merge all the layers in the document before saving the edits back into the Smart Object.

- **Retain Layers:** If you'd like to retain the layers you've added, type **Command-S** (Mac) or **Ctrl-S** (Win), which will present you with the Save As dialog box. Save the image in a file format that supports layers (like TIFF or Photoshop file format). After closing the newly saved document, you'll be prompted with the warning that indicates the Smart Object must be rasterized. At that point, just click Cancel to abort the editing process. Then, once you're back in the original document, choose **Layer>Smart Objects>Replace Contents** and point Photoshop to the layered file you just saved.

There's no doubt that these Smart Objects will have a dramatic effect on how we work with layers. Once you are comfortable with this feature, you will be able to accomplish highly complex tasks in a fraction of the time it took in earlier versions of Photoshop. And considering that it's fresh off the assembly line, Smart Objects is amazingly robust and full of useful complexity. There are some things I wish it could do better (such as making Layer and Vector Masks as smart as the Objects!), but overall I believe that the time you spend on this particular learning curve is well worth it.

Swan

Maria Gonzales

(303) 555-1919 • maria@swansoap.com

63 Lilypad Drive • Clear Lake, CO 88129

www.swansoap.com

Swan

Lucy Woo

555-1818 • lucy@swansoap.com

63 Lilypad Drive • Clear Lake, CO 88129

www.swansoap.com

Swan

Bennie Smith

555-1717 • bennie@swansoap.com

63 Lilypad Drive • Clear Lake, CO 88129

www.swansoap.com

Chapter 5
Variables

IF YOU FIND YOURSELF NEEDING to create dozens or even hundreds of documents that have a common underlying design, and in which the only variables are the text and graphic elements (business cards, invites, packaging or awards, for example), then you'll go nuts for Photoshop's new Variables feature, which can only be called a miracle of automation.

Variables allows you to create templates that contain placeholder text and graphics. The placeholder elements can be quickly switched out with the contents of a simple text file that lists the text and graphics you wish to use for alternate versions of the document. This enables you to automatically produce multiple graphic files that are variations on the template design. Still not with me? Here's an extreme example of how this feature could save you days of work.

Imagine that you're the sole designer for a large corporate behemoth. The muckety-mucks on the top floor order a complete redesign of the corporate identity. Excited at the opportunity, you labor away creating fresh designs for business cards, letterhead and envelopes. After having your design approved, you're given the task of preparing press-ready files for all 20,000 employees! Knowing how to use Variables, you request a text file that lists all employee names and other vital information. You feed the file to Photoshop and leave on a three day vacation as Photoshop processes the data and automatically creates no less than 60,000 graphic files!

Here's an overview of what's involved when working with Variables:

- **Create Template** to define the overall design of your document.
- **Define Variables** to determine which layers should change between the individual documents.
- **Create Data Sets** to control which images and text should be used for each document you'd like generated.
- **Preview Results** to make sure everything is working as expected.
- **Generate Graphics** by having Photoshop automatically produce separate graphic files for each entry in the Data Set used.

Variables have been a part of ImageReady since the version that shipped with Photoshop 7, so it isn't exactly a new feature, but it is new to Photoshop. Photoshop users who don't bother with ImageReady may be delighted to discover what they've been missing.

A Brief Overview of Variables

To produce multiple graphic files that have a common underlying structure:

1) Create a template file that contains placeholder text and graphics (like a business card that contains a fake name, address, phone number and e-mail address) and defines the general look of the finished files you desire (fonts, colors, size, position of graphic elements, etc.).

2) Make the placeholder layers changeable by assigning each one a unique name (this is how you define them as Variables). The unique names should reflect the purpose of each layer (for the business card example, you might call them 'name,' 'address,' 'phone,' 'and e-mail').

3) Create a specially formatted text file that lists all the Variables (the unique names mentioned above) and the text and graphics (file names for graphics stored on your hard drive) that should be swapped out for the layers that were used to create the template file (separated by commas). This text file can only contain plain text (no formatting instructions like font size or color) since the style that will be used is defined by the template file. The contents of these text files are rather simple: The first line simply tells Photoshop the order in which the content will be presented by listing the unique names that were assigned to each layer ("name, address, phone, e-mail" for example). All subsequent lines list the content that should populate those layers ("Ben Willmore, 7157 Magnolia Drive, 555-555-1212, book@digitalmastery.com" for example). Each line that contains content is known as a Data Set.

4) Feed that special text file into Photoshop to have separate graphic files created for each Data Set contained in the text file. There is no practical limit to the number of entries that can be in the text file and therefore no limit to the number of graphic files Photoshop can generate.

name	address	phone	email
Ben Willmore	7157 Magnolia Dr.	303-555-3191	book@digitalmastery.com
Regina Cleveland	63 Longmont Dam Rd.	303-555-1234	regina@digitalmastery.com
Nik Willmore	18 110th St	212-555-1418	nik@e-dot.com
Nate Willmore	12 Main St.	303-555-4467	doesnt@haveone.com

This spreadsheet shows Variable names in the top row and four Data Sets in the rows below.

```
name,address,phone,email
Ben Willmore,7157 Magnolia Dr.,303-555-3191,book@digitalmastery.com
Regina Cleveland,63 Longmont Dam Rd.,303-555-1234,regina@digitalmastery.com
Nik Willmore,18 110th St, 212-555-1418,nik@e-dot.com
Nate Willmore,12 Main St.,303-555-4467,doesnt@haveone.com
```

The same file viewed as a comma-delimited text file ready to be fed to Photoshop.

Template file with four Variables assigned to four different text layers (name, address, phone, e-mail).

One of the four graphic files produced by applying the text file shown above.

Create Template

The first step to implementing Variables is to create a template file. This is just an everyday Photoshop file (**File>New**) that will contain placeholder text and graphics that you'd like to later swap out with other content.

Design Considerations

You'll need to create a separate layer for each item you want to be able to swap out. Using a business card as an example, you'll likely end up with separate layers for Name, Title, Address, E-mail, Telephone Number, Fax Number, and Web Site, as well as one for the company logo (if it needs to vary between cards). Here are some things to keep in mind when creating templates:

Leave extra space so text can vary in length without being truncated or bumping into other graphic elements (just because your sample data is short doesn't mean that the replacement text will be the same length).

Consider graphic orientation by planning for both horizontal and vertical images. Using square placeholder graphics will leave room for replacement graphics regardless of their orientation.

Avoid using the Background for items you want to vary. The Background layer cannot be controlled with a Variable, so whatever is on the Background will be consistent between documents.

When creating a template file, use seperate layers for each item that you want to define as a Variable. The Layers palette shown here is for the example image shown on the previous page.

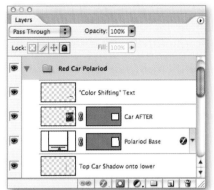

The visibility of the four layers inside this Group can be controlled by a single Variable.

Show/hide multiple layers by placing them into a Group (which looks like a folder and used to be known as a Layer Set). A single Variable can control the visibility of a group and hence all the layers that are contained within the group.

Plan for multiple templates by incorporating all the layers that will be needed collectively for all the templates. If you plan to create multiple template files that will be used with the same data (such as business cards, letterhead and envelopes that all use the same text and graphics), then create a single template document that incorporates all the layers that will be needed for all the templates. For instance, if you start by creating a template for your corporate envelopes (which normally contain just the company logo and address), you'd still want to include layers for information such as e-mail address, phone number and title, even though you don't want them visible on the envelope. Then, after defining the Variables (which we'll talk about in a moment), duplicate the first template and use it as the basis for other templates by simply hiding any layers that you don't want to have visible in each template. That way all the templates can be used with the same data since they all share a common structure of Variables.

Now that you know what's involved with creating templates, it's time to define which layers should vary by assigning Variables to some of the layers that make up the template.

Define Variables

The next step is to tell Photoshop which layers you want to be able to change by defining them as Variables and specifying what should be changeable (contents or visibility). Do this by choosing **Image>Variables>Define**, and select the name of the layer you want to use from the **Layer** pop-up menu (or use the arrows next to the menu to cycle through all the layer names).

Choosing a Variable Type

Once you've found the layer you'd like to define as a Variable, it's time to decide between the three types of Variables that are available:

Visibility

This method allows you to show or hide the contents of a layer. Example: you're designing business cards for a real estate firm where some employees are certified brokers and others are not. The design for everyone's cards will be the identical, but some should display a certification graphic and others should not. Once you've turned on the *Visibility* checkbox, then enter a name that describes the purpose of the layer (such as "certified_logo_visibility").

If your template contains complex multi-layered graphics that you need to show or hide, then place the layers within a Group (which looks like a folder) and define the Group as a Variable.

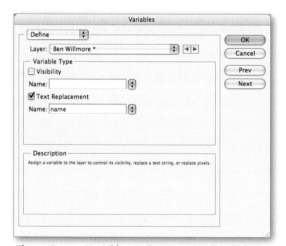

Choose Image>Variables>Define to access this dialog.

Text Replacement

This method allows you to replace a string of text with alternate text from an external file (we'll talk about those text files soon). This type of Variable is essential when creating a series of business cards or other documents that need to be personalized for each employee in a company.

Pixel Replacement

This method replaces the contents of a pixel-based layer with an external image file. Since the size of images can vary widely, Photoshop offers four methods for scaling the imported graphics to fit the space defined by the placeholder image (known as the layer's bounding box):

Fit will scale the graphic until it fits within the bounds of the placeholder image while maintaining the width/height proportions of the replacement graphic file. This is the setting I use for about 90% of the graphics I work with because all the other methods have the potential to crop or distort the images.

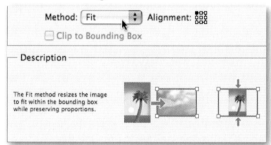

The Fit Method.

Fill will scale the graphic until it completely fills the space taken up by the placeholder image, while still maintaining the width/height proportions of the replacement graphic file. That can cause the replacement graphic to become larger than the placeholder image, which will create layout problems. You can hide the areas of the graphic that extend beyond the placeholder image by turning on the *Clip to Bounding Box* checkbox. I mainly use this setting with organic looking images (water, bark, etc.) or patterns (brick, fabric, etc.) where it's more important to have consistently sized graphics and it doesn't matter how the image ends up being cropped.

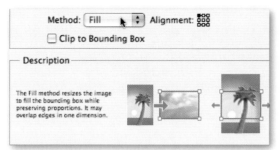

The Fill Method.

As Is will not scale the replacement graphic at all. I only use this setting when it's important to display the image at a specific size (as when demonstrating the exact size of a product). If you'd like to hide any areas that extend beyond the placeholder image, then turn on the *Clip to Bounding Box* checkbox.

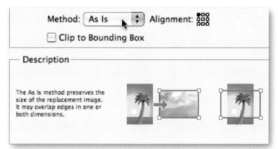

The As Is Method.

Conform will scale the replacement graphic until it takes on the same dimensions as the placeholder image without concern for the replacement graphic's original width/height proportions. I almost never use this setting since it will distort the image unless it perfectly matches with the width/height proportions of the placeholder image.

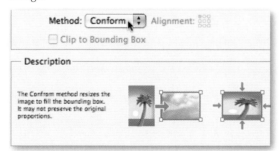

The Conform Method.

Once you've determined the scaling method, you should indicate whether the replacement graphics should be centered or aligned to one of the edges of the placeholder image. You can do that by clicking on the corresponding square in the alignment grid that is displayed to the right of the **Method** pop-up menu. (The Conform scaling method does not offer an alignment setting.)

Assigning Multiple Variable Types to a Layer

You're not limited to defining a single Variable type to each layer. For instance, you might want to assign a Text Replacement Variable to the e-mail address text on a business card template and also assign a Visibility Variable so you can easily hide the text for people who do not have e-mail addresses. The only time you won't be able to assign two types of Variables is when the layer to which you're assigning a Variable does not contain text or a graphic (an Adjustment Layer, for example). In those cases, you'll only be able to assign a Visibility Variable.

Naming Variables

If you're anything like most Photoshop users I encounter, then your layers most likely have creative names like 'Layer 1' because you're either too efficient or too lazy to spend the time to think about layer names. You definitely don't want to continue with this practice when naming Variables, because later you're going to have to type the names into other programs. Here are a few tips to use when naming a Variable:

NOTE

Which Are Variables?
You can easily tell which layers have been defined as Variables and which ones haven't by clicking on the Layer pop-up menu at the top of the Define Variables dialog box. Layer names with an asterisk (*) next to them have Variables attached, while those with no asterisk, have no Variables attached.

Use a descriptive name so it's easy to figure out what the Variable refers to (for instance, "logo visibility" is much better than the default "VisibilityVariable1"). This becomes essential when you start creating the Data Sets that are used to define the replacement text and graphics.

Stick with lower case since the Variable names are case sensitive and the names between the Variable and the Data Set must match perfectly, otherwise you'll receive an error message. Sticking with all lower case letters will ensure that you never receive an error message due to a capitization mismatch between files.

Use short names because you'll need to remember the names when switching back and forth between Photoshop and the program you use to define the Data Sets that determine the text and graphics that will replace your placeholders.

Replace spaces with underscores because Variable names cannot contain spaces (for instance "e-mail address" becomes "e-mail_address").

Watch the first letter because Variable names cannot start with a number, a period or a hyphen.

Don't use special characters because Variable names are limited to letters, numbers and only the following special characters: periods (.), hyphens (-), underscores (_) and colons (:).

All this might sound a bit complicated, but if you simply stick to using letters and numbers and use underscores whenever you'd usually use a space, then you should be fine.

Special Considerations

Below are two situations when you'll need to think outside the box when defining Variables:

File Name Variable

In the end, the purpose of using Variables is to have Photoshop quickly create numerous graphic files. At some point Photoshop will have to figure out what names to use for all those graphic files. If you don't think ahead, you'll end up with names like "business card 1." To avoid overly generic names, I suggest you create an extra text layer and hide it in the Layers stack by turning off the eyeball icon for that layer. You can then define a Text Replacement Variable for that layer that will be used to define the file name of the graphic files Photoshop will generate. That way you'll be able to get custom names for each graphic file and end up with more useful names like "Ben Willmore's

Business Card." I'll show you how to define the file names near the end of this chapter.

Linked Variables

If you want to use an element (text or graphic) in multiple areas of the template (let's say a logo is used in two places of the template), then you'll want to link the Variable assigned to one layer to other layers that should contain the same content. You can do that by clicking on the pop-up menu that appears to the right of the Variable name field and choosing the name of a Variable that is already being used by a different layer. Once you've done that, a link symbol will appear to the right of the Variable name indicating that the layer is using the same Variable as another layer.

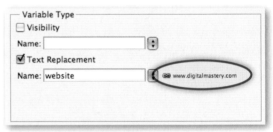

The link symbol indicates that two layers have the same Variable assigned and will therefore be replaced with the same text or graphic.

Now that you know how to properly define Variables, let's take a look at how you define the text and graphics that will be used to replace the placeholders you have in your template file.

Create Data Sets

Once you have a template file created and have defined as many Variables as you see fit, it's time to define the text and graphics that will be used to replace your placeholder layers. All Photoshop needs is a simple text file, but creating the beast isn't as easy as you might expect. Rather than talking you through it while you attempt to construct a file in your head, I think it will be easier to understand what's needed by looking at a simple sample.

name	displaylogo	mugshot
Ben Willmore	TRUE	ben.jpg
Regina Cleveland	TRUE	regina.jpg
Nik Willmore	FALSE	nik.jpg
Nate Willmore	FALSE	nate.tif

This spreadsheet file contains data that will be used to control a Text Replacement Variable, a Visibility Variable and a Pixel Replacement Variable.

```
name,displaylogo,mugshot
Ben Willmore,TRUE,ben.jpg
Regina Cleveland,TRUE,regina.jpg
Nik Willmore,FALSE,nik.jpg
Nate Willmore,FALSE,nate.tif
```

The same sample file viewed as a tab-delimited text file looks a lot more complicated even though it contains the exact same data.

Take a look at the example shown above. The first line is a simple list of the three Variables that were defined in a template file (matching the exact spelling and capitalization perfectly). Each of the lines below the top one is known as a Data Set. This text file is first imported into the template file, and then exported, creating separate graphic files for each Data Set.

Three types of Variables are getting their data from this file. The left-most column is a Text Replacement Variable called 'name,' the middle column is for a Visibility Variable called 'displaylogo' (an entry of TRUE causes the layer to be visible, while FALSE causes the same layer to become hidden), and the right-most column is for a Pixel Replacement Variable called 'mugshot' (where the text matches the file names for images that are stored in the same folder as the text file).

The order of the columns is unimportant as long as the Variable names match the position of the data that is appropriate for each Variable. That's nice for those times when you can obtain a text file that contains that data you need (like an employee directory) because all you have to do is tailor the first line so that it corresponds to the proper data in the file.

So far the concept might seem simple (because it is), but there are some things that can make the creation of a proper text file more difficult. First off, Photoshop needs a text file where entries are separated by either commas or tab characters (the commas and tabs are known as 'delimiters,' and the text files we will be working with are referred to as comma-delimited or tab-delimited files). The example above has everything organized into nice columns and was prepared in a word processor using tabs to delineate between the columns. It was then saved as a text file, as opposed

to the word processor's native file format. Let's see what the same data looks like when it's saved as a comma-delimited text file. If you compare the two examples, you'll see that it's essentially the same data.

Now let's look at some special situations you might run into when creating a text file:

Watch for commas that are part of addresses or other text entries. "7157 Magnolia Drive, Nederland CO, 80466" is a properly formatted street address, but since Photoshop thinks of commas as things that separate one entry from the next, it will read the text as "7157 Magnolia Drive" in one entry, "Nederland CO" in a second entry, and "80466" in a third entry. To prevent this problem, enclose the entire address in quotes. When quotes are used, Photoshop ignores any commas, tabs or carriage returns that appear between the quotation characters.

Watch for line breaks. A return character indicates a new Data Set, so if you have a multi-line address like the one below, it will break into multiple entries. So, again, be sure to enclose the entire address in quotes.
"1060 West Addison St.
Chicago, IL 60612"

Watch for quotes because as you've just learned, Photoshop will treat them as an instruction to ignore commas and tabs and will not display them as part of a text replacement layer. So, if your friend is known as Ben "Pixelhead" Willmore, the entry will come into Photoshop as Ben Pixelhead Willmore with no quotes. The solution is to use double quotes by surrounding the entire entry with another set of quotation marks like this "Ben "Pixelhead" Willmore". That will cause Photoshop to leave the text between the outer quotation marks unchanged.

Spaces are ignored if they appear immediately before or after a comma or tab character that separates entries. If you really need a space at the beginning or end of an entry (where the commas would appear), then enclose the entire entry in quotes.

Watch for empty entries where two commas appear with nothing in between them. Every Variable must have a value, so you can't use ",," to indicate that you don't want to replace a string of text or a graphic file.

Watch for capitalization differences between the Variable name as it was defined in Photoshop and how it is used in the text file. The two must match perfectly. A single capitalization difference is enough to prevent the entire process from working. For that reason, I once again suggest you stick with lowercase and use short and simple descriptive names.

Empty equals an error because all entries must contain data, so if you'd like to leave a Text Replacement Variable empty, be sure to place a space between two quotation marks (" ") so Photoshop doesn't ignore the space altogether. You can use the same trick for a Pixel Replacement Variable when you want to prevent a graphic from being replaced.

Location is everything when it comes to graphics files. Using a name like "ben.jpg" will cause Photoshop to assume that the referenced graphics file is in the same folder as the text file that's being fed to Photoshop. If the graphic file is located elsewhere, you'll have to include the path needed to find the file (for example: Hard Drive/Users: Ben/Documents/ben.jpg).

The first Variable is important because it is the only Variable that will be used to give each Data Set a name. That name will be part of the final file name (more on this later). I like to use a hidden layer for this first field so I'm free to put any content into it without fear of that content appearing in the final graphic files that are generated.

For the clean, trouble-free text files, I suggest that you create your Data Sets text file using a spreadsheet program (like Excel). Spreadsheet programs don't try to add spaces after commas and check for punctuation errors like many word processors do (which can wreak havoc on a cleanly formatted text file). Just make sure that when you're done you save the file as a tab or comma-delimited text file .

Okay, we've gone through the steps needed to create a proper text file, so now let's see what's involved with loading it into Photoshop and previewing the results you get when the data replaces the placeholder text and graphics in your template file.

Preview Results

To preview the results of applying a text file to a template image, choose **Image>Variables>Data Sets**. This allows you to load a text file, examine and edit its contents, preview the resulting graphic files and add additional Data Sets, all from a single dialog box.

To load a text file of Data Sets, click the *Import* button that appears on the right side of the dialog box. That will cause the Import Data Set dialog box to appear. That's where you can specify the location of the file you'd like to load, indicate if the first Variable should be used to name the individual Data Sets (as I mentioned earlier, this feature is useful when you want to control the final file name, amongst other things) and decide if you'd like to replace the Data Sets that were previously loaded (you should be able to get away with leaving the encoding pop-up menu to **Automatic**).

The Import Data Set dialog box can be accessed by choosing Image>Variables>Data Sets and then clicking on the Import button in the resulting dialog box.

When you click the OK button, Photoshop will attempt to match up the data in the text file with the Variables that have been defined in your template file. If all is successful, you'll get a preview of the first graphic file that is based on the first Data Set in the text file, and you'll be able to cycle through the Data Sets (using the right and left arrow buttons near the top of the dialog box).

Possible Errors

Alas, success is not guaranteed, so let's look at the error messages you might encounter and how to get around them:

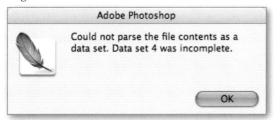

This message will appear when your text file does not contain enough data for all the Variables defined.

Incomplete Data

This error message will appear if your text file does not contain enough entries to feed all the Variables that are defined in the template file. There are two main culprits that usually cause this message to appear: Either you didn't list all the Variables in the first line of the text file, or one of the entries in one of the Data Sets is empty (two commas with nothing in between them). Fortunately, the message will usually indicate which Data Set is deficient so you don't have to check the entire file. In the example message shown on this page, it's Data Set #4, which means the fifth line of the text file needs to be checked (remember, the first line is just a list of Variable names and the second line contains the first real data).

Too Much Data

This error message will appear when there are either more Variable names listed in the first line of the text file than there are Variables defined in the template file, or when one or more of the Data Sets contains too many commas. This is

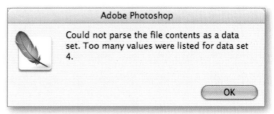

This message will appear when your text file either contains too many Variable names, or too many commas.

very common when addresses contain commas and they have not been placed between quotation marks (see the section on creating Data Sets for more information). As with the previous error message, this one will usually let you know which Data Set is the culprit.

This message will appear when the Variable names listed in the first line of a text file do not perfectly match the Variables defined in the template file.

Variable Name Mismatch

This error message will appear when a Variable name found in the first line of the text file either doesn't perfectly match the name of a Variable in the template file (keep on eye on capitalization in that case), or is nonexistent in the template file.

The Data Sets portion of the Variables dialog box after a successful import of data from a text file.

Check for Data and Layout Problems

Once you've successfully imported a text file, you should see how it is interacting with the placeholder layers of the template file. You can do that by cycling through the different Data Sets (using the right and left arrow buttons to the right of the **Data Set** pop-up menu). While you view the different Data Sets, keep on eye on your template file to see if any text is being truncated, or if there are any typos in the data that's being applied (make sure the *Preview* checkbox is turned on, otherwise you won't see any results). If you encounter any problems, you can modify the Data Sets by choosing the Variable you'd like to work with and modifying the Value field that appears just below the Variable's name. You can also click the *Apply* button to embed the Data Sets into the template file and then click OK to return to your template (just clicking OK without clicking *Apply* would trash the Data Sets and force you to re-import them before being able to preview the file again). Then you can adjust the layout to accommodate problems like lengthy text that you didn't anticipate when creating the template.

Once you are confident that everything is working correctly, you can stop previewing and actually create individual graphic files for each Data Set.

> ### NOTE
>
> **Manual Data Sets**
> *You can add Data Sets to a template file within Photoshop (they don't have to come from an external text file). To add a Data Set to the active template file, choose* **Image>Variables>Data Sets**, *click on the New Data Set icon (it looks like a floppy disc and is located to the left of the trash can icon. Ths is a very inefficient method for entering a lot of data, so I mainly use it when I notice that an external text file does not contain a Data Set that I need.*

Generate Graphics

If you were able to successfully preview the Data Set within the template file, you should be ready to have Photoshop create individual graphics files for each Data Set found in the text file.

Exporting Data Sets

To start the process, choose **File>Export>Data Sets As Files**. If you find that the menu is grayed out, then it means that there are no Data Sets currently loaded (you most likely clicked OK without clicking the *Apply* button in the last dialog box). If that's the case, then choose **File>Import>Variable Data Sets** and feed it your text file just as you did in the Data Sets area of the Variables dialog box (the thing you did earlier where you could have clicked *Apply* to attach the Data Set to your template file).

Save Options

The top portion of the dialog box allows you to specify where you would like the resulting graphic files to be saved. You also have the choice of creating files for all the Data Sets that were contained in the text file, or only exporting a single Data Set as a graphic file (I always leave the Data Sets pop-up menu set to **All Data Sets** because I could have applied a single Data Set using the **Image>Apply Data Set** command).

File Naming

This section allows you to specify a file naming convention for the group of images that will be saved. I usually enter a descriptive name in the first field (like "Business Card"), choose either

The Export dialog box allows you to specify the file names you wish to be used for creating multiple graphic files.

Space or Underscore for the second field and then set the third file to Data Set Name (which will insert the name of each individual Data Set into the end of the file name).

Once you click the OK button, Photoshop will start processing the data from the text file you imported and will create a separate graphic file for each of the Data Sets that were contained in the text file. Each of these files will be a layered Photoshop file format image that will be saved to the location you specified at the top of the dialog box.

You can apply the same text file to multiple template files (business card, letterhead and envelope, for example). Just make sure all the templates contain all the Variables that are defined in the Data Set (simply hide layers that shouldn't be part of the final image).

NOTE

Flattened Files
If you need flattened versions of the graphics files, consider making an action that simply flattens the image and then apply it through the new Image Processor feature that is covered in Chapter 10 (which allows you to quickly apply the action and then automatically save the file in TIFF or JPEG file format.)

Consider ImageReady
You can also process your template file from ImageReady (which comes bundled with Photoshop). This will allow you to save the images in any of the following file formats:

JPG   GIF
PNG   SWF

I'd like to say that if you feel a little befuddled after trying to digest all of this in one sitting, I wouldn't worry too much. Once you've given this thing a thorough test drive, you'll see for yourself how all the elements interact with each other, and it should be a lot less confusing. The time you spend learning this feature is priceless, because when you've got a project that is a good candidate for Variables, this incredibly powerful tool can save you hours if not days of your life.

Chapter 6
Small Gems
For Design

THIS CHAPTER IS FOR THOSE of you who appreciate taking the time to dig up those little nuggets that can make your life in Photoshop easier, and hopefully more pleasurable. The engineering that went into these features was obviously intended for the person who has, until recently, been Photoshop's favored child—the designer.

Even though designers now have to play nice and share more of their sandbox with photographers, there's nothing measly about these new design related features. Those who earn their bread and butter using Photoshop should get a lot of use out of what's in this chapter. And if you happen to use the holy trinity of Adobe design applications (InDesign, Illustrator and Photoshop together), you'll get even more out of what's offered here, especially when it comes to the new color swatches support and integrated stock photo service.

If you create web graphics, I expect you're going to be seeing a steady migration of features uprooting themselves from ImageReady and moving into Photoshop. CS2 has brought over the first emigrant—the Animation palette.

Here's a preview of some of the small but valuable goodies you'll find in this chapter:

- **Thumbnails View** allows you to see a preview of images you're about to open without having to launch Bridge.
- **WYSIWYG Font Menu** allows you to see a sample of each font from within the menu, making font selection a piece of cake.
- **Smart Guides** make it much easier to align layers by causing them to snap when aligned.
- **Animation Palette** has been transplanted from ImageReady, nudging Photoshop one step closer to its goal of becoming a full-featured web graphics application.
- **Save Swatches for Exchange** allows you to exchange color swatches between Photoshop, Illustrator and InDesign.
- **Support for PDF-X Format** allows you to save PDFs suited for high-end prepress output.
- **Adobe Stock Photos** makes it easier to work with on-line stock photo vendors by letting you download a low resolution comp and later purchase a high resolution version.

Thumbnails View

This feature allows you to see thumbnails of images using the **File>Open** command. It's not really new, but in past versions of Photoshop you had to enable the Version Cue feature in your preferences (that setting is turned on by default in CS2), so not a lot of people knew about it.

Viewing images as thumbnails in the Open dialog box.

Now that this feature is turned on by default, you'll see a *Use Adobe Dialog* button in the Open dialog box. Clicking that button will switch to another dialog box which offers a View pop-up menu. There you'll find choices for Details, Icons, Thumbnails and Tiles. The Thumbnails view is nice since it allows to you see a preview of the images that are in the folder you're currently viewing. My only complaint with this feature is that it does not create thumbnails for Raw format images. If you don't like using this newer, alien dialog box for opening your images, you can always get back to the plain old vanilla version by clicking the *Use OS Dialog* button.

The choices available under the View pop-up menu determine what your images will look like when viewed in the Open dialog box.

WYSIWYG Font Menu

If the mega-acronym in the heading above stumps you, it stands for What You See Is What You Get, and it is pronounced Wizzywig. In this case it simply means that the font menu in Photoshop will show you what a font actually looks like in the menu itself, as opposed to forcing you to select the font and see what your text looks like in the main window. If you take a look at the font menu (you'll find it on the left side of the Options bar at the top of your screen when the Type tool is active) you'll see three elements for each font: a symbol on the left that indicates which type of font it is, the font name and then a sample of the font shown in its actual typeface.

Determining Font Type

There are three different symbols that can appear to the left of a font name. The 'double T' indicates a *TrueType* font, the 'a' indicates a *Postscript Type 1* font and the 'O' indicates an *OpenType* font.

From top to bottom: TrueType, Postscript Type 1, OpenType.

If you want to know a little about the font formats, here's the skinny (from oldest to newest):

Postscript Type 1 was developed by Adobe in the late 80's and was designed to provide high quality output on Postscript language printers (which are used by most commercial printing companies). Each font included both a screen version and an outline version that was used for high quality printing. There were different versions for Mac and Windows, so you couldn't interchange them between platforms. Adobe charged license fees for these fonts, which naturally irritated some of the font companies who created fonts in this format.

TrueType was developed by Apple in partnership with Microsoft in the early 90's, largely because they wanted to create an open standard that didn't require license fees. This format combined the screen and outline versions of the font into a single file, which simplified file management, but you still needed different versions for Mac and Windows which was a giant pain in the patooty for users who wanted to share files between the two platforms. Of course once the TrueType format was available, Adobe stopped charging license fees in an attempt to block the advance of the TrueType standard.

OpenType was developed in the late 90's when Adobe and Microsoft got together and decided to end the font wars by merging the TrueType and Postscript Type 1 standards. This new format offers all the features of the previous two formats and is a cross-platform standard (finally!) which allows the same font file to be used on both Mac and Windows platforms. This format also offers a wider range of characters (like true small caps characters), and offers better compression than the other formats.

In the end it doesn't matter which of these formats you use in Photoshop. OpenType is still relatively new and there are still quite a few programs that don't fully support it. We'll most likely see all three formats being used for the years to come, but as support for OpenType expands, I think we can expect font companies will standardize on the OpenType format.

Now that we've covered the meaning of those cryptic font symbols, let's look into the previews that show up to the right of each font.

Selecting Font Preview Size

Choosing **Preferences>Type** from **Photoshop** (Mac) or **Edit** (Win) will present you with the new Type Preferences dialog box. This is where Adobe has consolidated all the type related settings that used to be found in the General Preferences dialog box. The only thing new about it is the *Font Preview Size* setting. You can choose between three preview sizes: Small, Medium and Large.

The *Font Preview Size* setting also affects the size of the font name. The Small and Medium settings will leave the font name small just like it appeared in previous versions of Photoshop, but

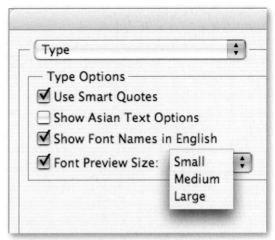

The Font Preview Size pop-up menu determines the size at which the font samples will appear in the menu.

Viewing the fonts with the preview size set to Small.

Viewing the fonts with the preview size set to Medium.

Viewing the fonts with the preview size set to Large.

Viewing the fonts with the font preview turned off.

changes the size of the actual preview to small or medium. The Large setting will cause both the font name and font preview to appear larger.

If you don't like the new font previews and find them bothersome, just turn off the checkbox next to the *Font Preview Size* setting.

Smart Guides

If you've ever struggled with aligning layers, you'll enjoy using the new Smart Guides. This new feature aligns multiple layers by having one layer snap to the edge or center of another.

Start by choosing **View>Show>Smart Guides** to allow these special guides to become visible when multiple layers align (a checkbox next to the *Smart Guides* choice indicates they have been enabled). Also, choose **View>Snap To>Layers** to cause the layers to snap when they align.

It's much easier to see this feature in action than to read about it. The images at the top of the next column illustrate how the Smart Guides allow you to quickly align one layer to the edges of other layers in the document. The pink guides only show up when the active layer is aligned with one or more layers in the image. When the Smart Guide is visible, the active layer is snapped to the guide so that its movement is limited. These two options are independent of each other: you can still snap to the Smart Guides even if they are not visible, or you can view the guides while not snapping to them. If you want to temporarily disable the snapping behavior, then hold down **Control** (Mac or Win) when dragging.

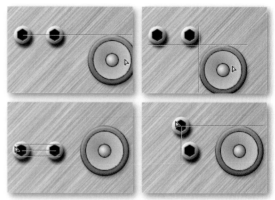

The pink lines indicate how the layer that is being moved is aligning to other layers. The top, bottom, left, right, or center of the active layer can align with the same areas of any surrounding layers. If the layer aligns with more than one layer, the pink line is extended to indicate how many layers are being aligned.

The Smart Guides ignore any Layer Styles that have been applied to the active layer (Drop Shadow, Outer Glow, etc.) and when working on soft-edged layers, they consider areas that are at least 50% opaque to be the 'edge' of the layer. They also appear when creating or moving selections, Shape layers and other features. I find them to be especially useful when creating a series of shapes that must relate to each other (like a web site interface).

You can choose which color is used for the Smart Guides by choosing **Preferences>Guides, Grid & Slices** from the **Photoshop** menu (Mac) or **Edit** menu (Win).

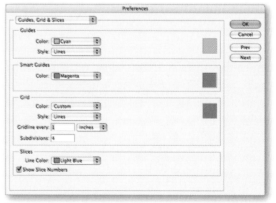

You can change the color of the Smart Guides in the Guides, Grid & Slices dialog box.

Animation Palette

Photoshop has always had a somewhat clumsy relationship with ImageReady (the web graphics application that has been bundled with Photoshop since version 5.5). When new features were introduced they usually made it into one of the two programs, but seldom both. Adobe has started to integrate some of ImageReady's features into Photoshop and has for the most part stopped developing ImageReady. I'm guessing that the next release of Photoshop (CS3?) might not ship with ImageReady since they will have integrated all of its functionality into Photoshop.

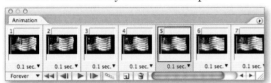

The Animation palette is now available within Photoshop as well as ImageReady.

This time around they snagged the Animation palette from ImageReady and plunked it into Photoshop (they did the same with Variables, but that's the subject of another chapter). I'm not going to cover the actual process of creating animations since the Animation palette has been available in ImageReady since the days when Photoshop 5.5 was on the market. This transplanted palette works just like the one found in ImageReady, but a few features had to be moved since there were animation related choices in the Layers menu and other areas of ImageReady. Let's take a look at where these features ended up:

Animation related icons always appear at the top of ImageReady's Layers palette. You can control when those icons will appear in Photoshop by selecting from the **Animation Options** found in

The side menu of the Layers palette allows you to choose when the animation icons will be visible.

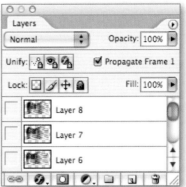

The icons related to animations only apppear while the Animation palette is visible (unless you change the Animations Options setting from the side menu of the palette).

the side menu of Photoshop's Layers palette. The *Automatic* choice will cause the icons to only appear when the Animation palette is visible, which is both the default setting and the setting that I prefer to use.

Propagate Frame 1 Changes found in both the Layers menu and side menu of the Layers palette of ImageReady now appears as a checkbox at the top of the Layers palette in Photoshop.

Match Layer Across Frames used to appear as a choice called *Match*, both in ImageReady's Layers menu and the side menu of the Layers palette. It is now found in the side menu of the Animation palette in Photoshop.

Next/Previous Frame icons used to appear at the bottom of the Layers palette in ImageReady. You'll now find those icons at the bottom of the Animation palette in Photoshop.

Optimized View was available as a tab at the top of the document window in ImageReady. Photoshop doesn't offer this view, so you'll have to choose **File>Save for Web** to see an optimized view of your animation. Next Frame, Previous Frame and Play icons can now be found in the Save for Web dialog box.

There's only one critical flaw that I've found in the implementation of the Animation palette: Photoshop will fail to recognize the animation contained in pre-existing animated .gif files. In order to have Photoshop recognize the animation frames, you have to open the .gif file in Image-Ready and then click on the Edit in Photoshop

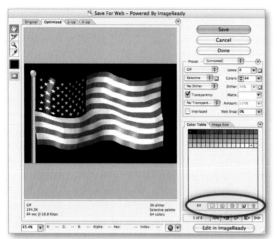

The animation controls appear below the Color Table in the Save for Web dialog box.

icon at the bottom of the Tool palette. That means that the new Animation palette is a lot less useful when working with pre-existing animations. The only time I use it is when creating an animation from scratch and even then I'm very careful to remember to save my in-progress image in Photoshop file format so that the animation frames will appear in Photoshop. If I need to work with pre-existing .gif animations, then I work strictly in ImageReady.

Save Swatches for Exchange

You can now use the same color swatches in Photoshop, Illustrator and InDesign. Each of those programs used to use a different format for color swatches, but the Save Swatches for Exchange feature (available from the side menu of the Swatches palette) saves in the new .ASE format, which allows the swatches to be loaded into multiple Adobe applications. This makes it much easier to create consistent designs using more than one Adobe application. For instance, the red color used in the major headings of this book was created in InDesign, and if I wanted to, I could import the color swatch into Photoshop and use it to create images that incorporate the same color.

Click on the side menu of the palette to access the Save Swatches for Exchange command.

Support for PDF-X Format

Many magazines and newspapers require that ads be submitted in a standardized format. The format of choice is fast becoming PDF/X. PDF/X is a normal PDF file that has limits placed on which settings can be used to save the file. This helps to eliminate problems and guesswork at the printing stage. There are two main versions of PDF/X available. Here are the fundamental differences between the standards:

PDF/X-1a is the oldest of the two formats and will automatically convert any RGB or Lab modes images into CMYK mode (based on the profile chosen in the **Destination** pop-up menu of the Output section of the Save Adobe PDF dialog box). This format also supports spot colors and is preferred over PDF/X-3 by most U.S. publications that require PDF/X files.

The new Save Adobe PDF options dialog box.

PDF/X-3 is a newer creation that allows for RGB, CMYK and Lab mode images that have embedded color profiles. This format is useful when an image will be reproduced under multiple printing conditions (newspaper, magazine, etc.) and is much more popular in Europe than in the U.S.

When PDF/X format is required, be sure to ask which settings should be used when saving the file, otherwise you might end up with a PDF/X file that is incompatible with the publication.

To save an image as a PDF file from Photoshop, choose **File>Save** and choose Photoshop PDF from the **Format** pop-up menu.

Adobe Stock Photos

You stock photo hounds no longer have to launch a web browser to find your stock images. The new Adobe Stock Photos feature within Bridge allows you to search for, browse and purchase stock photos from the online libraries of five major stock photo companies.

Once you've found images that you like, you are welcome to download a low resolution watermark free version of the images (usually no larger than 500x500 pixels). These images are known as comping images and are to be used for experimentation before purchasing a high resolution version of the image (you are not allowed to use them for commercial projects, unless it's simply to show a preview to your client). Let's take a look at how the whole process works.

Bridge allows you to search for & browse stock photos.

Search By Keyword

Start in Bridge by choosing Adobe Stock Photos from the Favorites tab, or Search Stock Photos from the **Edit** menu. Once you've done that, you'll find a search field at the top of the Bridge window where you can search for images based on keywords (simple words that describe the contents of a photograph). Clicking the Start Search icon (the binoculars icon) will cause thumbnails to appear in the area below. If you don't see what you want in the first list of results, click the More Results arrow in the upper right.

Advanced Searches

I prefer to use the Advanced Search feature (it looks like a pair of binoculars with a plus sign (+) next to it). That's where you can tell Bridge to ignore illustrations or black and white images and specify if you're looking for a portrait, landscape or panoramic oriented photographs.

As anyone who works with stock images already knows, the value of a stock service doesn't lie just with the quality and quantity of its images, but also with the sophistication of its database and intuitiveness of its search engine. You can have the greatest images in the world, but if someone hasn't taken the time to identify the images with proper keywords, the entire catalog is almost

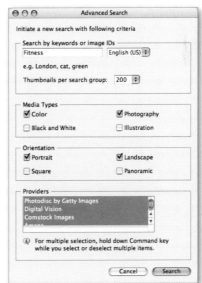

The Advanced Search dialog box allows you focus your search on specific styles and orientations of images.

useless to a professional user. When I tested this new service from Adobe, I didn't stumble across many major search bloopers when using very simple search words like 'dog,' 'house,' 'car,' etc., but when I entered the phrase, 'red house,' I got tons of images with red in them, but very few red houses. So, as it is with most stock providers, you'll need to experiment a bit to find your way with their search capability.

Downloading Comps

Once you've found some images you like, you can click the *Download Comp* button that appears above the thumbnail area to download a low resolution version of the image. To view and open the comps, click on the Downloaded Comps choice in the Favorites pane in the upper left of the Bridge dialog box.

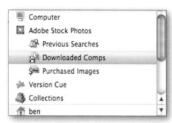

To view comps you've downloaded, click on the Download Comps choice in the upper left of the Bridge window.

These comp images are especially useful when working with Adobe InDesign and Adobe Illustrator. In those programs, you can place the comp images and use them when creating your initial design. Then, once you've decided which images will make the final cut for your project, you can **Control-click** (Mac) or **Right-click** (Win) on the image within your layout and choose *Purchase This Image* (which will automatically launch the Adobe Stock Photos section of Bridge and place the image in your shopping cart). Once the image has been purchased, you can re-link the newly downloaded high resolution version of the image and continue with the design process. Unfortunately, the same elegant integration isn't available when you're working in Photoshop, so you'll have to settle for using Bridge as a simple image browser and purchase mechanism that is somewhat independent of Photoshop.

Purchasing An Image

Once you've found an image you'd like to purchase, click the *Get Price & Keywords* button that appears above the thumbnail images. That causes a dialog box to appear that lists the cost associated with purchasing the image. The cost usually varies based on the resolution of the image (the higher the resolution, the higher the price). Clicking the shopping cart icon next to any price will add the image to your shopping cart so you can purchase it when you close your cart.

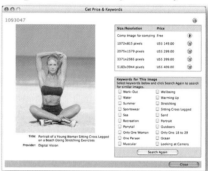

The Price & Keywords dialog box is where you can add an image to your shopping cart.

This is also where it will present a list of keywords that are associated with this image. Clicking on the checkbox next to any of the keywords and then clicking the *Search Again* button should produce similar images.

Checking Out

Once you've added one or more photos to your shopping cart, you can click the cart icon that is found in the upper right of the Bridge window to view the contents of your cart. If you're ready to purchase the images in your cart, then click the *Checkout* button.

The shopping cart will list all the images you've indicated that you'd like to purchase.

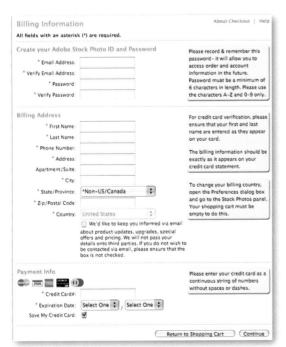

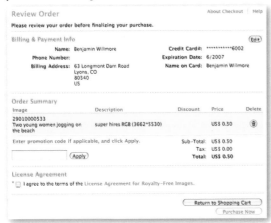

Be sure to remember the password you specify since you'll need it to login at a later date.

The Review Order screen is the last place where you can make changes before purchasing an image.

Creating An Account

The next step is to create an account by filling in your name, address and credit card information. You should only have to go through this process once. When you want to purchase additional images in the future, you'll be able to sign-in using your e-mail address and password.

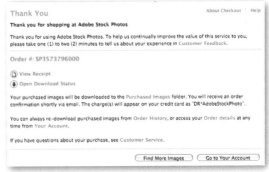

This final screen is an order confirmation.

Reviewing Your Order

Once you've created an account, you'll be sent to a screen that allows you to review all the details of your order. At this point you haven't actually purchased anything. That will happen only after you click the *Purchase Now* button that's found at the bottom of the window.

The Download Status dialog box allows you to monitor the progress of your downloads.

Downloading Your Images

The next screen is a simple one that thanks you for placing your order. This is also where you'll find the *Open Download Status* button, which will cause another dialog box to pop open. The Download Status dialog box will list all of the images you just purchased and includes a *Download* button that allows you to immediately start downloading your newly purchased images.

Viewing Purchased Images

Once you've downloaded your images, click on the *Purchased Images* choice under the Favorites tab in the upper left of the Bridge window to view thumbnails of your images. Double-clicking on an image should open it in Photoshop.

To view the images you've purchased through the Adobe Stock Photos service, click the Purchased Images choice under the Favorites tab.

File Management

All images that relate to the Adobe Stock Photos service are stored in your **Documents/AdobeStock-Photos** folder on a Mac or the **My Documents/AdobeStockPhotos** folder in Windows. That's also where any downloaded comp images are stored along with purchased images and the thumbnails viewed from previous searches. You can manually navigate to this area using the Folders tab in Bridge.

Thumbnail vs. Comp
Thumbnail images can only be viewed within Bridge (unless you access the image from Photoshop's alternative Open dialog box). Double-clicking on a thumbnail image will cause Bridge to download a comp version of the same image and open it within Photoshop. Thumbnail images are approximately 1/3 the size of comp images.

You can also access stock photo files via the Folders tab in Bridge.

You'll find one of three small icons below any images that relate to the Adobe Stock Photo service. These icons indicate if the file is a thumbnail, comp or high resolution image.

Left to right: Thumbnail, Comp, High Resolution

Bridge will retain all of the thumbnails you've ever viewed from previous searches, which can start taking up a big chunk of your hard drive space. To remove some of those previous search

results, navigate to the Previous Searches folder in Bridge (as mentioned above), select the folder that contains the search results you'd like to remove (the folder name is the same as the keywords you searched) and **Control-click** (Mac) or **Right-click** (Win) on the folders within the thumbnails pane of Bridge and choose **Move to Trash** from the pop-up menu that appears.

Re-downloading Images

If you ever misplace a purchased image, you can re-download it by returning to the stock photos area within Bridge and clicking on the Accounts icon (which looks like a tiny person and is found in the upper right of the Bridge window). Once you've logged into that area, click on View Order History. From that screen you'll be able to click on any image you've purchased and then click the download link to re-download the image.

Click View Order History to get to the screen that allows you to re-download an image.

Setting Preferences

If you'd like to change the number of thumbnails that appear after a search, prevent warning dialog boxes from appearing or change other settings related to working with stock photographs, choose **Preferences** from the **Bridge** menu, (Mac) or **Edit** menu (Win) and click the *Adobe Stock Photos* choice found on the left side of the resulting dialog box.

I like to set the *Thumbnails per search group* setting to 200 so that a good number of thumbnails display after performing a search. Doing that makes clicking the *More Results* button a much less frequent requirement. The *Adobe Stock Photos Folder Location* setting is useful if you prefer to store your stock photographs on an external

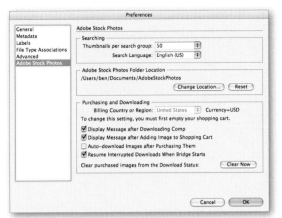

The Adobe Stock Photos pane of the Bridge Preferenecs dialog box showing the default settings.

As you read through this chapter I hope you were able to glean some goodies that will make a difference in your daily work. Sometimes it's all about small moves, and I think the ones in this chapter are worthwhile additions to Photoshop.

drive. I find the many confirmation dialog boxes that Bridge displays (after downloading comps or adding images to my cart) annoying, so I like to turn off both the *Display Message after Downloading Comp* and *Display Message after Adding Images to Shopping Cart* checkboxes. I also prefer to turn on the *Auto-download Images after Purchasing* checkbox so I don't have to make additional clicks each time I purchase an image.

As you might imagine, prices range wildly in the universe of stock photography. Adobe's chosen vendors fall in the middle to high range of pricing, which I find to be a bit excessive when I'm looking for an image that is relatively easy to find (like a wrench, for example). However I probably wouldn't mind paying the price if the image was exceptional and unique to that vendor. There are a number of vendors, like www.istockphoto.com and www.photospin.com, who offer prices far below that of Adobe's stock providers. Using the example of a wrench, I found wrench images in Adobe's service to range from $49 to $409 (varying with resolution). However, with the more competitive vendors I just mentioned, I could buy a high-resolution wrench for as low as $2.00 per image. So be sure to check your other options before you spend too much money with the Adobe Stock Photos service.

uptospeed

Section III
Photography

Chapter 7
Camera Raw 3

Camera raw got the superstar treatment with CS2. The makeover is loaded with so many improvements that even the most jaded digital photographer should feel a little breathless when they see what Adobe has cooked up for them. From making it much easier to work with large numbers of images to adding a new level of precision to adjustments, Camera Raw 3.0 is definitely one of the cornerstones of the CS2 upgrade.

Let's take a look at a quick list of what's new in Camera Raw 3 and then we'll explore each one of these features in-depth.

- **Automatic Tonal Adjustments:** For faster adjustments and better initial thumbnails.
- **Shadow & Highlight Clipping Warnings:** To see where you're losing detail without having to change the view of the entire image.
- **Image Rotation and Straightening:** To fix off-kilter horizon lines.
- **Non-destructive Cropping:** Useful when creating web photo galleries and contact sheets.
- **Color Sampler Tool:** For precise camera calibration and image adjustment.
- **Curves Tab:** Allows for more precise adjustment of brightness and contrast.
- **Multi-image Support:** To efficiently adjust dozens or hundreds of images.
- **Save Multiple Images:** To quickly save images in common file formats.
- **Bridge Integration:** Improved the workflow used when adjusting multiple images within Bridge (the replacement for CS' File Browser).

Where's My Stuff?

While Adobe was performing plastic surgery on Camera Raw, the dialog box got rearranged somewhat. Before we dive into the latest features, let's prepare ourselves so we don't trip and fall in Camera Raw's new living room. Here's what you need to know:

- **Contrast Change?** If you're surprised by how different unadjusted images look in Bridge and Camera Raw, then you've just noticed the effects of the new *Auto* checkbox. You can toggle it on and off by typing **Command-U** (Mac) or **Ctrl-U** (Win). Later in this chapter I'll show you how to turn it off permanently.
- **Update Button Not Available:** Holding **Option** (Mac) or **Alt** (Win) in CS changed the OK button to *Update*. Clicking the button attached the adjustment settings to the Raw file without actually opening the image in Photoshop. That feature has been replaced with the *Done* button that is now found in the lower right of the Camera Raw dialog box.

- **Sudden Appearance of .xmp Files:** Camera Raw settings are now automatically saved in sidecar .xmp files with the original images. If you prefer the old way, just choose **Preferences** from the side menu of the Camera Raw dialog box and set the **Save image settings in:** setting to **Camera Raw database**.

- **Preview Not Working as Expected:** They've changed the *Preview* checkbox so that it only previews the settings in the currently active tab (Adjust, Lens, etc.). To toggle a preview of all your adjustments, choose **Image Settings** from the **Settings** pop-up menu and then type **Command-Z** (Mac) or **Ctrl-Z** (Win) to see before and after. Just make sure you finish with the menu set to **Custom** to retain the adjustment.

- **Can't Find Tool Icons:** The tool icons from Camera Raw 2.0 have been consolidated at the top of the window.

- **Basic/Advanced Toggle Missing:** The old *Advanced Mode* just made all the tabs visible and offered **Preferences** as a choice from the side menu. All the tabs and the preferences are now available by default.

- **Selected Image Setting Missing:** The **Selected Image** choice in the **Settings** pop-up menu would always allow you to get back to the adjusted version of your image if you had changed the menu to a different setting. That option has been renamed **Image Settings** because you can now have multiple images selected within the Camera Raw dialog box, so the old name no longer made sense.

Automatic Tonal Adjustments

Ok, we're done with quick lists. It's time to pop the hood and get some grease under our fingernails. The first thing you'll notice about Camera Raw 3.0 is that the thumbnail images for unadjusted Raw images have much more contrast. That's due to the new *Auto* checkboxes in the Camera Raw dialog box. These checkboxes automatically adjust each image to ensure that it has bright highlights, dark shadows and a good

The Auto checkboxes are on by default. Moving the corresponding slider will instantly turn off the checkbox.

amount of brightness and contrast all based on the content of each individual image. That means that you'll no longer see your images turning to mush as Bridge (formerly known as the File Browser) builds thumbnails and previews for each image (in previous versions a JPG preview from the camera was used before a high quality preview could be created).

Auto Isn't Always Great For Your Images

This new feature (the *Auto* checkbox) is really a mixed blessing; on the one hand it give us better looking thumbnail images, but on the other hand it makes it next to impossible to see the difference between different exposures taken of the same scene (bracketed exposures). In effect, it normalizes each image so they look as if they were all taken with similar exposure settings.

Changing Your Camera Preferences

Fortunately, Adobe made it easy to turn off the *Auto* setting. If you're a photographer who often brackets exposures and want to see more of what you captured (as opposed to an already adjusted image), do the following:

1) Double-click on any Raw file to open the Camera Raw dialog box.
2) Set the **Settings** pop-up menu to **Camera Raw Defaults** if it isn't already.
3) Choose **Use Auto Adjustments** from the side menu of the dialog box to toggle it off (or type **Command/Ctrl-U**).
4) Choose **Save New Camera Raw Defaults** from the same side menu as above.
5) Repeat the process for Raw files from other cameras you own (the preferences are camera specific).

Top: Images with differing in-camera exposure settings. Bottom: The same three images after auto adjustments.

Left: Exposure clipping view, Middle: Shadow clipping view, Right: Resulting image.

Toggling Auto

Moving any one of the sliders that has an associated *Auto* checkbox will automatically turn the checkbox off so you can easily apply custom settings. If you'd like to quickly toggle all of the *Auto* checkboxes off and back on again, just type **Command-U** (Mac) or **Ctrl-U** (Win) a few times. It's really a personal preference; I use *Auto* when I want to quickly create a web photo gallery or contact sheet (via the **Tools>Photoshop** menu in Bridge) and I end up manually adjusting each image when I'm going to use them for an important project.

Shadow & Highlight Clipping Warnings

When manually adjusting Raw files, it's very easy to lose detail in the bright or dark areas of your image by moving the Exposure or Shadows sliders too far. In the past, you could hold **Option** (Mac) or **Alt** (Win) and move those sliders to get what's known as a 'clipping display' (which is still available). This special mode would indicate where you were losing highlight or shadow detail. To understand what that special mode does, you'll want know that your image is made out of three components behind the scenes; red, green and blue light. When an area shows up in color, that indicates that you're losing detail in one or two of those three components, but still have some detail in at least one component, so the area hasn't quite become white or black yet. Areas that show up as white (when moving the Exposure slider) have lost all detail and are solid white, while areas that show up as black (when

moving the Shadow slider) have lost all detail and have become solid black. That feature is still available and now you have an alternative.

Highlight/Shadow Detail Warning

At the top of the Camera Raw dialog box you'll find the new *Shadows* and *Highlights* checkboxes. The *Highlights* checkbox will place a bright red color over any bright areas that are starting to lose detail by becoming too close to white. The *Shadows* checkbox does a similar thing to the darkest areas by placing a bright blue color over areas that are that are starting to lose detail by becoming too close to black. When I say 'too close to black' and 'too close to white,' I mean that you're losing detail in one, two or all three of the three compo-

> **NOTE**
>
> **Toggling Checkboxes**
> *If you don't want to move your mouse to the top of your screen to turn the Highlights and Shadows on or off, try typing **U** to toggle the Shadows checkbox or **O** to toggle the Highlights checkbox.*

The red color in the upper right of this image is caused by the Highlight checkbox in the Camera Raw dialog box, while the blue in the center of the image is caused by the Shadows checkbox.

nents that make up your image. That means that this new feature doesn't differentiate between the areas that would show up in color versus black or white in the clipping display feature that was available in previous versions of Photoshop. So what does that mean to you? Well, don't freak out if you see a lot of color showing up on your image. Saturated colors will often max out one of the components that make up your image, causing the color to show up when you still have plenty of detail. If you're concerned, hold **Option** (Mac) or **Alt** (Win) and click on the Exposure slider (if the color overlay is red), or Shadows slider (if the color overlay is blue) to see if you've really trashed all the detail or not.

When It's Okay to Lose Detail

I think it's okay to completely lose detail in the bright part of your image if that area is limited to where you see a light source or a reflection of the light source on a shiny object (like glass, water or metal). In those cases, making the area white will make it jump off the page and look brighter than anything else in the image, which is usually appropriate for light sources. When it comes to partially losing detail, you have to be careful. Overly saturated colors (usually indicated by losing detail in one or two components of your image) often look unnatural, so I usually toggle the checkbox off and then examine the area to see if that's the case. If you need maximum detail in an area, make sure no color appears on top of it and you shouldn't have a problem.

Image Rotation and Straightening

If you have an image with a cockeyed horizon line, then you'll be happy to learn about the new Straighten tool in Camera Raw. The tool is found just to the left of the Rotate Left and Rotate Right icons at the top of the Camera Raw dialog box. To straighten a horizon (or for that matter any line that you'd like to make perfectly horizontal or vertical), click on the Straighten tool and then click and drag across the line that you'd like to

The cropping rectangle indicates the angle of rotation and which areas of the image will be displayed when the image is opened in Photoshop.

straighten. Once you release the mouse button, you will see a cropping rectangle that indicates which portion of the image will be loaded into Photoshop when you decide to open the file.

Unlike the Crop tool in Photoshop, the Straighten tool in Bridge has no *Done* button to show you the end result. Instead, you have to actually open the image in Photoshop to see the end result of your rotation (you can cheat a little if you open multiple images in Camera Raw... more on that later in this chapter).

> **NOTE**
>
> **Use a Crosshair**
> I find that the cursor you get in this tool is less than helpful when trying to be precise, so I usually press **Caps Lock** on my keyboard to transform the cursor into a crosshair. That makes it much easier to determine where you're clicking with the tool.

If you mess up on your first try, just click on the tool a second time and try again (no need to remove the cropping rectangle that appears). You can also move your mouse just beyond one of the corner points and drag to rotate the cropping rectangle. If you decide to completely start over, then press **Delete** (Mac) or **Backspace** (Win) to remove the cropping rectangle (you can also press **Esc** or click on the Crop tool and choose **Clear Crop**).

Non-Destructive Cropping

Camera Raw 3.0 also offers a Crop tool which allows you to specify which area of the image you'd like to use when the image is opened in Photoshop or saved in a different file format. This Crop tool can be found just to the left of the Straighten tool. When the Crop tool is active,

Dragging over an image while the Crop tool is active will create a cropping rectangle.

you can click and drag across your image to indicate how you'd like to crop the image. After you release the mouse button, you can drag any of the corner handles to fine-tune the crop.

Click on the Crop tool to access the Crop Tool Options menu, and choose Custom to enter precise values.

The area of your image that will be discarded will be ghosted back compared to the area that will remain. I call this non-destructive because no matter what you do with the Crop tool, all the original data in your Raw file remains even though you've effectively cropped the image.

If you want to crop your image to a specific size or width/height ratio, then click on the Crop tool and hold down the mouse button to access the Crop tool pop-up menu. The **Normal** choice doesn't restrict the size or proportions of the crop, while the section below limits the width to height ratio. My favorite feature is the **Custom** choice, which allows you to enter en exact width and height in pixels, inches or centimeters (or a custom ratio). When you drag within your

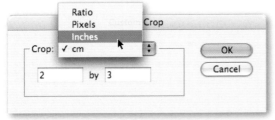

You can access the Custom Crop dialog box by choosing Custom from the Crop tool pop-up menu.

image, Photoshop is smart enough to figure out if you want a horizontal or vertically oriented image based on how wide or tall you make the cropping rectangle. I love this feature because it allows me to enter a size like 8x10 inches, draw a cropping rectangle and then quickly save that size image as a TIFF, JPG or PSD file via the *Save* button (more on that button later). I just wish I could save preset sizes so they would show up in the Crop tool's pop-up menu.

If you're sneaky enough, you'll be able to copy a cropping rectangle to multiple images and effectively use a preset, but we'll have to make it through a few more features before you learn about Multi-image Support, which is where we'll start playing those tricks.

Color Sampler Tool

To the left of the Crop tool is the new Color Sampler tool. When you click on that tool and then click on your image, you'll add a 'sample point' to your image, which looks like a crosshair. At the same time, an RGB readout will be added just above the image which will indicate how much Red, Green and Blue light is being used to create the color that appears under the sample point. By clicking on multiple areas of your image, you can add up to nine of those crosshairs and corresponding readouts. Each sample point is labeled with a number so you can easily see which RGB readout corresponds to which sample point. You can also add a sample point by **Shift-clicking** while the White Balance tool is active (which is loacted to the left of the Color Sampler Tool). To delete a point, hold **Option** (Mac) or **Alt** (Win) and click on a sample point while the Color Sampler tool is active, or click the Clear Samplers button to delete them all.

What To Use It For

If you're not used to using the Color Sampler tool within Photoshop itself (it's hidden in the same slot as the Eyedropper tool in Photoshop's Tool palette), then you might not have an idea as to what these sample points are used for, so let's take a look:

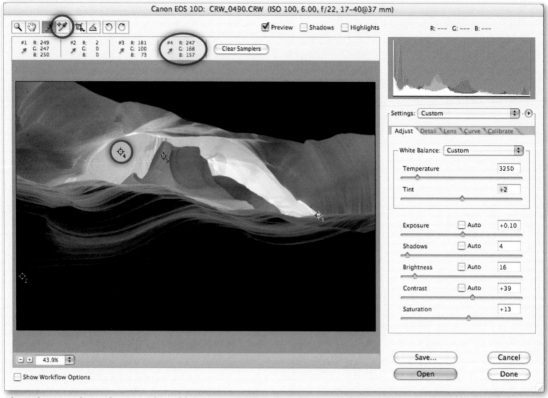

The Color Sampler tool was used to add four 'sample points' and four matching RGB readouts above the image.

- **All three numbers reach zero** indicates a solid black area with no detail at all. This is useful when adjusting the Shadows slider to determine if detail is being lost in an important area.
- **All three numbers reach 255** indicates a solid white area with no detail. This is useful when adjusting the Exposure slider to determine if detail is being lost in an important area.
- **All three numbers higher than 240** indicate an area that is so bright that you can't rely on being able to see detail in it even though the area is not solid white. This is useful when adjusting the tonal controls (Exposure, Brightness or Contrast) to determine if detail will be visible in important areas.
- **All three numbers lower than 25** indicate an area that is so dark that you can't rely on being able to see detail in it even though it is not solid black. This is useful when adjusting

the tonal controls (Shadows, Brightness or Contrast) to determine if detail will be visible in important areas.
- **Balanced RGB numbers** indicate an area that does not contain color (a shade of gray), which is useful in determining if a white or gray object is contaminated with color and might need to be clicked on with the White Balance tool to neutralize a color cast.
- **A single number reaching 0 or 255** in a saturated color indicates the area is starting to lose detail but hasn't gone all the way to black or white. This is useful when determining if the Saturation slider is so high that detail is being lost in saturated colors.
- **RGB values** define the color that appears in an area and the numbers can be useful when calibrating a digital camera using the Calibrate tab in Camera Raw (that technique is not new and so is beyond the scope of this book).

The color samples can also be useful when using the new Curves tab in Camera Raw. They are used with the same general concepts as I mentioned above; the only difference is the feature that's being used to change the overall brightness and contrast of the image. Don't worry if you don't end up using the Color Sampler tool. I'm guessing that less than 10% of Photoshop users are big enough gearheads to find it to be worthwhile.

Curves Tab

The adjustments found under the Adjust tab are great for defining how your image will look overall, but at the same time most of them have more sophisticated equivalents in Photoshop. However, due to a few special qualities of Raw files, it's best to get the most out of your image while you're in the Camera Raw dialog box before unleashing Photoshop's tools on your image.

Camera Raw vs. Photoshop

So what makes a Raw file so special that the Camera Raw dialog box can often give you better results than Photoshop? The simplest explanation I can give you is that files opened in Photoshop are built to closely reflect how our eyes perceive color and tonality, while your digital camera perceives color and tonality quite differently. If you want to know the nitty-gritty, then please read on. When you double the amount of light entering your eyes, your brain doesn't perceive things are being twice as bright. Sure things would be quite a bit brighter, but it doesn't actually look twice as bright. A digital camera on the other hand isn't that sophisticated. It simply measures how much light enters the lens and when the light doubles, it considers that to be twice as bright. When you open a Raw format image in Photoshop, the Camera Raw dialog box does the conversion between how your camera perceives color and how it thinks your eyes perceive color (which is what gets loaded into Photoshop). Many adjustments will produce better results when Photoshop is thinking like your camera (specifically controls found under the Adjust, Curve and Calibrate tabs). White Balance is the

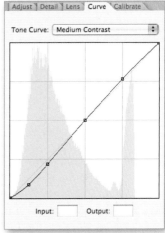

The controls found under the Curves tab allow you to precisely adjust the brightness and contrast of different tonal ranges within your image.

largest benefit to working in Camera Raw since there really isn't a similar adjustment in Photoshop that can produce anywhere near the quality you can get from using that feature in Camera Raw. It's a good thing to get as much out of your image while in the Camera Raw dialog box before taking the image into Photoshop.

The Curves tab is new to Camera Raw 3.0 and it allows you much more control over the tonality of your images than you would have if you limited yourself to the choices that are found under the Adjust Tab (Exposure, Shadows, Brightness and Contrast). For example, in the image below I'd like to darken the building without making the surroundings too dark. If I only know how to use the controls found under the Adjust tab, then I'm probably going to start by trying the Brightness slider. But that slider brightens or darkens everything except black and white in the image, so not only will the building become darker, but its surroundings will also. The same is true of the Exposure and Shadows sliders. When you work with the Adjust tab controls, you're lim-

Left: original unadjusted image, Middle: brightness slider adjustment, Right: Curves adjustment.

ited to affecting the image overall. But, switch over to the Curves tab and you can easily isolate and adjust the brightness or contrast of different brightness ranges without affecting others. Let's see how it works.

Curves Crib Notes

Since Curves is not new to Photoshop (you can find it under the **Image>Adjustments** menu) and attempting to cover it all here would cause this chapter to be more about Curves than Camera Raw, I've decided to give you some short tips on using Curves in Camera Raw. If you want to really learn how to think about Curves, then I suggest you check out the chapter on that topic in my *Photoshop Studio Techniques* book. Let's jump in and see what we can learn about Curves without getting too overwhelmed by the topic.

The Circle is Your Guide

If you hold **Command** (Mac) or **Ctrl** (Win) and hover over your image (but don't click the mouse button), you should notice a circle appearing on the curve. That circle indicates the part of the curve that will affect the brightness level that's currently under your mouse. You can move across an area and watch the circle jump around to see how much of an area on the curves line you'll need to manipulate in order to affect the area you're mousing over.

Height Determines Brightness

If you click the mouse button on your image while holding **Command** (Mac) or **Ctrl** (Win), then you'll add a dot to the curve. Once you've done that, you can use the **up arrow** key to add light to the image and cause it to become brighter, or use the **down arrow** key to take away light and cause the image to become darker. The diagonal gray line represents the original brightness of the image. The more you stray from that gray line, the more radically you will brighten or darken the image.

Angle Determines Contrast

If you'd rather make changes to the contrast of your image, then start making the curve steeper (more toward vertical), or flatter (more toward

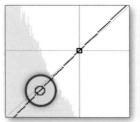

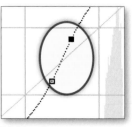

Hold Command (Mac), or Ctrl (Win) to see a circle while mousing over your image.

Making the curve steeper than the gray line will add contrast to an area.

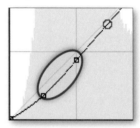

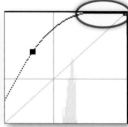

Moving the curve below the gray line will darken the image.

If the curve ever goes completely flat, then you've lost detail in an area.

Saving a curve as a settings subset will cause the preset to appear in the Tone Curve pop-up menu.

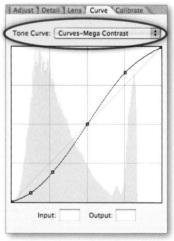

horizontal). The steeper you make the curve, the more contrast you'll have in an area of your image. To pump up the contrast in a particular area, hold **Command** (Mac) or **Ctrl** (Win) and move across the area without pressing the mouse button. While you're dragging, keep an eye on the curve to see where that circle jumps around. That's the area you want to make steeper to gain contrast.

Opening multiple images in Camera Raw will cause each image to be displayed as a thumbnail image.

I usually try to avoid making the curve too flat because that reduces contrast and can quickly turn your image to mush. If you ever end up with part of your curve going completely flat, then click on the curve in the middle of the flat area and drag the dot that you just added toward the dot that's farthest away (of the two dots that surround the problem area), and then finesse the position of the dot until the curve is no longer flat.

If you've already used Curves, then you might wish that you could add your own presets to be used again later. Well, Adobe thought about that. After creating the curve you want to save, choose **Save Settings Subset** from the side menu of the Camera Raw dialog box, set the **Subset** pop-up menu at the top of the dialog box to **Tone Curve** and then click the *Save* button. Now whenever you'd like to use your newly saved curve, just choose the name you gave it from the **Tone Curve** pop-up menu that appears just below the Curve tab.

> **NOTE**
>
> **Selecting Points**
> *You can type **Control-Tab** to cycle through the points that make up a curve, type **Shift-Control-Tab** to cycle backwards, or type **D** to deselect all the points. While a point is active, use the **up** and **down** arrow keys to reposition the point.*

Multi-Image Support

Now that we've seen the major new features in Camera Raw, let's see how they can be quickly applied to multiple images. With more than one image selected in Bridge, you can type **Command-R** (Mac) or **Ctrl-R** (Win) to open the images in Camera Raw. You'll see each image as a thumbnail on the left side of the dialog box. You can click on the individual thumbnails to switch which image is visible in the main image pane of the Camera Raw dialog box. That means that you can quickly adjust multiple images by clicking on the first thumbnail, changing the adjustment settings and then moving on to the next thumbnail.

Adjusting Multiple Images Simultaneously

If you'd like to apply identical adjustments to multiple images, do one of the following before changing the adjustment sliders:

- **Select Individual Images** by **Command-clicking** (Mac) or **Ctrl-clicking** (Win) on the thumbnails you want selected.
- **Select Multiple Images** by clicking on one image and then **Shift-clicking** on a second image thereby selecting all the ones in between.
- **Select All Images** by typing **Command-A** (Mac) or **Ctrl-A** (Win) or clicking on the *Select All* button that appears above the thumbnails.

Once you have multiple images selected, moving any slider will apply the settings from all the sliders to the selected images (even if you only moved one slider). Or, if you've already adjusted one of the images and want to apply those settings to the others, then select the images you'd like to work with and click the right or left arrow icon that appears at the bottom of the main image pane until the image that has the settings you want to apply is visible in the main image page (the image being viewed will have a blue outline around its thumbnail to show it's not only selected but visible in the main window). Now you're ready to click the *Synchronize* button to apply the settings from the visible image to all the selected images. Clicking that button prompts a dialog box to appear asking which settings you'd like to copy to the other images. Once you click OK, then those settings will be applied to all the selected images. If you'd rather not see that dialog box, then hold **Option** (Mac) or **Alt** (Win) when clicking the *Synchronize* button to use the last settings you specified in the Synchronize dialog box.

Once settings are applied to an image, a small icon will appear on the affected thumbnails to indicate they have been adjusted.

Clicking the Synchronize button will cause Camera Raw to prompt you for settings.

Rating and Labeling Images

You can also quickly rate (on a five star scale) or add color labels to images within Camera Raw. These ratings will also appear within the Bridge application. When you have multiple images open, type one of the following keyboard shortcuts (to remove a color label, just type the keyboard shortcut a second time):

The thumbnail above has been cropped (left icon), adjusted (right icon), rated (stars) and labeled (color).

RATING AND LABELING SHORTCUTS		
Mac	**Win**	**Result**
Cmd-1	Ctrl-1	1 Star Rating
Cmd-2	Ctrl-2	2 Star Rating
Cmd-3	Ctrl-3	3 Star Rating
Cmd-4	Ctrl-4	4 Star Rating
Cmd-5	Ctrl-5	5 Star Rating
Cmd-, (comma)	Ctrl-, (comma)	Increase Rating
Cmd-. (period)	Ctrl-. (period)	Decrease Rating
Cmd-6	Ctrl-6	Red Label
Cmd-7	Ctrl-7	Yellow Label
Cmd-8	Ctrl-8	Green Label
Cmd-9	Ctrl-9	Blue Label
Shift-Cmd-0 (zero)	Shift-Ctrl-0 (zero)	Purple Label

Tricks To Play on Multiple Images

There are a bunch of interesting things you can do when you have multiple images selected within Camera Raw:

- **Zoom to Matching Magnifications** by typing **Option-Command-0** (Mac) or **Alt-Ctrl-0** (Win) so you can use the arrow keys at the bottom of the main image area to cycle through the images and inspect the same area in each image. This is useful when reviewing bracketed exposures.
- **Use Identical Crop Settings** by creating a cropping rectangle. This feature is also useful when using the Exposure Merge feature (covered in *Chapter 8: HDR Imaging*) because every image needs to be cropped exactly like

the others to make sure they still line up after being merged. If you used a Custom Crop setting (like 8x10 inches), then you can effectively apply a preset sized cropping rectangle to all the selected images. Then you can click on individual thumbnails and adjust the cropping rectangle to specify different areas in each file to turn into an 8x10 image.

- **Preview Crop/Rotation Results** using thumbnails. Do you remember that I was going to tell you something special about the crop/rotate feature when we got to multi-image support? If you recall it is a wee bit frustrating to crop and rotate an image in Camera Raw because you don't actually get to see the final result of the crop/rotate until you open the image in Photoshop (all you see is a cropping rectangle at an angle). However, if you open multiple pictures in Camera Raw, you will see the results of your crop/rotate in the small thumbnails that appear on the left of the Camera Raw dialog box (but not the main image pane), so at least you have a small indication of the final result.
- **Apply Ratings or Labels** to multiple files with a single keystroke.

As you can see, adjusting multiple images within Camera Raw is fast and easy. When we get on to the subject of Bridge integration, I'll show you other methods of applying Camera Raw settings to multiple files. But first, let's explore the difference between opening Raw files in Bridge and Photoshop.

Bridge or Photoshop—Any Difference?

My next topic is a very cool aspect of CS2. For those of you who fell in love with the File Browser (now known as Bridge), you'll be thrilled to know that it now opens independently of Photoshop. You can also cause it to launch by clicking its icon in the Options bar or choosing **File>Browse** from within Photoshop. That means you now have two distinctly different routes into the Camera Raw dialog box. And—this is the really important part, so pay attention—the route you take to Camera Raw determines how much

background processing you can get away with. Here's how it works. You can either open your Raw images from within the Bridge application (by typing **Command-R** or **Ctrl-R**) or have them sent directly to Photoshop (by double-clicking or typing **Command-O** or **Ctrl-O**). In both cases, you'll be presented with the Camera Raw dialog box and the general functionality is identical, but there are some advantages and disadvantages to each approach:

- **Batch Process Files in Photoshop** by applying an action to a folder full of images while you simultaneously adjust Raw files using Bridge.
- **Background Process File Conversions** in Bridge by clicking the *Save* button for multiple images. The saving of the files will happen in the background even if you close the Camera Raw window and continue working within Bridge (Camera Raw via Photoshop stops background processing as soon as the dialog box is closed).
- **Work with Bridge on a Second Monitor** so that you can continue working in Photoshop as you monitor Bridge's progress on batch saving images.
- **Files Open Faster From Photoshop** by typing **Command-O** (that's an Oh, not a Zero). That sends the file directly to Photoshop's Camera Raw dialog box instead of having to send the data to Bridge's Camera Raw dialog box and then make an extra jump to get the info into Photoshop.

Save Multiple Images

Once you've adjusted your images within Camera Raw, you have four options:

- **Click Cancel to Discard Settings**, close the files and leave them in the same state they were in before they were opened. Use this option when you feel your adjustments have done more harm than good and you want to leave the images untouched.
- **Click Done to Update Settings** by attaching them to the Raw file without opening the image in Photoshop. Use this option if you plan to adjust the image in Camera Raw but

don't need to open the files in Photoshop until later, or if you'd like to create a web photo gallery or contact sheet using the commands from the **Tools>Photoshop** menu within Bridge.

- **Click Open to View the Image in Photoshop**. Use this option when you plan to continue working on the image using Photoshop's adjustment and retouching tools.
- **Click Save to Convert to Another File Format** such as TIFF, JPG or PSD. Use this option when you need to either use the image in a program that doesn't support Raw files (such as a page-layout program), or need to send the file to a friend or client.

You can save multiple images by selecting the images you'd like to save and then clicking the Save X Images (the X represents the number of images selected). There is no need to wait for Camera Raw to finish saving the images. You're welcome to return to Bridge, open, adjust, and continue saving more images. You'll see a progress report line appear just above the *Save* button that will reflect how many images are left in the cue to be saved.

The Save Options Dialog Box

Clicking the *Save* button in the Camera Raw dialog box will present you with a window full of choices. Let's explore them one at a time:

These buttons are found in the lower right of the Camera Raw dialog box.

Destination

Choosing **Save in Same Location** will place the saved files in the same folder as the original Raw files. You don't have to worry about overwriting the original Raw files because the newly saved images will have a different file extension. I usually choose the **Save in New Location** setting and then click on the *Select Folder* button to specify my desktop. That way I can process dozens or

hundreds of images without having to remember where the original Raw files were stored. Holding **Option** (Mac) or **Alt** (Win) when clicking the *Save Image* button in Camera Raw will cause it to use the last settings you specified, which is another advantage of using the desktop as a standard save location.

File Naming

This area allows you to automatically change the name of the saved files so that they end up as a numbered series such as Hawaii Vacation 01.jpg, Hawaii Vacation 02.jpg, etc. If you'd like to keep the original file name, then just leave the first field set to **Document Name** and leave the rest of the fields alone.

Format

The Format area allows you to choose one of four file formats (DNG, TIFF, JPG or PSD) and any compression options offered by the format.

I find that the combination of saving Raw files as JPG's and TIFF's and the new Crop tool (using a custom size setting) makes Camera Raw a very effective production tool. I can easily save 8x10 inch TIFFs ready to be sent off for printing, or save 100-pixel-wide JPG's ready to be emailed to a client, all without leaving the Camera Raw dialog box. If you like the new multi-image support within Camera Raw, then wait until you see what you can do in Bridge!

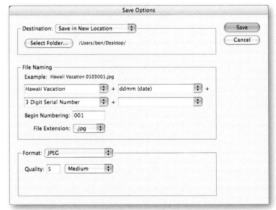

The Save Options dialog box will appear after clicking the Save button within the Camera Raw dialog box.

Bridge Integration

I covered the major changes of Bridge back in *Chapter 1*, but I skipped over the new Raw functions within Bridge, so let's cover them here.

File Status Icons

A quick glance at the thumbnails in Bridge will reveal which images have been adjusted in Camera Raw (they show an adjustment icon) and which ones are just being displayed using the default settings. You'll also find a Crop icon on any image that has been cropped within Camera Raw. These icons make it very easy to figure out which images you've adjusted and which you haven't. You'll also notice a document icon on any images that are currently open in Photoshop (but only in Thumbails or Filmstrip view).

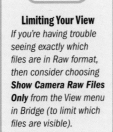

NOTE

Limiting Your View
If you're having trouble seeing exactly which files are in Raw format, then consider choosing **Show Camera Raw Files Only** *from the View menu in Bridge (to limit which files are visible).*

Apply Camera Raw Settings

In the previous version on Photoshop, you could **Control-click** (Mac) or press the right mouse button (Win) on a Raw file within the File Browser and choose **Apply Camera Raw Settings**, but the choices were somewhat cumbersome. With Bridge, Adobe has made slight refinements that make it much easier to quickly apply settings to a multitude of images.

You can now copy and paste Camera Raw settings between Raw files. There are three ways to access the copy/paste functionality:

- Choose **Apply Camera Raw Settings** from the **Edit** menu within Bridge.
- **Ctrl-click** (Mac) or press the right mouse button (Win) while hovering over the desired Raw file in the thumbnail area of Bridge.
- Type **Option-Command-C** (Mac) or **Alt-Ctrl-C** (Win) in an active file to copy settings and then select other files and type **Option-Command-V** (Mac) or **Alt-Ctrl-V** (Win) to paste the settings.

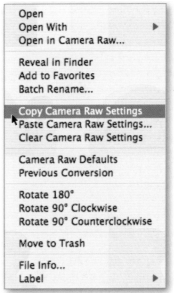

Control-clicking (Mac) or pressing the right mouse button (Win) will allow you to choose from the menu shown here.

The idea is to choose **Copy Camera Raw Settings** while the desired file is active, then to select all the files you'd like to apply those settings to and choose **Paste Camera Raw Settings** to apply the settings.

When you access the **Apply Camera Raw Settings** menu, you'll also find choices for clearing settings, using the previous conversion, or applying the Camera Raw default settings. Let's look at what each of those choices will do to your images:

- **Previous Conversion** applies the settings used for the the last image that was opened or updated from within Camera Raw.
- **Clear Camera Raw Settings** does literally what it says by removing all hints of any adjustments. This will cause Bridge to create a new preview image using the default Camera Raw settings but will not mark the image as being adjusted.
- **Camera Raw Defaults** applies the current Camera Raw default settings and marks the image as being adjusted.

Those last two options might sound a little too similar for comfort. Both choices will cause Photoshop to create a new thumbnails which are based on the current Camera Raw defaults. The **Camera Raw Defaults** choice actually attaches the current default settings to the file, which means the image will look consistent even if it's viewed on a machine that has different default settings than yours. Using **Clear Camera Raw Settings** does not attach the *current* Camera Raw default settings to the file and therefore will cause the thumbnails to be regenerated if you change the default settings or open the images from a different machine.

Smart Objects

Photoshop CS2 offers a brand new type of layer that can be useful to anyone who shoots in the Raw format. This new layer type allows you to embed the original Raw file within a layered Photoshop file. I covered all the details of Smart Objects back in *Chapter 4: Smart Objects*, so if you plan on incorporating your Raw images into layered Photoshop files, then go check out that chapter, I think you'll like what you see. For now, I just want to let you know that you can select a Raw file and then choose **File>Place>In Photoshop** to convert a Raw file into a special layer within the currently open file.

Tiny Tweaks Make All The Difference

I know we've covered a lot in this chapter, but if you think that's all Adobe did when updating Camera Raw, you underestimate their commitment to beefing up Camera Raw. Below is a list of even more (but perhaps a bit smaller) tweaks you'll find in the new Camera Raw:

- **The Show Workflow Checkbox** at the bottom of the dialog box allows you to make more room for the preview image.
- **Renamed Chromatic Aberration Sliders** (Lens Tab) makes it easier to figure out which colors will be affected. The sliders are not new, but the naming has been improved. These sliders are designed to reduce or eliminate colored halos that are caused by light bending as it passes through the lens on your camera...

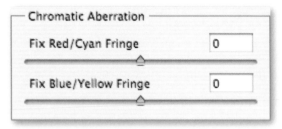

just like going through a prism, white light becomes a micro rainbow of colors. This can cause halos of color on the edges of high contrast edges.

- **Moved the Camera Raw Plug-in** because it is now used by two programs (Bridge and Photoshop) and Adobe wanted to make sure both programs use the same version of Camera Raw. The new location on a Mac is **Library/ Application Support/Adobe/Plug-ins/CS2/File Formats** and on Windows is **C:/Program Files/ Adobe/Plug-ins/File Formats**. If you buy a new digital camera and have to download a newer version of the Camera Raw plug-in, you now know where to put it. You can also search for 'Camera Raw' on your hard drive to find the location.
- **Added Export Settings Option** to the side menu of the Camera Raw dialog box. This option allows you to save the adjustment settings for the active image as an .xmp file. This is useful when you are using the Camera Raw Database preference but would like to share an image and the Raw settings associated with it with others.
- **Updated Camera Profiles** are available for select cameras (Canon 1D Mark I, Nikon D100 and Nikon D1X) that allow for more accurate color reproduction than the older profiles provided. You can switch between the older version of the camera profile (which is useful if you need to duplicate the results you were getting from earlier versions of Camera Raw) by setting the **Profile** pop-up menu in the Calibrate tab to 2.4 and use the new, more accurate version by choosing 3.0. If you don't find a 3.0 profile for your camera, that simply means that Adobe has not been able to improve on the original profile for your particular camera

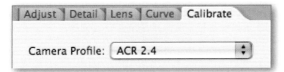

model (in other words, they did a great job the first time around).

- **Changed the Preview Checkbox Behavior** so that it in effect shows a before/after of only the setting used in the active tab (Curves for instance). To see a before and after of all the adjustments combined, choose **Image Settings** from the **Settings** pop-up menu and then type **Command-Z** (Mac) or **Ctrl-Z** (Win) multiple times to toggle between the original settings (before adjustment) and the current settings (after adjustment).

- **Added Megapixel Count to Size Pop-up** menu. The '(1.6 MP)' after a menu item would indicate that the file contains approximately 1.6 million pixels (or megapixels). I don't find this info to be useful, but some people might like to use it to determine how many additional pixels are need to scale an image up or down.

- **Added Symbols to Size Pop-up** menu. As usual, a **+** indicates scaling an image up (adding info) and a **-** indicates scaling an image down (throwing away info), but now you might find a * next to the default size or a **#** to indicate the size that would produce the highest quality result. These symbols will only show up when using certain camera models (some Fuji's and the Nikon D1X for example).

- **Added Crop and Adjustment Icons to Bridge** that indicate which files have been cropped and adjusted within Camera Raw. That makes it very easy to figure out which files have been adjusted and which ones are still virgin files straight from your camera.

CRW_5567.CRW

- **Changed Preference for Sidecar Files** so that Camera Raw settings are saved as .xmp files in the same folder as the each Raw file instead of being stored in a central database. The previous versions defaulted to using the database, which caused problems when images were opened using different copies of Photoshop or when they were saved to CD's (the Raw settings didn't go with them). If you notice .xmp files with the same name as your Raw files, keep those two files together because the .xmp file contains the Raw adjustment that has been applied to the Raw file.

- **Added Warning Triangle** to the upper right of the image window to warn when the on-screen appearance is not accurate.

- **Added Camera Raw Cache Preference** that allows you to set a limit on the cache's size and specify its location on your hard drive. This cache helps make Camera Raw open faster, makes switching between thumbnail images faster and improves the speed at which Bridge is able to create thumbnail and preview images after you adjust files in Camera Raw. Each Raw file takes up about five megabytes in the cache, so the default setting is ideal for folders that contain 200 or less Raw files. If you commonly work with folders that contain more files, just multiply the number of files in a folder by five megabytes to determine the ideal cache size for your situation. Purging the cache does not cause any image data to be lost and can be done when you need to free up hard drive space.

- **Added Multiple Undo/Redos** keyboard shortcuts. You can now type **Option-Command-Z** (Mac) or **Alt-Ctrl-Z** (Win) to undo multiple steps and type **Shift-Command-Z** (Mac) or **Shift-Ctrl-Z** (Win) to redo what you just undid.

I'm known to be notoriously picky, but I have to say that Adobe obviously worked very hard to improve Camera Raw in a multitude of places. With their continued support, digital photography marches on unimpeded and I'm quite happy with the changes I see.

KEYBOARD SHORTCUTS		
Feature	**Mac**	**Win**
Zoom Tool	Z	Z
Hand Tool	H	H
White Balance Tool	I	I
Color Sampler Tool	S	S
Straighten Tool	A	A
Crop Tool	C	C
Preview Checkbox	P	P
Shadows Checkbox	U	U
Highlights Checkbox	O	O
Rotate Image Right	R	R
Rotate Image Left	L	L
Toggle Auto Checkboxes	Cmd-U	Ctrl-U
Camera Raw Preferences	Cmd-K	Ctrl-K
Cycle Curves Points	Cmd-Tab	Ctrl-Tab
Save Image	Cmd-S	Ctrl-S
Save Image w/o Dialog	Opt-Cmd-S	Alt-Ctrl-S
Open	Cmd-O	Ctrl-O
Open without updating	Opt-Cmd-O	Alt-Ctrl-O
Cancel	Esc	Esc
Reset Image Settings	Opt-Esc	Alt-Esc
Select All Thumbnails	Cmd-A	Ctrl-A
Deselect Thumbnails	Shift-Cmd-A	Shift-Ctrl-A
Increase Number by 1	Up Arrow	Up Arrow
Increase Number by 10	Shift-Up Arrow	Shift-Up Arrow
Decrease Number by 1	Down Arrow	Down Arrow
Decrease Number by 10	Shift-Dn Arrow	Shift-Dn Arrow
Undo/Redo	Cmd-Z	Ctrl-Z
Multiple Undo	Opt-Cmd-Z	Alt-Ctrl-Z
Multiple Redo	Shift-Cmd-Z	Shift-Cmd-Z
Fit in Screen	Cmd-0 (zero)	Ctrl-0 (zero)
Zoom to 100%	Opt-Cmd-0	Alt-Ctrl-0
Zoom In	Cmd-+ (plus)	Ctrl-+ (plus)
Zoom Out	Cmd– (minus)	Ctrl– (minus)
Mark for Deletion	Delete	Delete
1—5 Star Rating	Cmd-1—5	Ctrl-1—5
Increase Rating	Cmd-, (comma)	Ctrl-, (comma)
Decrease Rating	Cmd-. (period)	Ctrl-. (period)
Red Label	Cmd-6	Ctrl-6
Yellow Label	Cmd-7	Ctrl-7
Green Label	Cmd-8	Ctrl-8
Blue LabelCmd-9	Ctrl-9	
Purple Label	Shift-Cmd-0	Shift-Ctrl-0
Camera Raw Preferences	Cmd-K	Ctrl-K

Chapter 8
High Dynamic Range Imaging

FILM AND DIGITAL CAMERAS CAPTURE a very limited tonal range. In a single shot it's often impossible to get the full scope of detail in scenes that contain extreme swings between light and dark. We are forced to choose where we want to retain detail: in the intensity of a sunset or its shadowy surroundings; in the interior of a dimly lit room or the radiance of the world outside its window. It's usually a game of favoring one or the other, but almost never both. High Dynamic Range imaging is designed to change all that.

The difference between the brightest and darkest areas of a scene is known as its *dynamic range*. Until now, we've been limited to working on *Low Dynamic Range* (LDR) images in Photoshop. LDR images are limited to a brightness range that is typical of what a camera or scanner can capture in a single pass, which is much more limited than what your eyes experience in an average day.

High Dynamic Range (HDR) images are designed to contain the full brightness range of a scene no matter how wide that range might be. That means that a single HDR image is capable of containing detail in something as dazzling as the sun at high noon while at the same time retaining detail in the inky depths of a cave! This is only possible by taking multiple exposures of a scene and combining those shots into a single HDR image.

Here's an overview of what's involved with working with HDR images:

- **Exposing for HDR:** Taking multiple exposures of the same scene allows you to capture a wider range of brightness levels than you can get in a single shot.
- **Merging Exposures:** Merging is the process of combining multiple exposures of the same scene into a single HDR image that contains the full brightness range of the scene.
- **Working with 32-bit Images:** This new mode is designed specifically for HDR images. It allows you to improve the quality of a few filters, and make new, unique adjustments.
- **Converting to 16-bit:** Only 8 or 16-bit images can be printed or saved in file formats that can be opened by common graphics software.

The Evolution of an HDR Image

An HDR image starts with a scene that contains a brightness range that is beyond that which your camera can capture in a single shot. Multiple exposures are taken to capture the entire brightness range of the scene and then those exposures are merged into a single 32-bit HDR image. Once the exposures are merged into a single file, the on-screen view is less than optimal even though the file contains the full brightness range of the scene. The HDR file must be converted to 16-bit mode in order to print the image and to gain access to most of Photoshop's retouching and adjustment tools. When converting to 16-bit mode, Photoshop allows you to intrepret the 32-bit image (which can contain over one billion brightness levels) to produce a more useable 16-bit version of the image (which can contain just over 30,000 brightness levels). Only 256 brightness levels (also known as 8-bit) are necessary to view or print an image at the highest quality our computer displays and printers are capable of producing. The extra brightness levels in a 16-bit image allow you to perform extreme adjustments in Photoshop in an attempt to produce the most pleasing interpretation of the high dynamic range image. When you're done adjusting the image, it can be converted to 8-bit mode to save a considerable amount of space on your hard drive. In this case, the six original exposures took up 29MB on my hard drive. Merging the exposures into a single 32-bit HDR image produced a 17.8MB file. Converting to 16-bit mode and adding multiple adjustment layers produced a 28.4MB file and the final 8-bit flattened image was 4MB. The layered 16-bit file was retained as the master image file.

This image is the result of enhancing the 16-bit conversion of the HDR image using Photoshop's Adjustment Layers. Once the image was finalized, it was converted to 8-bit mode to produce a smaller file size.

The tonal range of this scene is more than a camera can capture in a single shot. A bracket of four exposures was needed to capture the full tonal range, but a total of six exposures were taken to avoid posterization.

This image was created by merging six exposures into a single HDR image. Viewing such a wide dynamic range using the limited brightness range of a computer display causes it to look noticeably flat and dull.

This image is the result of converting the HDR image to a 16-bit file. In the process, the image was interpreted to obtain a more optimal version that can be viewed or printed using the limited brightness range available on most displays and printers.

Exposing For HDR

HDR imaging is essential when a scene contains a wider dynamic range than your camera can capture in a single shot. In those cases, you can capture the full brightness range by taking multiple exposures of the same scene (also known as a bracket). This is possible with either a film or digital camera, but with a film camera it can be hit or miss unless you are skilled with a light meter.

Some digital cameras offer the advantage of a bar chart that's known as a histogram. The histogram indicates when a scene is beyond the range your camera is capable of capturing and can be very helpful when bracketing exposures.

Histograms

Most medium to high-end digital cameras provide a histogram display. When viewing a histogram, imagine that there is a gradient below it that contains all the brightness levels from black (on the far left) to white (on the far right). I've added such a gradient to the histogram on the right. The bars on the histogram indicate which of the shades in the gradient are used to make up the image. The height of the lines indicate how prevalent each brightness level is within the image. If you ever find one-pixel-wide spikes on the absolute ends of the histogram, that indicates that you have a large area of solid black (spike on the left), or solid white (spike on the right). It's only the absolute left and right ends where spikes are important. A spike in the middle of the histogram is not a problem. Only the extremes of black and white will cause detail to be lost.

A spike on the far left of the histogram indicates that the exposure setting used to capture the

> **NOTE**
>
> **Finding the Histogram**
> Camera manufacturers are not consistent in how they choose to toggle the visibility of a histogram. On my Canon 20D, I simply press the Info button on the back of the camera when reviewing a shot to toggle the histogram. You'll have to review your camera manual if you can't figure out how to display a histogram.

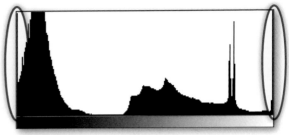

A spike on the far left of the histogram indicates a large area of solid black, while a spike on the far right indicates a large area of solid white.

image has caused the image to become so dark that the darkest areas of the image have become solid black (no shadow detail). A spike on the far right indicates that the exposure setting used caused the image to become so bright that the brightest areas of the image have become solid white (no highlight detail). A spike on both ends of the histogram indicates that both the shadows (spike on the left) and highlights (spike on the right) do not contain detail. If you're not able to find an exposure setting that prevents spikes at the ends of the histogram, then the scene is beyond the range the camera is capable of capturing in a single shot and is a good candidate for an HDR image.

The way to capture the entire brightness range of a scene that creates spikes on one or both ends of the histogram is to take multiple exposures of the same scene (a bracket), each exposure with a varying brightness level.

Bracketing Your Exposures

Here are some guidelines for capturing the full brightness range in a scene:

- **Use a tripod** so that all the exposures will align with one another (and consider using a cable release to prevent camera shake).
- **Use Aperture Priority or Manual** mode and only vary the shutter speed between exposures. Changing the aperture setting changes the depth of field, which will cause the focus in each image to be different, resulting in a less sharp HDR image.

Choosing an Aperture Setting

Be sure that the aperture setting you've chosen will allow for a wide enough range of exposures (before you run into the limitations of your camera equipment). In the example below, the camera that was used had a maximum shutter speed of 30 seconds. An arbitrary aperture setting of f/16 was chosen without thinking of how the setting would affect the bracket of exposures. Using f/16 at the maximum shutter speed of 30 seconds was not enough to push the dark part of the image toward the middle of the histogram. A similar problem can occur when shooting a bright scene when using a low f-stop setting (shooting 'wide open'); you can find yourself bumping into the minimum shutter speed of your camera before the highlights are near the middle of the histogram. In that situation, either use a higher aperture setting (closing down the lens), or use a neutral density filter in front of the camera lens to reduce the amount of light entering the lens. In the image below, only three expsoures were needed to avoid spikes on the histogram, but more were taken to ensure a non-posterized HDR image.

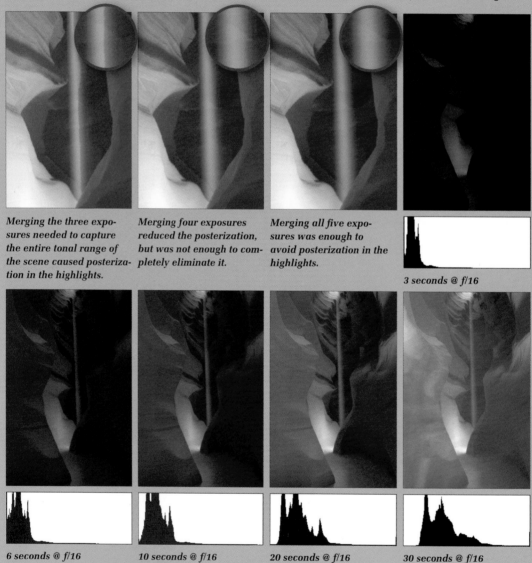

Merging the three exposures needed to capture the entire tonal range of the scene caused posterization in the highlights.

Merging four exposures reduced the posterization, but was not enough to completely eliminate it.

Merging all five exposures was enough to avoid posterization in the highlights.

3 seconds @ f/16

6 seconds @ f/16

10 seconds @ f/16

20 seconds @ f/16

30 seconds @ f/16

- **Use Manual Focus** mode to ensure a consistent focus point throughout all the exposures. Auto-focus cameras are infamous for changing the focus point between exposures, even when the camera and subject remain stationary. Varying focus points can cause slightly soft looking HDR images.
- **Use one stop increments** between exposures. Using more or fewer exposures can cause posterization or other undesirable results.
- **Expose for the highlights** by underexposing until no spike appears on the far right of the histogram and then go one more stop beyond that for safe measure (two stops would be even better). The safety is needed because the histogram does not always accurately reflect what will be captured in a Raw file (because it's based on a contrast-adjusted JPEG image).

The spike indicates bown out highlights (no detail).

The lack of a spike indicates good highlight detail.

- **Bracket until shadows become midtones** by increasing the shutter speed on each shot until the left edge of the histogram appears to the right of center in the histogram (don't worry about any spikes on the right side of the histogram because you captured highlight detail in the step above). This is ideal because digital cameras capture fewer shades in areas that are close to being black (that's also where all the noise shows up). Exposing until the shadows become midtones will usually result in noise-

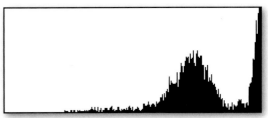

Ideally the brightest exposure would keep the histogram away from the far-left side.

free captures that have many more brightness levels in the shadows that wouldn't otherwise be present if you didn't push them until they become midtones.

- **There is no practical limit** on the exposure range you can capture. There's nothing wrong with using 5, 15 or 20 shots to capture the full brightness range of a scene (as long as it's necessary to avoid spikes on the ends of the histogram). The example on the opposite page shows only five shots, but it would have been better to capture at least three more so that the shadow area (left side of histogram) would end up closer to the middle of the histogram.
- **Avoid motion** at all costs. Objects in motion will cause areas of the image to appear blurry or might produce ghosted double images.
- **Consider using Auto Bracketing** on your digital camera. If your camera has this feature and allows for one stop differences between exposures, then this can help to reduce camera shake since you won't have to touch the camera between exposures.
- **Use Mirror Lockup** if you want the absolute sharpest image possible. I don't do this for most shots, but I'd consider it if I was going for the sharpest image possible.
- **Record the Exposure settings** if you're shooting film (digital cameras automatically include this info with each shot). Photoshop will need to know the film speed (ISO), shutter speed, and aperture setting for each shot.

Now that you have an idea of how to capture the full range of brightness levels in a scene, let's look at what's involved in merging those exposures into a single HDR image.

Merging Exposures

An HDR image is created by merging a minimum of two exposures (but ideally three or more). Let's see what's involved in merging multiple exposures into a single HDR image.

Merge to HDR

Open Bridge and select the images you'd like to merge and then choose Merge to HDR from the **Tools>Photoshop** menu. If you are using scanned images, then Photoshop will prompt you for the exposure settings used to capture each image (digital cameras attach this info to each image so that Photoshop doesn't have to ask). Once Pho-

toshop has the correct settings in hand, it will start preparing your images for merging (opening each one, pasting each them into separate layers in a single file, etc.). Once Photoshop is done processing the images, it will present you with the Merge to HDR dialog box.

NOTE

Camera Raw Settings
Make sure any Camera Raw settings used are applied to all of the images. The following Camera Raw settings would degrade the quality of an HDR image and are therefore ignored:
Exposure
Brightness
Shadows
Contrast
Curve

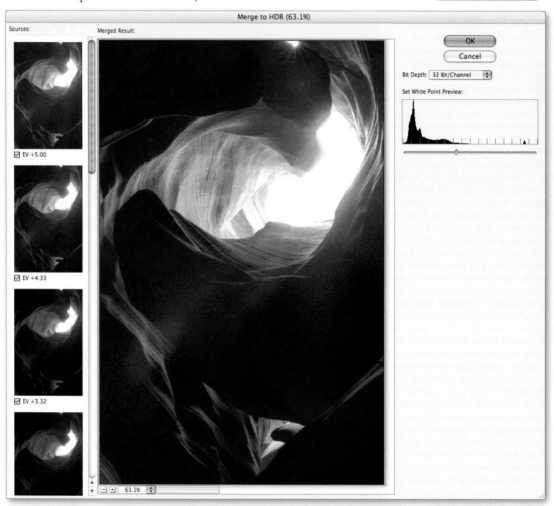

To access the Merge to HDR dialog box, choose Tools>Photoshop>Merge to HDR from within Bridge.

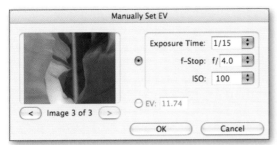

When merging scanned images, you will be asked for the exposure settings used to capture each image.

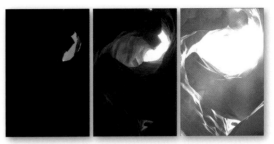

The White Point Preview slider allows you to see how much detail is lurking in the shadows of the image.

A Quick Tour

On the left side of the dialog box you'll find thumbnails of all the images you selected in Bridge. Under each thumbnail will be a number that indicates how many stops there are between exposures. Ideally there would be a single stop between each image, but you may find quite a bit of variation in the numbers. The checkboxes under each thumbnail tell Photoshop which exposures to use to create your HDR image, which is displayed as the large image preview in the middle of the dialog box.

On the right side of the dialog box, you'll find a histogram that reflects the contents of your composited image. The red tick marks at the bottom of the histogram represent EV (exposure value) stops. As you look from right to left, each mark represents half as much light as the previous stop. Here's how you can think about stops: Starting with the brightest area of the image, one stop down from that would be an area that contains half as much light as the brightest area, another stop down would be half again as much light and you could continue thinking that way until you'd made it through five stops total. A single shot from a digital camera usually contains a little over five stops of information. If you count the number of red tick marks, you can see how many stops of light you have in your newly created HDR image... it should be a lot more than the five your camera would deliver in a single shot.

Moving the slider that appears below the histogram will determine the brightness range you can see on-screen. Move the slider all the way to the right to view the entire brightness range contained in the image. Viewing the full range will usually cause the image to look noticeably flat. That's because your image contains a much wider brightness range than your computer displays. If your display were to accurately render the full brightness range of your image, then the white would potentially have to be as bright as the sun! To see the true detail in your image, move the slider to the left while you view the large preview image. That will slowly reveal more and more shadow detail at the expense of highlight detail (by showing bright areas as solid white). As you move the slider to the left, the areas of the histogram that appear to the right will become white.

> **NOTE**
>
> **16-bit For Best Results**
> The Merge to HDR command will respect the last Depth setting that was used at the bottom of the Camera Raw dialog box. Be sure to use the 16 Bits/Channel option to obtain the highest quality. That will cause it to use 128 times the amount of data as 8 Bits/Channel.

Optimizing HDR Merge Settings

Now let's take a look at how you can obtain a high quality HDR conversion. None of these steps are required, but the more of them you follow the more likely you are to obtain superior results:

- **Look for spikes** at the absolute far right and left of the HDR histogram. If you find a tall spike at either end, it's an indication that you don't have a wide enough range of exposures to capture the full brightness range of the original scene (consider re-shooting).

- **Check the EV values,** ideally there should be 1 stop between each exposure. If some are much less than 1, try turning off the checkboxes for in between exposures and move the slider that appears below the histogram to see if that produces smoother transitions in the image.
- **Check for Posterization** by moving the Set White Point Preview slider across its full range. If posterization is evident, try turning off the checkbox for one or more images within that brightness range and then test the slider again to see if you've improved the results. You can often get away with some posterization, but ideally the full range of brightness levels would display smooth transitions.

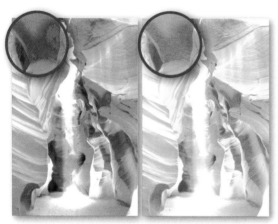

Left: Posterization is usually caused by having the exposures more or less than one stop apart.
Right: A good exposure bracket prevents posterization.

- **Set White Point Preview** by moving the slider under the histogram all the way to the right so you can see the full brightness range in the image.
- **Choose Bit Depth** from the pop-up menu that appears above the histogram. **Choose 16 Bit/ Channel** (unless you're in the movie industry, a 3D guru or just a bleeding edge photographer who wants to push the boundaries more than most people have time for—in those cases, choose 32-bit/Channel).

Choosing Between 16 and 32 Bit Modes

A 32-bit image is a different beast than anything we've had to wrangle with in the past (that is, in Photoshop's past). These images can contain over one billion brightness levels. By comparison, 8-bit images offer a few hundred brightness levels and 16-bit images offer a few thousand brightness levels. 8 and 16-bit images are also limited to containing brightness levels that range from black on the dark end to white on the bright end. 32-bit images on the other hand can easily contain areas that are darker than black and areas that are many times brighter than white. Now mind you, Photoshop doesn't have the means to display areas that are darker than black or brighter than white, but that concept is very useful if you're in the movie or 3D business.

The idea is to choose a brightness range that will be visible in Photoshop (via the **View>32-bit Preview Options** menu) and then load the image into a 3D program. The 3D program can then shine virtual lights on the image to reveal detail in areas that appear to be black in Photoshop. Or, through something like virtual sunglasses, the program can view areas that are brighter than white, again revealing detail that couldn't be seen in Photoshop. The same is done in movies when compositing something like a car that has tinted windows or headlights into another scene where the car interacts with the background.

Photoshop's support for 32-bit images is so limited and the tools that are available are so crude, that I'd argue against working in that mode, unless you've got an agenda that includes 3-D animation, high-end movie work, or you're using more than a dozen exposures to capture the full brightness range of a scene. Otherwise, if you're working on 2-dimensional images that will only be printed or viewed on-screen, my opinion is that you're wasting your time with 32-bit. If you've decided to save your sanity and go the 16 Bit/Channel route, you can breathe a sigh of relief and skip over the next section and go straight to the section that covers converting to 16-bit mode. For the rest of you high-tech maniacs, read on.

Working With 32-bit Images

A 32-bit image contains a brightness range that is beyond what your monitor is capable of displaying, so there has to be a way to choose which brightness range should be visible in Photoshop. To do this, you'll be working with a preview of the image that might seem strange at first because you can't see all the detail on-screen. At times, this might make you feel like you're fumbling around in the dark, but while you're fumbling you can be assured that although you can't see all the detail at once, the 32-bit technology makes it so that areas that appear as black or white on-screen will still maintain detail in the file itself.

Choosing the Visible Range

The **32-bit Preview Options** choice found under the **View** menu will determine the range of brightness levels that will be visible on-screen. The settings that you specify are saved with your file and will be used each time you open the image. You can change this setting as many times as you'd like because these settings are not destructive. When adjusting images in 32-bit mode, think of these settings as creating a preview of the results you'll get after converting the image to 8 or 16-bit mode. The settings will be transferred into the 32-bit Conversion dialog box when you change to 8 or 16-bit mode.

Highlight Compression

This choice will cause the brightest area of an image to appear white even if that area is actually an order of magnitude brighter than white in the

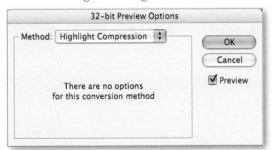

The 32-bit Preview Options dialog box set to the Highlight Compression method.

actual 32-bit file. This can be useful if you want to see detail in the brightest areas of the image without radically changing the contrast of the image (which can often happen when using the Exposure and Gamma method described below).

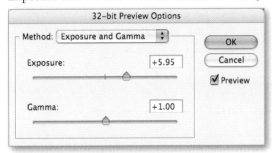

The 32-Bit Preview Option dialog box set to the Exposure and Gamma compression method.

Exposure and Gamma

Photographers often get excited about the *Exposure* setting in Exposure and Gamma because it literally allows them to change the exposure used to display the image as if the shutter speed setting was changed at the time the photo was taken (this doesn't apply to the time-stopping or blurring quality that comes along with different shutter speeds). Moving the slider toward the right will make it look as if a longer exposure time was used and will result in a brighter image. This brightening effect is weighted toward the bright portion of the image so be sure to keep an eye on what's happening to your highlights.

The Gamma slider controls how much darker the shadow areas will be when compared to the highlights in the image. Moving the slider toward the left will darken the shadows, while moving it toward the right will brighten them.

The only difference between these three images is the Exposure setting used.

The only difference between these three images is the Gamma setting used.

Revealing The Hidden Detail

If you click on the triangle icon that appears at the bottom edge of the document window and choose **Show>32-bit Exposure**, you'll cause an Exposure slider to appear at the bottom of your document window. Moving this slider will temporarily brighten or darken everything in the image an equal amount, allowing you to see if there is detail in areas that appear as solid black or solid white on-screen (but might still contain detail). Moving the slider toward the right will brighten the image (just like the Exposure slider in the 32-bit Preview Options dialog box). This slider is designed to temporarily show the effects of an exposure change. This setting is not saved with your image and can prevent you from being able to maintain the current look of your image if

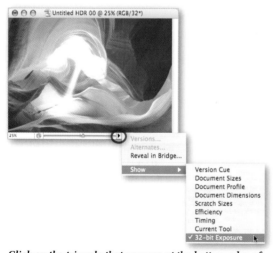

Click on the triangle that appears at the bottom edge of your document window and choose Show>32-bit Exposure from the resulting pop-up menu.

it's converted to 8 or 16-bit mode. When I'm done messing with this slider, I always double-click on the slider to reset it back to the center (default) position so that I can assume my view of the image is one that I can easily maintain when converting to an 8 or 16-bit image.

> **NOTE**
>
> **The Disappearing Menu**
> *The document information menu will only show up if the window is wide enough to allow room for the menu. If you don't see the pop-up menu, just drag the lower right corner of the document window to expand the window.*

If you want to permanently adjust the Exposure, then do so by choosing **Image>Adjustments>Exposure** (instead of using the slider at the bottom of the document window).

So, now that we've explored how to control which areas of your HDR 32-bit image are visible on your LDR screen, let's look at how we can manipulate the image using the tools and adjustment features in Photoshop.

Adjusting 32-bit Images

There are only three adjustment choices available when working with 32-bit images: Exposure, Photo Filter and Channel Mixer. That's because most of Photoshop's 'normal' adjustment choices can't deal with the 32-bit floating point numbers that make up these images. Let's start by exploring the one adjustment choice that was designed specifically for 32-bit HDR images.

Exposure

Choosing **Image>Adjustments>Exposure** will present you with a dialog box that contains settings for *Exposure*, *Offset* and *Gamma*. Two of those controls work very much like the ones we just finished talking about, but unlike the preview controls, these sliders actually change the data that makes up your image. That means that they can be destructive by changing the contrast in your image in such a way that two areas that used to differ in brightness become identical. So if you clicked OK and then re-adjusted the image, you would not be able to get that detail back.

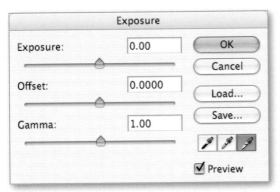

Unlike the 32-bit Preview Options, the Exposure adjustment makes destructive changes to the image.

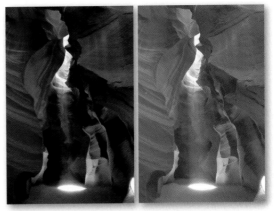

Left: A negative Offset setting darkens the shadows.
Right: A positive Offset setting lightens the shadows.

There's nothing really wrong with applying adjustments that have the possibility of destroying data, it's just that you need to be careful when you use them. You want to make sure you don't regret decisions after you've gone beyond the point that you can undo the changes.

Exposure and Gamma: The Exposure and Gamma sliders work much like the ones we talked about in the 32-bit Preview Options dialog box.

Offset: You'll also find an *Offset* setting in the Exposure dialog box. The position of the Offset slider determines which areas of your image will end up being black. The farther you move the slider toward the left, the more the dark areas of the image will turn black. It's somewhat similar to the upper left slider in Photoshop's Levels dialog box, but small moves of the Offset slider can quickly force large areas of your image to solid black. Moving the slider toward the right will

lighten the darkest areas of your image and eventually force than to lighter and lighter shades of gray (much like the lower left slider in Photoshop's Levels dialog box). Moving the Offset slider can feel like using a sledge hammer to apply a thumb tack, so keep your moves under control.

The Eyedropper Tools: The Exposure dialog box offers White, Gray and Black Eyedropper tools. Clicking on the Black eyedropper and then clicking within your image will cause the clicked area to become very dark, but will not often produce black. That's because (behind the scenes), your image is made out of red, green and blue light and the Black Eyedropper will darken the image until one of those three colors goes to zero, but will not make all three of them go to zero (which would produce black). The White Eyedropper works on a similar principal, forcing one of the red, green and blue components of your image to white, but not allowing all three to go to white

NOTE

Precision Sliders

If you find that the sliders in the Exposure dialog box are a bit too sensitive to tiny movements of your mouse, then try this: hover over the number associated with a slider, and hold down **Option and Command** *(Mac), or* **Alt and Ctrl** *(Win). Then click and drag to the left or right to adjust the slider within 1/10th the sensitivity of a normal slider. Dragging in this way will cause the number associated with each setting to increase as you drag toward the right. This can feel counter-intuitive because dragging to the right will cause the Gamma slider to move toward the left (which is what's necessary to cause the gamma setting to increase).*

Result of clicking in the circled area using the White (left), Gray (middle) and Black (right) eyedroppers.

and therefore possibly retaining detail. The Gray (middle) Eyedropper changes the area clicked on to approximately 50% brightness without shifting the color of the image.

The eyedroppers are simply an alternative method for adjusting the Exposure, Offset and Gamma sliders in the Exposure dialog box. Clicking with either the White or Gray eyedroppers will cause the Exposure slider to change position, while using the Black Eyedropper will cause the Offset slider to move.

These tools might look the same as the ones found in the Levels or Curves dialog boxes, but they differ in one important way—they will not shift the color of an area and therefore they cannot be used to perform color correction (unlike the Levels or Curves eyedroppers).

It's not all that often that I use the Eyedropper tools, but there are some instances when they can be useful:

- **Experiment With Exposure** by clicking around your image with the Gray Eyedropper tool. If an area is way too bright, then you might click on it with this eyedropper to force it to a medium brightness level.
- **Check if Offset is trashing detail** by clicking with the Black Eyedropper in a dark area that should retain detail. If the offset value shifts from a negative number to one that is closer to zero, then the area being clicked on was going to lose detail with the previous offset setting.
- **Maximize saturation** by clicking in a colorful area with the White Eyedropper tool.

The Eyedropper tools are much more useful when applying adjustments through a selection or when painting with the History Brush. We'll cover those techniques later in this chapter.

Now that we've looked at the one adjustment that is specifically designed for 32-bit HDR images, let's move on to a few adjustments that have been available in Photoshop for some time.

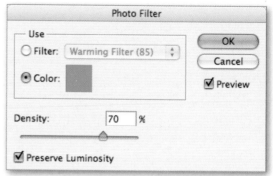

The Photo Filter adjustment using a custom color.

Photo Filter

Choosing **Image>Adjustments>Photo Filter** will allow you to simply shift the colors in your image toward the color you choose. It has the same effect as placing a colored filter in front of a camera lens. You choose the color you'd like to use either by selecting it from the pop-up menu of presets, or by clicking on the color swatch and picking a custom color. After you've chosen a color, you can adjust the Density slider to control the strength of the color shift. If you find that the image is becoming too dark after shifting the color, then consider turning on the *Preserve Luminosity* checkbox to force Photoshop to not change the brightness of the image.

Photo Filter adjustments can be used to make an image appear more warm (red/orange/yellow), more cool (blue/green), or to remove a color cast and make the image feel neutral (no color bias). If your image is too blue, too yellow or too orange, all you have to do is find that color from the edge of a standard color wheel and then look directly across to the opposite side of the color wheel

A standard color wheel can help to determine which color is needed to remove a color cast from an image.

Left: Before. Right: After removing a color cast.

to find the color that's needed to neutralize the color cast. Just choose that color in the Photo Filter dialog box and then adjust the *Density* setting until the color cast has been minimized.

Channel Mixer

The last choice available from the **Image>Adjustments** menu is the Channel Mixer. You can use the Channel Mixer to shift the overall color of your image (making it feel warm or cool), but it's not as predictable as when you use a Photo Filter adjustment. Choosing Red from the **Output Channel** pop-up menu at the top of the dialog box will allow you to shift things toward red or cyan, setting it to Green will allow you to shift things toward green and magenta and setting it to Blue will shift things toward either blue or yellow. This adjustment is literally blending the contents of the red, green and blue channels that appear in the Channels palette in Photoshop. On occasion, I've been able to use a Channel Mixer adjustment

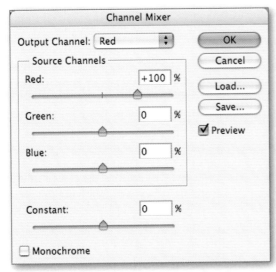

The Channel Mixer is useful for shifting the colors within an image.

to lessen the posterization that can occasionally plague a single channel (by mixing in one of the channels that does not have posterization).

Filter Support

If you're a filter junky, you'll be rather disappointed to learn that there are only 15 filters available when working on a 32-bit image. That's because the numbers that make up a 32-bit image are radically different than the ones that make up an 8 or 16-bit image and Adobe would have to completely reprogram the filters to make them work with 32-bit images. However, there are a few filters that use simpler math so these are available to 32-bit images and few have specific advantages when working with 32-bit images.

One category of filters that I feel does a better job on 32-bit images than on normal 8 or 16-bit images is the blur filters. The only problem with blur filters in 8 or 16-bit images is that they average surrounding pixels to figure out how bright or dark an area should be. That means that blurring any small light sources will usually cause them to become much darker than they were in the original image. If you were to blur an image by moving the camera as the photo was being taken, those same small light sources would be much brighter than the results you get in Pho-

32-BIT COMPATIBLE FILTERS
Menu Path to Filter
Filter>Blur>Average
Filter>Blur>Box Blur
Filter>Blur>Gaussian Blur
Filter>Blur>Motion Blur
Filter>Blur>Radial Blur
Filter>Blur>Shape Blur
Filter>Blur>Surface Blur
Filter>Noise>Add Noise
Filter>Render>Lens Flare
Filter>Sharpen>Smart Sharpen
Filter>Sharpen>Unsharp Mask
Filter>Video>De-Interlace
Filter>Video>NTSC Colors
Filter>Other>High Pass
Filter>Other>Offset

Left: Original image, Middle: 32-bit motion blur, Right: 8 or 16-bit motion blur.

toshop. That is, unless you apply the filter to a 32-bit image. That's when the light sources stay bright and look much more realistic.

Getting Tricky

If you explore the menus and tools within Photoshop while a 32-bit image is open, you'll quickly learn that many features are simply not available:

- No Layers (including Adjustment Layers).
- Only 15 out of over 100 filters are available.
- The most useful retouching tools are not available (you're limited to the Clone Stamp tool).
- You're limited to making selections using the Marquee and Lasso tools.

These limitations force you to get creative if you want to make extensive changes to a 32-bit image. The situation is almost identical to what it was like when 16-bit support was first introduced in Photoshop. They started with very limited support and then expanded it over the next few versions of Photoshop until now just about all of Photoshop's features are supported in 16-bit. So, you can see this section as a glimpse into the future, just like the original 16-bit implementation was a preview of how easy 16-bit editing is today.

Creating Selections

If you don't want to be limited to using the Marquee tool and Lasso tool to make selections, then you'll have to learn to work with a duplicate image that is in 8 or 16-bit mode. Here are the steps involved:

1) Choose **Image>Duplicate** to create an identical file to be used for making selections.

2) Choose **Image>Mode>16 Bits/Channel** (using default settings) to convert the duplicate image into a mode that supports all the selection tools.

3) Make a selection using any method.

4) Choose the Marquee tool, click within a selected area, hold **Shift** and drag to the 32-bit image in which you'd like to use the selection. Holding **Shift** will ensure that the selection is in the same position in both documents.

5) To limit which areas of the image are affected, apply an adjustment while the selection is active.

6) Choose **Select>Save Selection** if you'd like to be able to retrieve the selection at another time. And use **Select>Load Selection** to retrieve a saved selection.

'Masking' Adjustments

If you're used to using Adjustment Layers and enjoy painting on the masks that come along with them, you'll be sorely disappointed to learn that 32-bit files do not support layers. But there is a way to get much of the same functionality by creatively using a few features.

If you created a list of the tools and features available to 32-bit images, it might look like slim pickins', but there is one standout that makes more sophisticated adjustments possible.

TOOLS AVAILABLE IN 32-BIT FILES		
Marquee	Lasso	Move
Crop	Slice	Rubber Stamp
History Brush	Type Mask Tool	Pen Tool
Annotations		

The History Brush: The History Brush will allow you to selectively undo just about anything you can do to change your image (the exceptions are cropping, resizing and changing modes). The idea is that the History palette (found under the **Window** menu) gives you a list of the last 20 operations you've performed on your image (after all, you're becoming a digital surgeon with

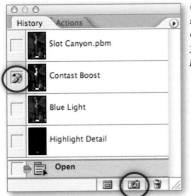

Create Snapshots of each adjustment you'd like to paint with.

this technique). The History Brush allows you to paint with any of those 'History States' to in effect selectively undo any changes you've made. You choose the state you'd like to paint with by clicking in the square area to the far left of the step you'd like to use.

Let's take a look at how you can use the History Brush and History palette to get more control over your 32-bit adjustments:

1) Merge multiple exposures into a 32-bit HDR image, or open a pre-existing HDR file.

2) Choose **Window>History** to access the History palette.

3) Adjust the image using either a Photo Filter, Exposure or Channel Mixer adjustment to optimize a particular area (regardless of how bad other areas appear).

4) Hold **Option** (Mac) or **Alt** (Win), click on the Snapshot icon at the bottom of the History palette (it looks like a tiny 35mm camera) and give this adjustment a name (something like 'Dark Sky' or 'Highlight Detail').

5) Type **Command-Z** (Mac) or **Ctrl-Z** (Win) to undo the adjustment and return to the original

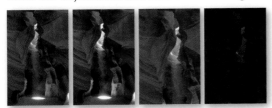

Left to right: original image, three adjustment results.

unadjusted image (the snapshot you took in the last step will be retained even though you specifically told Photoshop to undo your last action).

6) Repeat steps 3-5 until you have all the adjustments you'd like to use to perfect your image.

7) Choose the History Brush in the Tool palette (it looks like a brush with a partial circle around it and is located right below the normal Brush tool) and choose a soft-edged brush to paint with.

8) **Shift-Control-Click** (Mac) or **Shift-Right-Click** (Win) within the image, choose the name of the Snapshot you'd like to paint with and then paint on your image to 'apply' that adjustment.

9) Repeat step 8 until you are satisfied with the look of your image.

Now that you know how to get the most out of your 32-bit images, let's take a look at the file formats that are available when saving a 32-bit image.

Available File Formats

Most common file formats were designed before the days of 32-bit and therefore aren't readily available (unless you convert your image to 8 or 16-bit mode). If you plan to open your 32-bit images in programs other than Photoshop, you'll want to choose a file format that is compatible with the software you'll be using.

When saving a 32-bit image, you're presented with a total of six file formats. To test the formats, I created five 2048x3072 pixel 32-bit images that contained between two and six exposures. I then saved each file in the various file formats and compared the amount of time it took to save the image, how large the resulting file size was and how long it took to re-open each file. The results showed that it didn't make much of a difference how many exposures were merged into an HDR image because the file size varied less than 1MB for different numbers of exposures. Saving and opening time wasn't much of an issue with the exception of the TIFF file format, which I'll detail below. Let's take a look at your options:

Photoshop (.psd): This format is not able to compress 32-bit files to produce a small file size so I ended up with a 72MB file. I wouldn't consider using this format for 32-bit images because I usually reserve the Photoshop file format for layered files, and since 32-bit files don't support layers, I simply never use it for 32-bit files. That way I can tell at a glance what type of content I have just by glancing at the file type. I use .tif for low dynamic range images that don't contain layers and .psd for layered files.

Large Document Format (.psb): This format is an updated version of the .psd file format that Adobe designed to allow for features that are not supported in the .psd format (like images wider than 30,000 pixels). It offers no advantage over .psd files when saving 32-bit files and since it is not able to compress 32-bit files, it produced 72MB files in all my tests.

OpenEXR (.exr): This format was developed by Industrial Light and Magic (the same folks who give us the awesome Hollywood special effects). It is able to losslessly compress 32-bit files to save considerable space on your hard drive and produced images that ranged from 12.5 to 12.9MB in my tests.

Radiance (.hdr): This format is able to compress 32-bit files and produced files that ranged from 18.1 to 18.7MB in my tests. It seems to be the format that has the widest support among other programs that support 32-bit images (such as 3D programs).

Portable Bit Map (.pbm): This format does not offer compression and therefore produced 72MB files in my tests. I would only use it if I was going to use a program that does not support the other formats.

TIFF (.tif): The TIFF file format offers many types of compression and therefore produced a wide range of file sizes. Leaving the compression set to None produced 72MB files as expected. Using LZW compression, I ended up with files that ranged from 25 to 29.8MB while LZW combined with Predictor Compression produced files from 16.4 to 16.6MB. Using the ZIP compression scheme slowed down the saving speed considerably (it jumped from five seconds to over two minutes) and produced files that ranged from 16.3 to 20.4MB. Turning on Predictor Compression in addition to ZIP sped up the saving to around 30 seconds and produced files that ranged from 13.9

32-BIT FILE FORMAT COMPARISON				
Format	Extension	File Size	Pros	Cons
Photoshop	.PSD	72.0MB	None.	Produces overly large files and can easily be confused with 8 or 16-bit layered images.
Large Document Format	.PSB	72.0MB	None.	Produces overly large files
OpenEXR	.EXR	12.9MB	Produces small files.	Not compatible with all HDR applications.
Radiance	.HDR	18.7MB	Produces small files, offers the widest support among HDR applications, and makes for easy identification of HDR images with the .HDR file extension.	None.
Portable Bit Map	.PBM	72.0MB	None.	Produces overly large files.
TIFF	.TIF	14-72MB	Produces small file size with LZW compression	Can easily be confused with 8 or 16-bit flattened images.

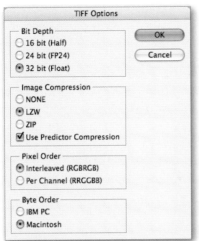

When saving a TIFF file, you will be prompted for many options.

to 14MB. If you choose to use the TIFF file format, I'd suggest you use a combination of LZW and Predictor Compression for a good balance of speed and file size.

Out of all the formats available, I've chosen to save my 32-bit HDR images in the Radiance (.hdr) format because it seems to have the widest support among 32-bit compatible software, it produces small file sizes (considering how much data can be in a 32-bit file) and having a file extension of .hdr makes it very easy to scan a folder and determine which files are 32-bit HDR's.

Converting to 8 or 16-bit

You'll have to convert your HDR images to 8 or 16-bit mode LDR images in order to print them or save them in a file format that is readable by most software programs. When you convert the image, Photoshop will present you with a dialog box that offers four methods (we'll talk about those in a moment) you can use to squish your high dynam-

> **NOTE**
>
> **Bits & Brightness**
> A 32-bit HDR image can contain well over one billion distinct brightness levels. Also, a 32-bit file can contain brightness levels that are darker than black or brighter than white. Converting a 32-bit image to 16-bit mode will result in an image that ranges from black to white and contains up to 32,000 brightness levels.

ic range image into a more limited low dynamic range 8 or 16-bit image. At the bottom of the dialog box is an exposure triangle that allows you to view a histogram of the HDR data. This area also offers an adjustment curve, that is visible no matter which conversion method you use, but is only functional when using the Local Adaptation option. Let's look at your conversion choices:

Exposure and Gamma

This choice presents you with the same Exposure and Gamma sliders that are found when you choose **View>32-bit Preview Options**. In fact, any adjustments made via the **View** menu will be transferred to the Exposure and Gamma sliders in the HDR Conversion dialog box to maintain the visual look of your image. We talked about the choices available under the **View** menu earlier in this chapter and since this conversion method offers identical choices, I'm not going to repeat an exact description of what the controls do here.

I mainly use this conversion method when I've modified an HDR image in 32-bit mode and want to retain the visual look of the image after converting to 8 or 16-bit. That might sound like what you'd want to do every time you convert an image and for some people that will be the case. But once you learn about the Local Adaptation method, you might change your mind.

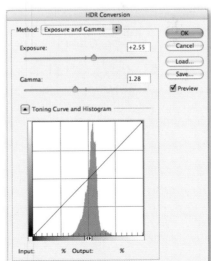

The Histogram in the Exposure and Gamma dialog box is non-functional.

Highlight Compression is an automated adjustment with no options.

Highlight Compression

This conversion method will make the brightest area of your HDR image white while darkening the rest of the image in an attempt to maintain a smooth transition between all the tones in the image (instead of making all areas that are brighter than white appear as solid white). This is a rather crude conversion method since it doesn't give you any control over the process. I mainly use this choice after editing a 32-bit image using the same setting specified in the **View>32-bit Preview Options** area. That way I can maintain the on-screen appearance of the image after converting to 8 or 16-bit mode. This mode will automatically be selected if you're using the equivalent setting for your **32-bit Preview Options** setting.

Equalize Histogram

This conversion method is very similar to the previous one but it also makes the darkest area of the image black. It will often produce more contrast (especially in images that have been brightened using **Image>Adjustments>Exposure**) than the Highlight Compression method but doesn't offer any choices and therefore is less useful than other methods of conversion. However, it can be helpful when you want to get a quick glimpse at what your image contains before switching to a more powerful method like Exposure & Gamma or Local Adaptation.

The Equalize Histogram option is an automated adjustment with no options.

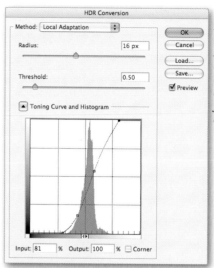

The Local Adaptation method is the only one that offers a functional curve.

Local Adaptation

The Local Adaptation method is special in that it's the only conversion method that allows you to apply a curve to an HDR image. Now Curves isn't something you learn how to use in just five minutes. You might want to review the section on Curves in *Chapter 7: Camera Raw 3* to get a better idea of how to think about Curves.

Adjusting a Curve

Since the concept of Curves isn't new to CS2 and would take considerable space to describe it in detail, I'm going to walk you through how I think of adjusting an image.

Setting The Range: I usually start by defining which areas of the image should be black and which areas should be white. You can do that by moving the dot that appears in the lower left corner toward the right (for black) and moving the dot in the upper right corner toward the left (for white).

NOTE

Learning Curves
*If you really want to learn how to use Curves, then go check out my other book: **Photoshop Studio Techniques**. I devote over 30 pages to the subject and describe all the concepts behind Curves. I consider Curves to be the most powerful adjustment tool offered in Photoshop.*

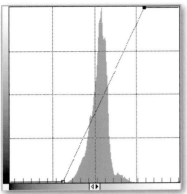

Moving the upper right and lower left dots toward the middle will define which areas become black and white.

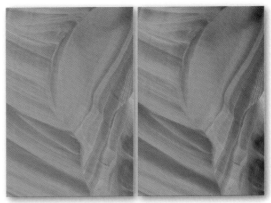

Left: original unadjusted image, Right: result of making the curve steeper to exaggerate detail.

Checking for Detail: While I'm adjusting the end points of the curve, I keep an eye on the histogram that is overlaid on the Curves area. If I move the dots so that they go beyond the beginning of the histogram, that's usually an indication that areas are becoming solid white or solid black, which means I'm starting to trash detail in the image. To see what's really happening to the image, I open the Info palette (via the **Window** menu) and move my mouse over important areas of the image. I set the palette to show 8-bit RGB values by choosing from the menu you see when you click on the eyedropper icon next to each readout. If all three numbers reach zero, then I've forced an area to solid black. If all three reach 255, then an area has become white. If you want to make sure an area has visible detail, don't let the numbers go above 240 or below 25 in important areas.

The numbers that appear in the Info palette show you if there is still detail in your highlights or shadows.

Pulling Out Detail: After I've defined which areas should be black and white, I start thinking about detail. If there's an area of the image where I'd like to see more detail, then I'll move my mouse over that area and click and drag across it. That will cause a circle to show up in Curves which indicates the part of the curve that would affect the area over which I'm dragging. I then add a dot to the curve at each end of the area the circle moved across. Making that part of the curve steeper will make it easier to see detail. If you move the upper dot that you added straight up, then you'll expose more detail by brightening the image. If on the other hand you move the lower dot down, then you'll darken the area. You're also welcome to do both if you'd like to brighten the highlights and darken the shadows.

Adjusting Brightness: If I notice an area that is too bright or too dark, I'll drag over it with the mouse held down to figure out which part of the curve would affect that area. Then I click on the curve to add a dot to that general area and move it up to brighten or down to darken.

Left: original unadjusted image. Middle: darkened by moving the curve down. Right: brightened by moving the curve up.

Avoid Flat Spots: While I'm messing with the curve, I'll always keep in mind that making the curve flat *Flat areas on a curve indicate that a portion of the image is losing detail.* (horizontal) will make the image look like mush (a gray, low contrast blob). So after adjusting the image using the ideas mentioned above, I glance at the curve looking for areas that are becoming flat and I experiment to see if there's a way to finesse the adjustment to avoid the flat spot.

Before we move on, let's look at a few tips for working with the curve:

- Type **Control-Tab** to move to the next point on the curve and **Shift-Control-Tab** to move to the previous point.
- Once you've added a new point to the curve, use the **up** and **down arrow** to move the dot (this allows you to be more precise than using a mouse). Add **Shift** to the above keyboard shortcut to move the dot a large distance
- If you are purposefully making an area flat to hide detail, then consider turning the points on each side of the flat spot into Corner points. Do this by clicking the *Corner* checkbox while the points are active. This can sometimes prevent the rest of the curve from bending in unusual ways.

Once you get the general look you were going for, you can start adjusting the *Radius* and *Threshold* settings. Let's take a look at what they do.

Radius
The curve in this dialog box is a bit different than the one you can apply to an 8 or 16-bit image via the **Image>Adjustments** menu. Changes you make to this curve will not just affect the range a circle runs across when you drag on your image. Instead the *Radius* setting allows the adjustment to affect a small surrounding area. The higher the *Radius* setting, the wider the surrounding area that will be affected.

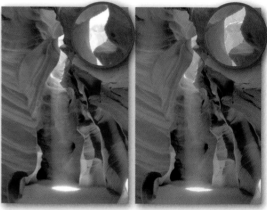

The only difference between these two images is the Radius setting used (inspect the highlights).

Threshold
The Threshold slider helps to prevent the halos that come with using higher *Radius* settings. After you've adjusted the *Radius* setting, take a careful look around the edges of high contrast areas within your image and see if you can detect a bright halo. If you do, then move the Threshold slider toward the left until the halo is no longer obvious.

Adjusting the Radius and Threshold is not an exact science. It really depends on the specific image you're converting and on the strength of your Curves adjustment.

The only difference between these two images is the Threshold setting used (look for halos).

Now that we've covered our conversion options, let's look at how 8, 16 and 32-bit images can be transformed to create high quality prints.

HDR Is Just The Start

You can think of merging multiple exposures into a 32-bit HDR file as only the first step in producing a high quality image. The features available in 32-bit mode are so severely limited that working in 32-bit mode is impractical for the majority of users.

Converting to 16-bit mode allows you to enhance the image using adjustments and tools that are not available in 32-bit mode. Editing a high dynamic range image in 16-bit mode is preferred over 8-bit because it offers 128 times the number of brightness levels available in 8-bit mode. Those extra brightness levels can't be seen on-screen and are not used when the image is printed, but they can help to produce higher quality adjustments. Just imagine an image where the most important detail is contained in the darkest 10% of the image. In a 16-bit image you can have over 320 brightness levels in the darkest 10% of the image, while you'd only have 26 shades in an 8-bit image. Adjust that area so that the darkest area becomes black and the brightest area becomes white and the 8-bit version might not look smooth while the 16-bit version would have more than enough information to produce a smooth looking image.

> **NOTE**
>
> **16-bit Enhancements**
>
> *This chapter does not cover the process of enhancing 16-bit images because the features needed to accomplish that are not new to Photoshop CS2. My book* **Photoshop Studio Techniques** *covers all the techniques necessary to obtain the highest quality images.*

> **NOTE**
>
> **Compatibility and File Size**
>
> *When saving layered 16-bit files in Photoshop file format, you'll be asked if you want to use Maximum Compatibility. Turning on that checkbox will save a flattened version of the 16-bit file so that programs that are not capable of opening layered 16-bit files might still be able to open the image. This checkbox also prevents Photoshop from applying lossless compression to the image, which will result in a larger file size. For example, a 2048 x3072 pixel 16-bit image takes up 36MB without any layers (Photoshop doesn't allow you to turn off the compatibility checkbox for images that do not contain layers), while the same image with six Adjustment Layers ballooned to 61.7MB with the Maximum Compatibility checkbox turned on. The same layered file was only 26.3MB with the checkbox turned off. That's right, it was smaller than the flat version of the image due to the compression Photoshop was able to use.*

The additional shades available in 16-bit mode are only useful when adjusting an image. Once you're done working on the file, you can convert the image to 8-bit which will produce a much smaller file while still containing enough data to display and print the image at its highest quality. Just make sure that you flatten the image when converting to 8-bit, otherwise any adjustment layers in your image will not be able to take advantage of all the data that was in the 16-bit file.

As you can see, there is a lot to know about working with HDR images, but spending some time learning the ins and outs of HDR images can help you produce much higher quality images.

Unadjusted 16-bit HDR image with detail in darkest areas of the image.

Adjusted in 16-bit mode, flattened and then converted to 8-bit mode.

Adjusted in 16-bit mode and converted to 8-bit without flattening.

Chapter 9
Retouching & Filter Enhancements

THERE ARE SO MANY JUICY new features in this chapter, it's like trying to figure out which present to open first on Christmas morning. My personal favorites include the ever-so-amazing Vanishing Point filter, the Lens Correction and Surface Blur filters, and the brilliant little Spot Healing Brush.

Retouching and Filters are covered in a single chapter because the vast majority of the new filters happen to be useful for retouching. Here's a sampling of what you'll learn in this chapter:

- **Spot Healing Brush:** Allows you to quickly remove scratches, dust and other small artifacts without having to choose a sample point.
- **Red Eye Tool:** You can now remove red eye with one click of the mouse.
- **Vanishing Point:** This remarkable filter lets you edit, clone, and retouch images in near-3D perspective.
- **Lens Correction:** Allows you to correct for common problems caused by various camera lenses: barrel distortion, vignetting, etc.
- **Reduce Noise:** A much smarter way of reducing the noise that is inherent in digital files.
- **Blur Filters:** Learn about the three new blur filters: Box Blur, Shape Blur and Surface Blur.
- **Smart Sharpen:** You can now control how much sharpening is applied to shadows and highlights.

Where's My Stuff?

Adobe did a minor bit of housekeeping with the filters and retouching tools. Here's how things have been rearranged:

- **Color Replacement Tool:** Adobe simply moved this tool and gave it a new icon. It can now be found in the same slot as the Paintbrush tool. They also replaced the Continuous, Once, and Background  Swatch choices (that used to be found under the **Sampling** pop-up menu) with three icons.
- **Healing Brush Not Acting Right:** The default is now the Spot Healing Brush, which looks suspiciously like the regular Healing Brush, but with a small dotted circle behind it. Just click and hold on that tool so you can see the regular Healing Brush hiding in the same slot in the Tool palette.

Spot Healing Brush

If you're accustomed to using the Healing Brush tool to remove specks of dust, small scratches or other small defects from your images, then you'll be happy to learn about the new Spot Healing Brush (a transplant from Photoshop Elements). It works just like the normal Healing Brush but does not require you to **Option-click** (Mac) or **Alt-click** (Win) on an area from which you'd like to clone. Instead, it intelligently selects an area from the surrounding image.

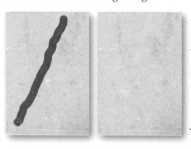

Left: The paint initially appears as a dark stroke. Right: Releasing the mouse button heals the area using texture from the surrounding area.

The idea behind the Spot Healing Brush is that Photoshop will copy the texture from a surrounding area and blend it into the brightness and color that surrounds the area you are painting. The result is that detail in the area in which you paint is replaced with texture appropriate for the area. If the results are less than satisfying, then simply paint over the area a second time and Photoshop will clone texture from a different area of the surrounding image.

The *Type* setting tells Photoshop where to go to copy the texture. Using the *Proximity Match* setting causes it to clone texture from an area close to where you are painting. The *Create Texture* setting will cause Photoshop to create its own texture, instead of copying it from the surrounding image. Use that setting when there is a lot of fine detail in the surrounding image that would not be appropriate for the area you are attempting to retouch.

Left: Original. Middle: Area healed using Proximity Match setting. Right: Area healed using Create Texture.

Red Eye Tool

This new tool is another welcome transplant from Photoshop Elements. It's a one trick pony designed to quickly and easily remove red eye. All that's required is that you center the tool over the red area of an eye, click the mouse button and bingo! No more red eye.

Options bar settings available for the Red Eye tool.

Pupil Size

This setting tells Photoshop how large the red pupil area is when compared to the rest of the eye. The default setting should work for most images. If the darkening effect of the Red Eye tool encroaches too far into the surrounding areas, just lower the Pupil Size setting to reduce the area that will be darkened.

Darken Amount

This setting determines how dark the pupil area will become as a result of applying the Red Eye tool. Lower this setting if the pupil ends up looking solid black and lacks detail.

Left: Original. Right: Result with the Red Eye tool.

Options bar settings available when the Spot Healing Brush tool is active.

Vanishing Point

Up until now, Photoshop thought that the world was flat. It could only think about a two dimensional representation of the three dimensional world we live in. However, it's no stretch for you to realize that equally sized objects appear to get smaller as they are moved further away from a camera. Or that most rectangular walls won't be perfect rectangles in a photograph due to the effects of perspective. Photoshop, on the other hand, has had no clue about these simple concepts that we take for granted every day...until now. Like Galileo insisting that the world is round, the new Vanishing Point filter gives Photoshop an entirely new perspective on the world and its three dimensions.

Photoshop Versus Vanishing Point

Before we get into the nitty gritty of how Vanishing Point works, let's take a look how it changes the way Photoshop approaches simple tasks. (In the examples, Photoshop's results are shown on the left and Vanishing Point's are on the right.)

Making Selections: The Marquee tool in Vanishing Point conforms to the perspective of the plane over which you drag.

Moving A Duplicate: Moving an object in Vanishing Point causes it to become larger or smaller to reflect the perspective planes in the image.

Changing Perspective: Since Vanishing Point is aware of the effects of perspective, you can effectively drag an object around the corner of a building and it will bend the image to make it look appropriate for the new area.

Painting: When painting, Vanishing Point will scale the resulting stroke to match the perspective of the image.

Retouching: When retouching an image, Vanishing Point not only scales your brush stroke, but also the contents you are cloning, allowing them to line up with areas as you move closer to the vanishing point of the image (the point at which lines converge into a single point).

Now that you have a sense of what Vanishing Point is capable of, let's looks at what's necessary to take advantage of this new way of thinking.

Before you can start using its painting and retouching tools, you have to educate Vanishing Point so that it can recognize objects as being three dimensional. This is done by drawing a rectangle across each face of an object so that Vanishing Point knows how to interpret the perspective of the objects you intend to manipulate. Each of those rectangles will be filled with a grid and is referred to as a *Perspective Plane* (which I'll refer to from here on as a 'grid' because that's what it looks like).

Defining Planes

After choosing **Filter>Vanishing Point**, choose the Create Plane tool (which I'll refer to as the Grid tool because that's what it creates and what its icon looks like) and click on your image to start creating a Perspective Plane. The idea is to click on the four corners of any rectangular object that appear on the surface you'd like to manipulate (such as the window in the example below). Holding down **X** will temporarily magnify the image, making it easier to precisely define the shape (press **Delete** (Mac) or **Backspace** (Win) if you need to remove the last point you added).

The resulting grid will appear in one of three colors, depending on how confused you've made Photoshop. The goal is to end up with a blue grid, which is an indication that Photoshop is having no problem figuring out how the grid could match the perspective that an object has in the real world.

If the grid starts out red, then Photoshop can't figure out how to create a 3D surface out of the shape you've created. This won't prevent it from manipulating your image, but it is an indication that the results might not look all that realistic. The Edit Plane tool (which I'll refer to as the Arrow tool because that's what it looks like)

allows you to adjust the corner and side points that define the grid. On your journey from a red grid to a blue one, you might encounter a yellow grid. Yellow is an indication that Photoshop is still having problems with your grid, but that your results might look acceptable using the current grid. Once you've achieved a blue grid, you can rest easy knowing that all is well with your perspective.

Once you have an acceptable grid (yellow or blue), you can expand it to cover the entire surface of the object (by pulling on the side points using the Arrow tool). After extending the grid, you might find that it doesn't perfectly match the photo. When that's the case, adjust the shape of the grid by dragging each corner using the Arrow tool. If the corners of the grid end up beyond the edge of your document, then type **Command-Minus (-)** (Mac) or **Ctrl-Minus (-)** (Win) to zoom out on your image and reveal the corner handles.

After expanding the grid to cover a large area, you might notice that it doesn't align with the image.

Zoom out if you need to pull the grid beyond the edge of the image while attempting to align it with the image.

The grid/outline will change between red, yellow and blue to indicate the status of the plane.

You don't have to create a grid for every surface of an image. You only need grids to define the surfaces you plan to manipulate in Vanishing Point (often you'll be able to get away with just one grid). To create additional grids, choose the Grid tool again, and repeat the process mentioned above. Once you have defined the perspective grids, you can use the retouching tools in the upper left of the dialog box to perform retouching on those 3D surfaces (we'll go into how to use each tool in a moment).

NOTE

Perpendicular Surfaces
When one surface is at a 90 degree angle from another, they're perpendicular to each other. To emulate that angle, use this shortcut: Create a grid that matches one of the surfaces. Then use the Grid tool to drag one of its side handles (not corner handles) to create another grid for the perpendicular area.

This image has five surfaces defined, but only two would need to be defined to copy the windows from the left side of the building and move them to the wall on the right.

Choose Filter>Vanishing Point to access the Vanishing Point dialog box (this image has only two grids defined).

Painting & Retouching

Now that you know how to define the flat surfaces that make up your image, let's take a look at how the Brush and Stamp tools can be used to manipulate your images to conform to the perspective of those areas.

Brush tool

The Brush tool allows you to paint with a solid color while your brush tip scales up or down to conform to the perspective of the grid you paint over. I find that this tool is mainly useful for adding straight lines to an area. Attempting to paint a smooth curve will often produce a non-smooth result because Photoshop simply can't keep up with you.

Painting in perspective causes the paint stroke to become smaller as you move into the smaller end of a perspective grid.

Since there is no Brushes palette available in the Vanishing Point filter, you'll have to use the *Diameter* setting to control the size of your brush and the *Hardness* setting to control its edge quality. The color swatch shown on the far right of the brush Options bar indicates the color that will be applied. You can change the color by clicking the color swatch to access a color picker, or by clicking within the image while the Eyedropper tool is active. If you find the perspective grid to be distracting when painting on your image, then turn off the *Show Edges* checkbox to hide the edge of the perspective grid.

There is a unique Heal option available with both the Brush and Stamp tools. I don't find that option to be overly useful when using the Brush tool, so I'll hold off describing it until we start talking about the Stamp tool.

Stamp tool

The primary use for the Stamp tool is to retouch areas that are surrounded with lines or patterns that get smaller as they move away from the camera position (a wood deck or brick wall for instance). That's when the retouching tools in Vanishing Point become essential.

The Stamp tool combines the functionality of Photoshop's Clone Stamp and Healing Brush tools. With this tool, you **Option-click** (Mac) or **Alt-click** (Win) on the area you'd like to copy from, and then paint over an area you'd like to retouch, which will cause it to be covered with the copied information (after it's been scaled to conform to the perspective of the surface).

The bricks located near the bottom of this image were cloned and used to cover up the birds in the image. The end result (right) looks appropriate because the Stamp tool automatically scaled the bricks to the correct size to match the perspective grid defined for the brick road.

When using the Stamp tool, you can choose from the **Heal** pop-up menu above the image to control how your retouching will blend into the surrounding image. The *Off* setting will cause this tool to emulate the Clone Stamp tool from Photoshop, where no special blending is performed. When using that setting, you have to be very careful to make sure the *Hardness* setting is high enough to cause the retouching to blend into the area which surrounds it. The *On* setting will cause the tool to emulate the Healing Brush tool by copying texture from the cloned area and blending the result into the color and brightness values that surround the retouched area. I use this setting since it will almost always cause the retouched area to match the brightness of the

The options for the Stamp Tool appear at the top of the image preview area.

Heal settings used to retouch the image clockwise from upper left: Original image, None, Luminance, On

After making a basic selection of the left wall, it was duplicated and moved to the other wall.

surrounding area, which is essential when the lighting varies across a surface. The *Luminance* setting will cause the tool to copy both the texture and color from the cloned area and will blend the retouched area into the surrounding brightness. I use that setting when I need to apply the color of the cloned area and still have to blend into the brightness of the retouched area.

Selections

The Marquee tool is the only selection tool available in Vanishing Point. When you draw a rectangle, it will conform to the perspective of the grid you drag across. Let's take a look at what can be done after selecting an area.

If you want to duplicate an object and then move it within the surfaces you've defined, then hold **Option** (Mac) or **Alt** (Win) and drag from within the selected area while the Marquee tool is active. You can also move it to another area of the document. As you drag with the Marquee tool, the selected area will automatically transform according to the perspective grid over which you're dragging. Dragging from one surface to another will cause the image to snap to the perspective of the second surface.

Once you've moved an area of your image, you can control how it blends with the surrounding image by adjusting the *Opacity* and *Feathering* settings at the top of the dialog box. You can also scale or rotate the selected area using the Transform tool, which is only available when a portion of your image is floating above the rest of the image. To create a 'floating selection' either hold **Option** (Mac) or **Alt** (Win) when dragging a selection to create a duplicate, or type **Option-Command-T** (Mac) or **Alt-Ctrl-T** (Win) to float it without changing its position.

You can also select an area that you'd like to replace and then hold **Command** (Mac) or **Ctrl** (Win) and drag the selection to an area you'd like to copy from (the opposite of what we were doing above). That will cause the selected area to be interactively replaced with the contents of the area you drag to (similar to the Patch tool).

The possibilities are endless: Add windows to your home to preview a remodeling project, copy the brick facade from the front of your house and use it to cover the aluminium siding that graces the side of your home, extend that stone wall you never finished in your backyard, etc.

Left: Original. Right: Result of Option-dragging (Mac) or Alt-dragging (Win) when a selection is active.

Left: Original. Right: Result of Command-dragging (Mac) or Ctrl-dragging (Win) when a selection is active.

Vanishing Point Tips

Here are some tips and tricks to keep in mind when working with the Vanishing Point filter:

Correct Barrel Distortion First: This filter depends on having perfectly straight lines at the edge of each surface. If your image was shot with a wide angle lens, then be sure to inspect it for barrel distortion and correct the distortion using the new Lens Correction filter before proceeding to Vanishing Point.

Paste from Clipboard: You can import information from outside Vanishing Point by copying an image before choosing the filter. Then you can type **Command-V** (Mac) or **Ctrl-V** (Win) to paste the copied image as a floating selection that can be moved or transformed and will conform to the perspective grid when dragged onto a plane.

This can be useful if you have a photo of that fake brick siding you can purchase at the hardware store and you want to see what it would look like if you applied it to your living room wall. All you have to do is paste the image, drag it to the surface you desire and then use the Transform tool to scale it to the proper size.

Pre-existing Selections: If you need to use selections that are more sophisticated than those that are possible using Vanishing Point's Marquee tool, then consider making a complex selection in Photoshop before choosing **Filter>Vanishing Point**. The selection edges might not show up in Vanishing Point, but they are still being used to limit where the image can be changed.

Round Trips: You can return to Vanishing Point multiple times without having to re-define the perspective grids. Just make sure you click OK instead of Cancel after defining the grids. Photoshop will remember the existing grids the next time you choose **Filter>Vanishing Point**. This is especially useful when you want to work with many complex selections or when you need to paste multiple images into Vanishing Point.

Repeat Transformations: After Option-dragging a selection to move a duplicate, type **Shift-Option-**

Command-T (Mac) or **Shift-Alt-Ctrl-T** (Win) to move a duplicate of the selection an equal amount and create a repeated shape.

Render The Grid: You can hold **Option** (Mac) or **Alt** (Win) when clicking the OK button to add the grid to your image so you can create images similar to the one used at the beginning of this chapter.

Set Defaults: To save the current tool settings as the defaults, hold **Command** (Mac) or **Ctrl** (Win) and click on the *Cancel* button.

Watch Out for ESC and Return: When transforming a selection, try to resist typing Return or ESC because unlike in the rest of Photoshop these commands will affect the entire filter dialog box instead of only affecting the transformation.

Vanishing Point is a completely new way of working with your images and its 3D nature means that some practice is in order before you can really grasp its potential.

VANISHING POINT KEYBOARD COMMANDS		
Feature	**Mac**	**Win**
Arrow Tool	V	V
Grid Tool	C	C
Marquee Tool	M	M
Stamp Tool	S	S
Brush Tool	B	B
Transform Tool	T	T
Eyedropper Tool	I	I
Zoom Tool	Z	Z
Temp Zoom x2	X	X
Hand Tool	H	H
Undo	Command-Z	Ctrl-Z
Redo	Shift-Command-Z	Shift-Ctrl-Z
Deselect All	Command-D	Ctrl-D
Hide Selection/Plane	Command-H	Ctrl-H
Repeat Dupe/Move	Shift-Command-T	Shift-Ctrl-T
Float Selection	Option-Command-T	Alt-Ctrl-T
Dupe Float	Option-Cmd-Drag	Alt-Ctrl-Drag
Select Lower Grid	Command-click	Ctrl-click
Render Grid	Option-click OK	Alt-click OK
Delete Grid Node	Backspace	Backspace
Exit Grid Creation	Command-Period	Ctrl-Period
Full Canvas Plane	Double-click Grid Tool	

Lens Correction

In yet another nod to photographers, Adobe has bestowed upon us the new Lens Correction filter. It incorporates all of the lens related corrections that were only available in the Camera Raw dialog box, and supplements them with many new options. Most of the new features are designed to correct for distortion introduced by the lens or the angle at which the lens was pointing relative to the subject of the photograph.

A Quick Tour

To access the Lens Correction dialog box, choose **Filter>Distort>Lens Correction**. At the bottom of the dialog box, you'll find the *Show Grid* checkbox which will allow you to toggle the visibility of the grid that is overlaid on your image. This grid is useful when adjusting perspective and when attempting to correct for distortion. You can adjust the spacing of the grid lines by changing the *Size* setting. I like to adjust this setting using the *Scrubby Sliders* feature that was introduced back in Photoshop CS. To turn the Size setting into a Scrubby Slider, just click on its name and drag to the right or left until you have the setting you de-

sire. You can also change the color of the grid by clicking on the color swatch that's labeled Color in the lower right of the image preview area. If you want to reposition the grid, click on the Move Grid tool that's found near the upper left of the dialog box (it's the middle of the five tools available) and drag over your image.

You can zoom and scroll around the image by using the usual navigation keyboard shortcuts that are available in Photoshop, or by using the Zoom and Hand tools that appear in the upper left of the dialog box. Along the right side are the settings that affect the appearance of your image, along with the *Preview* checkbox (at the bottom) which allows you to switch between the original version of your image and the result of the adjustments you've made. Now that you've had a basic tour, let's jump in and see what can be done with the Lens Correction filter.

Pincushion & Barrel Distortion

Many wide angle and telephoto lenses produce distortion that causes straight lines occuring near the edge of the image to bend toward or away from the center of the image. Pincushion distor-

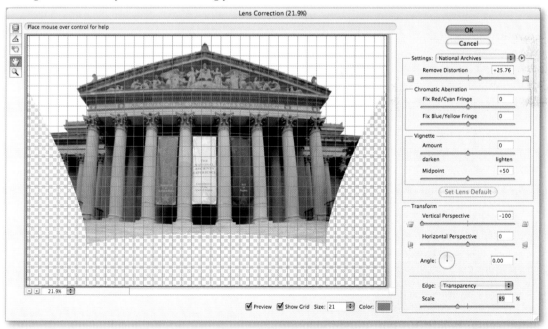

Choose Filter>Distort>Lens Correction to access the Lens Correction dialog box.

tion is when straight lines bend in toward the center of the image and is usually caused by telephoto lenses. Barrel distortion is when straight lines bend away from the center of the image and is caused by wide angle lenses.

Removing Distortion

To correct for pincushion and barrel distortion, either adjust the Remove Distortion slider that's found near the upper right of the Lens Distortion dialog box, or choose the tool of the same name and drag toward or away from the center of the image until the lines appear to be straight (use the grid to double-check that they are straight).

Left: Original, Right: Barrel distortion minimized (the image could still use some perspective correction).

Adjusting Scale and Edge Settings

Correcting for lens distortion will cause the edges of your (formerly) rectangular image to either push out beyond the edge of the document or pull in to produce a non-rectangular image. The *Scale* and *Edge* settings found near the lower right of the dialog box will allow you to adjust how the image fills the document. The *Scale* setting allows you to enlarge the image to fill the empty areas caused by correcting for barrel distortion, or reduce it to expose the areas of the image that were pushed beyond the edge of the document when correcting for pincushion distortion. The *Edge* setting determines what should fill empty areas of the image. Photoshop can either leave them empty (which looks like a checkerboard), fill them with the Background color, or repeat the edge pixels until they fill the area.

Edge Settings from left to right: Transparency, Background Color, Edge Extension

Left: Original, Right: Chromatic Aberration removed.

Chromatic Aberration

When white light passes through the various optical elements in a camera lens, it bends slightly, in a similar fashion to how light passes through a prism. This is known as Chromatic Aberration. It causes the white light to split into a spectrum of color that produces color halos around the edges of areas that should have crisp edges. It's most noticeable where a bright area bumps up against a much darker, well defined edge (like the leaves on a tree with sun shining between them). This problem is usually rather subtle, so you'll only notice it after zooming in on your image and inspecting high contrast edges.

If you notice a red or cyan halo around the edge of an object, then adjust the Fix Red/Cyan Fringe slider until the problem has been minimized. If you notice a blue or yellow halo, then adjust the Fix Blur/Yellow Fringe slider instead. On occasion you might need to adjust both sliders to completely remove the problem.

Vignetting

The barrel of a wide angle lens limits the amount of light that passes through the lens when that light is coming from an angle that is skewed. Just think what would happen if you shone a flashlight through a soup can that had both ends removed. If you shine the light straight through the can, then the vast majority of the light reaches the other side. But shine the same flashlight at an extreme angle toward the can and only a portion of the light makes it through to the other side. A similar effect happens when taking a photograph using a wide angle lens and a low f-stop. This results in an image that has dark corners, and is known as vignetting.

Left: Original

Right: Vignetting adjusted.

If your images exhibit this problem, then adjust the Amount slider until the corners of the image are as bright as the center of the image. Adjusting the Midpoint slider will change how far the brightening effect encroaches into the center of your image.

You can also draw the viewer's attention to the subject of your photo, by moving the Vignetting Amount slider toward the left, which will darken the corners of the image. Just make sure the *Midpoint* setting is low enough so that the effect will be subtle instead of obvious.

Perspective

We've all experienced the effect of taking a photo of a tall building, only to find that the top of the building appears much smaller than the bottom. That's perspective in action and you'll notice it any time you photograph a rectangular subject and allow the lens to be at an angle relative to the subject. That causes the areas of the subject that are closer to the lens to appear larger, while areas further away from the lens appear smaller. Architectural photographers sometimes overcome this by using a special tilt shift lens. They raise the front of the lens while leaving both the lens and the film plane parallel to the subject.

Left: Original, Right: Perspective adjusted.

You can correct for the effect of perspective by adjusting the Vertical and Horizontal Perspective sliders. I mainly use these sliders for straightening vertical lines that converge as they move further away from the camera.

Straighten

There are two ways to straighten a crooked image in the Lens Correction dialog box: either adjust the *Angle* setting that's found near the lower left of the dialog box, or, while the Straighten Tool is active, click and drag on an area that should be perfectly vertical or horizontal in the image.

A combination of more than one feature is often needed to completely eliminate the different distortions in your image. Also, you may need to apply this filter a second time if you've maxed out one of its sliders and the image still looks distorted.

Working with Presets

Once you've dialed-in the Distortion, Chromatic Aberration and Vignette settings for a specific lens or situation, you can save those settings as a preset by choosing **Save Settings** from the pop-up menu that appears to the right of the **Settings** pop-up menu. The settings found under the Transform heading are not saved as part of the preset because unique settings will be needed for each image.

You can quickly apply a saved preset by choosing its name from the **Settings** pop-up menu in the upper right of the dialog box. You can also save a preset that will be associated with the particular camera, lens, focal length and f-stop combination that was used to take the photo (assuming that information is available in the image's metadata) by clicking the *Set Lens Default* button. When working with other images that were shot using the same camera/lens setup, you can choose **Lens Default** from the **Settings** pop-up menu. If you'd rather not save your settings as a preset, then consider using the **Previous Conversion** setting found under the **Settings** pop-up menu, which will apply the same settings that were last applied to an image.

Reduce Noise

In previous versions of Photoshop, it was necessary to either use Blending Modes or to convert your image to LAB mode in order to effectively reduce or remove noise from an image. The new Reduce Noise filter makes those techniques largely obsolete by incorporating their general concepts into one central dialog box. Let's take a look at what you'll find after choosing **Filter>Noise>Reduce Noise**.

When I first get into the Reduce Noise dialog box, I usually set the Strength, Reduce Color Noise and Sharpen Details settings to zero so that they do not affect the image (using the *Remove JPEG Artifact* checkbox is not critical at this point).

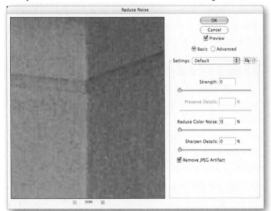

The Reduce Noise dialog box.

Reducing Color Noise

If your image is infected with multi-colored noise where areas that should be a solid color look like they contain a rainbow of colors, then you'll want to increase the *Reduce Color Noise* setting until you find the lowest setting that rids your image of that color variation.

Reducing Luminance Noise

Once you've taken care of any color noise, it's time to tackle the kind of noise that varies in brightness instead of color. Start by moving the Strength slider to a position above zero and then set the Preserve Details slider to zero so that the noise reduction will affect the entire image. Now

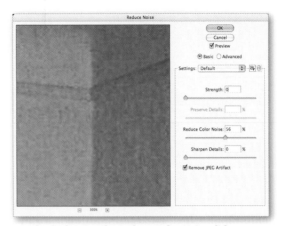

Result of adjusting the Reduce Color Noise slider.

adjust the Strength setting until you've removed as much of the remaining noise as possible. Then, to bring back some of the detail that was lost in the process, move the Preserve Details slider all the way to the right and then slowly lower the setting until you find the highest setting that gives you a good compromise between reducing noise and maintaining fine detail in the image.

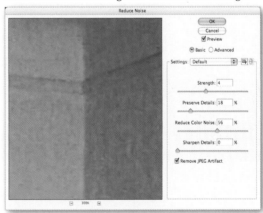

Result of adjusting the Strength and Preserve Details sliders.

Removing JPEG Artifacts

Saving an image in the JPEG file format will produce a very small file when compared to the other file formats that are available. This reduction in file size is mainly achieved by degrading the quality of the image by dividing it up into 8x8 pixel squares and generalizing the detail in the squares. If you zoom in on an image that was

Left: The original image. Right: Result of using the Remove JPEG Artifacts checkbox.

saved in JPEG file format, you might start to see the JPEG compression artifacts that are caused by those squares. Turning on the *Remove JPEG Artifact* checkbox will make Photoshop attempt to make those squares less obvious. Inspect the image closely to make sure you're not sacrificing too much fine image detail in your attempt to reduce those artifacts.

Working in Advanced Mode

In the Reduce Noise dialog box, you can work in one of two modes: Advanced or Basic. Behind the scenes your images are made out of Red, Green and Blue light (when in RGB mode). When working in Basic mode, the sliders in the dialog box will affect all three of those colors (also known as channels) in equal amounts. The problem is that most digital cameras produce more noise in the Blue channel, especially when shooting in low light situations. Therefore, adjusting the image while in Basic mode will often cause you to wipe out much of the fine detail in the image (because you are attempting to fix a problem that is primarily afflicting a single channel). To adjust the individual channels of your image, switch from Basic mode to Advanced mode at the top right of the dialog box, and then click on the Per Channels tab.

Before you start messing with the choices found under this tab, make sure you've set the *Strength* and *Reduce Color Noise* settings to zero under the Overall tab, otherwise the information shown under the Per Channel tab will not reflect the unfiltered state of the image.

Per Channel Noise Reduction

If the noise that's plaguing your image is primarily coming from two colors, then the problem can most likely be found in a single channel of your image. Red/Cyan noise originates in the Red channel, Green/Magenta noise comes from the Green channel, and Blue/Yellow noise is usually found in the Blue channel. You can inspect the three channels that make up your image by clicking on the Per Channel tab and then cycling through the choices that appear in the **Channel** pop-up menu.

Channels from left to right: Red, Green, Blue.

If you find that the noise is concentrated primarily in a single channel, then choose the afflicted channel from the **Channels** pop-up menu. Next, move the Strength slider toward the right and set the Preserve Details slider to zero. Now adjust the Strength slider until you've removed as much of the noise as seems practical. Move the Preserve Details slider all the way to the right and then back toward the left until you find the highest setting that produces a good balance between noise reduction and fine detail in the image.

If working on a single channel is not enough to completely remove the noise, then click on the Overall tab and adjust those sliders until you achieve a satisfactory result.

Left: Original image. Right: Noise reduction concentrated in the Blue channel, supplemented with minor adjustments to the settings found under the Overall tab.

Blur Filters

Because Adobe knows we love to blur, they added three new filters to the **Filter>Blur** menu in Photoshop CS2.

Box Blur

If you're looking for a fast, adjustable blur filter, then this is it. This filter runs two to four times faster than the Gaussian Blur filter (mostly noticeable with bigger sized files) and can be help-

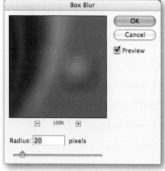

The Box Blur filter.

ful when applying actions to a large number of images. Visually it's not much different than the Gaussian Blur filter, however when you're blurring images that have high-contrast, distinct edges, Box Blur tends to leave a bit more edge than Gaussian Blur. It's a personal/artistic choice as to which filter you prefer.

Top Right:
Original image

Bottom Left:
Result of applying the Gaussian Blur filter

Bottom Right:
Result of applying the Box Blur filter.

Shape Blur

The Shape Blur filter will blur your image based on the shape that you specify. This can create some interesting effects when applied to text and other high contrast objects. The shape will also be pronounced in the highlights when applied to a photograph.

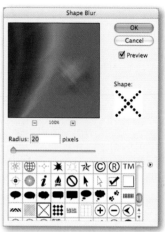

The Shape Blur filter.

Using various shapes with the Shape Blur filter.

Surface Blur

This filter will blur the fine detail in an image while maintaining crisp edges in the rest of the image. The Radius setting determines the amount of blurring while the Threshold setting determines the contrast range that will be blurred.

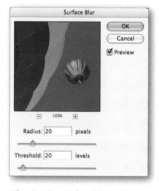

The Surface Blur filter.

This filter is great for making a photo look more like an illustration and can make many of Photoshop filters (such as **Filter>Sketch Find Edges**) more useful by feeding them less detail. I like the results I get when applying the Surface Blur filter to a copy of the image layer that has its Opacity set to somewhere around 60%.

Top Right: Original.

Bottom Left: Result of du-plicating the Background layer and applying the Surface Blur filter.

Bottom Right: Lowering the Opacity of duplicate layer to 60% effectively blended the Surface Blur result with the original image.

Smart Sharpen

The features available for sharpening images in Photoshop haven't changed in well over a decade. The old standard of the Unsharp Mask filter is now being challenged with the introduction of the Smart Sharpen filter in Photoshop CS2.

The Smart Sharpen filter borrows the *Amount* and *Radius* settings from the Unsharp Mask filter (but not the all-important *Threshold* setting) and throws a heap of options into the mix to give you precise control over the sharpening process. Let's take a look at each setting, one at a time.

The Smart Sharpen dialog box.

Basic Mode

The Smart Sharpen filter has two modes: Basic and Advanced. We'll start by exploring the settings available in Basic mode.

Amount

Sharpening is all about increasing the contrast on the edge of objects. Photoshop does this by first comparing two pixels that touch each other and then darkening the darker shade of the two, while brightening the brighter of the two shades right where they touch. That makes the edge more pronounced and therefore easier to see, all of which makes the image appear to be sharper. The Amount slider determines how much of a contrast boost will be applied to each edge.

Top Left: Original image, Top Right: Shape Blur, Bottom Left: Box Blur, Bottom Right: Surface Blur.

Left to Right:
Amount: 150
Amount: 250
Amount: 500

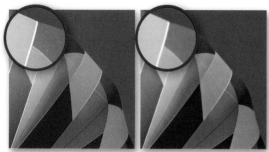

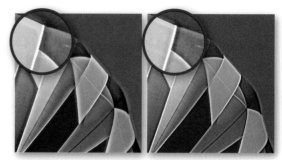

Left: Sharpened using a high Amount and low Radius.
Right: Sharpened using a high Radius and low Amount.

Left: Sharpened using the Gaussian Blur setting.
Right: Sharpened using the Lens Blur setting.

Radius

The *Radius* setting determines how wide of an area will be used for the contrast change that the *Amount* setting is causing.

If high values are used for both the *Amount* and *Radius* settings, then the halos caused by sharpening will be obvious (as seen in the images shown at the top of the next column). However, the sharpening goes unnoticed when a good balance has been achieved between the *Amount* and *Radius* settings (as shown above).

There are two approaches to creating that balance and the one that should be used will depend on the contents of the image:

Images with Visible Grain: For images that contain obvious grain, use a high *Radius* setting (between 10 and 20) and a low *Amount* setting (between 15 and 30). I usually start with the *Amount* and *Radius* both set at 20 and then fine-tune the results until the image appears to be sharp enough, but without obvious halos.

Fine Grained Images: If the image does not have obvious grain, then use a low *Radius* setting (between .5 and 1.5) and a high *Amount* setting (between 75 and 200). I usually start with the *Amount* setting at 100 and the *Radius* at 1. Then I adjust the *Radius* until fine detail looks natural, and fiddle with the *Amount* until I find the highest setting that looks acceptable.

Sharpening is more of an art than a science because what you see on your screen does not reflect the amount of detail that will appear when the image is printed. The amount of detail visible when the image is printed will vary depending on the type of printer used. For instance, printing an image in the newspaper will cause it to look much less sharp than it was on screen, while printing to an ink jet printer will more closely reflect the sharpness seen on screen. To get the most accurate view of the image, it's best to view your image at 100% magnification when sharpening.

Remove

The **Remove** pop-up menu determines how sophisticated the math will be that Photoshop uses to create the halos that effectively sharpen the image.

Gaussian Blur: This choice will produce the same results that would be obtained using the Unsharp Mask filter. The halos created will be more pronounced than those achieved using the *Lens Blur* setting. Because of this, I only use this setting when speed is more important than quality.

Lens Blur: This choice will produce less pronounced halos, allowing you to use higher *Amount* and *Radius* settings before the halos become obvious. I use this setting when quality is more important than speed.

Left to Right:
Radius: 1
Radius: 3
Radius: 5

Left to Right:
Gaussian Blur,
Lens Blur,
Motion Blur.

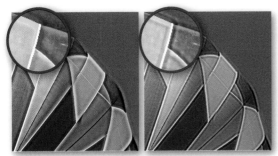

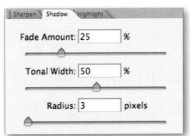

In Advanced mode, you can limit the amount of sharpening applied to the highlight and shadow areas of an image.

Left: Gaussian Blur with More Accurate.
Right: Lens Blur with More Accurate.

Motion Blur: This setting can be used to reduce the effects of camera motion that cause images to appear slightly out of focus. The key is to determine the direction of camera movement so that Photoshop can attempt to reduce the blur effect. I find that this choice is only useful when the motion blur is barely noticeable. When using this setting, it pays to spend time experimenting with the *Angle* setting because the direction isn't always immediately apparent.

More Accurate

This setting sharpens the image in two passes, which will cause the halos created by sharpening to be more pronounced. To see what I mean, squint when viewing the examples at the bottom of this page and compare them to the results obtained when the *More Accurate* checkbox was turned off. Since this setting causes Photoshop to effectively sharpen the image twice, the filter will take more time to process your image, but can produce a sharper looking result.

I find that the *More Accurate* checkbox is not helpful when an image contains noticeable grain or has been saved in the JPEG file format. That's because it tends to exaggerate the grain and unwanted JPEG compression artifacts (see the images above, which are exaggerated examples of this effect).

More Accurate Left to Right: Gaussian Blur, Lens Blur and Motion Blur.

Advanced Mode

Switching to *Advanced* mode near the top of the Smart Sharpen dialog box will cause the dialog box to be divided into three tabs: Sharpen, Shadow, and Highlight.

Shadow/Highlight Tabs

The Sharpen tab contains the settings that produce the sharpening effect, while the Shadow and Highlight tab settings determine the strength of the sharpening that will be applied to different areas of your image. Here's a rundown of the settings found under the Shadow and Highlight tabs:

Fade Amount: This setting will cause the sharpening to be applied to a lesser extent. It's the same as lowering the opacity on a layer where 100% causes the sharpening to be applied at full strength and 0% will apply no sharpening.

Tonal Width: This setting determines the range of shades that will be considered a shadow or highlight area and therefore the range where the sharpening effect will be lessened. Low settings limit the *Fade Amount* to affecting the darkest (shadow) and brightest (highlight) areas, while higher settings allow the *Fade Amount* to creep into the midtones of the image.

Radius: When using the *Fade Amount* setting, Photoshop will attempt to blend the fading effect into the surrounding image so that there is no obvious or abrupt transition. Once you've found the *Fade Amount* and *Tonal Width* settings that produce a satisfactory result, then adjust the *Radius* setting to control the transition between the sharpened and faded areas. The Radius setting determines how much of that area Photoshop will use to create this blend.

These settings are useful when the process of sharpening has caused the noise in the dark areas of the image to become more noticeable. In the Shadow tab, I start with the *Fade Amount* at 100% and the *Radius* set low to something like 3. I then adjust the *Tonal Width* until the noise is no longer being exaggerated, and I move the *Fade Amount* slider to see how much sharpening I can get away with in the dark area of the image. Finally, I adjust the *Radius* setting until I get a satisfactory transition.

Working with Presets

You can save a set of sharpening settings as a preset by clicking the Save icon (it looks like a floppy disk with a down arrow). After saving the preset, you can access those settings by choosing the preset name from the **Settings** pop-up menu.

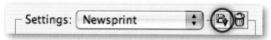

Clicking the Save button will create a preset that can be accessed via the Settings pop-up menu.

Fading with Luminosity

The halos introduced by sharpening will often end up being a color that is quite different than the object that is being sharpened (see the example below). To prevent this color shift, choose **Edit>Fade Smart Sharpen** immediately after applying the filter and set the **Mode** pop-up menu to Luminosity, which will prevent the colors from shifting.

I was surprised to see that a filter named 'Smart Sharpen' wasn't smart enough to know this trick, which has been used for years with the Unsharp Mask filter. I also find that I really miss the *Threshold* setting in the Unsharp Mask filter because it allows me to limit the sharpening applied so that it does not affect areas of slight contrast (like pores on people's faces). Conse-

quently, I still prefer to use the Unsharp Mask filter on many images.

I hope you'll be able to set aside the time needed to get these new tools working at their peak performance. Some of them do their job without any effort at all (like the red eye reduction tool), but others—like the new Vanishing Point filter—are going to take a bit of patience and some practice. However, if you invest the time, I think you'll find all of the features in this chapter will pay their way, again and again.

Left to Right: Original, Sharpened, Faded using Luminosity.

Chapter 10
Small Gems
For Photography

I T'S BEEN OVER TWO DECADES since the electronic publishing industry went hurtling into the digital universe. A similar revolution is currently underway in the photography field. Most of the headlines go to major advances in hardware and software, but it would be unwise to ignore the smaller changes that are slowly nudging the industry forward. This chapter is all about those features that will fail to grab headlines, but just might change how you work in Photoshop.

If you didn't just jump ahead to this chapter and actually went through the entire book to get here, you've surely noticed that Adobe made some major nods to photographers when they cooked up CS2. The features covered in this chapter may not be the biggest or sexiest part of the upgrade, but they are indeed worthy of your attention.

If you work with large quantities of images, you'll love the new Image Processor which automatically performs tasks that, until now, could only be accomplished with custom-made actions. For folks working in 16-bit mode, Adobe continues to expand its list of features that support that mode. And for all of you web-aholics wanting to get your photos online, you'll be pleased to see that you now have more options than ever to either create your own web photo gallery, or hand your photos over to someone else to do all the work for you!

Here's a preview of some of the small but valuable goodies you'll find in this chapter:

- **Image Processor:** Allows you to scale and save multiple images in different file formats all from a single, easy to use dialog box.
- **Improved 16-bit Support:** A few more features have been added to the list of what's available in 16-bit mode and by tweaking a few settings we can now reduce those 16-bit monster file sizes down to something manageable!
- **Web Photo Gallery:** Your design possibilities have been expanded with some cool new Web Photo Gallery templates. Adobe has even integrated Flash into some of the templates.
- **Adobe Online:** The new service allows you to share your images online and order prints. The sharing is free, the prints are not.

Image Processor

The new Image Processor allows you to quickly scale, save and apply actions to large numbers of images, all from one simple and easy to use dialog box. There are two ways you can access the Image Processor: **1)** If you're working from Bridge, select the images you'd like to process and then choose **Tools>Photoshop>Image Processor**, or **2)** If you already have some images open within Photoshop, choose **File>Scripts>Image Processor**. Let's look at each of the Image Processor's settings:

Select the Images to Process

This section allows you to tell the Image Processor where to go to grab the images that you want to process. When you start from Photoshop, you'll have the option of either using the currently open images, or pointing the Image Processor to a folder full of images. If you start from Bridge it will assume you want to use the image thumbnails that are currently selected.

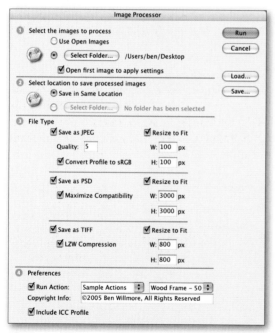

The Image Processor dialog box offers a multitude of options for saving and scaling your images.

The option called **Open first image to apply settings** is designed for working with Camera Raw files in the Image Processor even though it's still available when working with other file formats. If you don't work with Camera Raw files, you can skip to the next section. If you do, then click the **Open first image to apply settings** checkbox. This allows you to specify the workflow settings (color space, size, resolution, etc.) for any Raw format images you'll end up processing. But, instead of actually opening the first image in a folder, the Image Processor simply presents you with a standard Open dialog box that is pointing to your desktop and expects you to know what to do. Since the Image Processor is not sophisticated enough to automatically point you to the proper folder, you'll have to manually navigate to the folder you desire and choose the first Raw format image in the folder. After choosing a Raw file and clicking the Open button, you'll be presented with the Camera Raw dialog box.

Photoshop will use the Workflow settings you specify for this image and apply them to all the images you're processing. Be careful: because changing any of the adjustment sliders will affect all the images and will override any previous Raw adjustments applied to those images. Not only that, but changing a single slider will cause all of the settings found under that tab (the Adjust tab, for example) to be applied to the images. For example, increasing the Saturation setting will also cause all the other settings found under the Adjust tab to be applied to all the images that are being processed. Tabs that you don't modify will be ignored, causing the Image Processor to use any Raw settings that have been applied to individual images. For this reason, I usually limit my changes to the workflow settings that appear at the bottom of the Camera Raw dialog box.

When you're done specifying the settings you'd like to apply to all the Raw images, click the Open button to start processing the rest of the images. Now that we've covered the one feature that is specific to Raw files, let's get back to the features that work with all file types.

Select location to save processed images

This area is pretty straightforward. You're telling the Image Processor where to save your newly processed files. The Image Processor will automatically create a folder at the location you specify. You'll get one folder for each of the file formats you've chosen, so you don't have to worry about writing over the original images.

File Type

In this area, you specify the file formats in which you'd like to save your images. You're not limited to using just one format here. You can just as easily save JPEG's and TIFF's. I often use that because I want to e-mail a bunch of very low resolution JPEG's to a client, while uploading a bunch of higher resolution TIFF's to my ftp site so the client can download a larger, higher quality version if they like one of the images.

Resize to Fit

This setting allows you to scale each image so that it fits within the size specified. Entering the same dimensions in both the width and height fields will help if you're working with both vertical and horizontal images because it will cause the image to be scaled until the longest dimension matches your specifications.

I really wish Adobe would have allowed for different measurement systems in this area. I often want to save an 8x10 inch image that has a specific resolution setting. In order to accomplish that, you'll have to either work with images that have the proper resolution setting to begin with or work with Raw files where you can specify the resolution setting when opening the first file (via the checkbox I mentioned earlier). Then, to determine the number of pixels to enter into the Resize to Fit area, you have to multiply the dimensions you desire (measured in inches) by the resolution setting you're using. For example, if you have 300ppi images and want an 8x10 inch image: 8x300= 2400 and 10x300=3000. That means that you'd want to enter 3000 for both the width and height settings so that it can accommodate images regardless of their orientation.

Convert Profile to sRGB

I use this choice any time the images will be viewed in a web browser or other programs that are not designed to accurately reproduce colors (like databases and other non-graphics software). Most programs that are not designed to accurately display images assumes that your images are in sRGB color space.

NOTE

sRGB Problems
Using the Convert Profile to sRGB checkbox will cause the Image Processor to fail if it encounters an image that is already in sRGB. I primarily use this feature when processing high resolution Raw and TIFF files which all use the Adobe RGB color space. Hopefully Adobe will fix this problem in a future release.

The other options in the File Type area are standard settings that you'd see when saving files in those formats. The Maximize Compatibility checkbox saves a flattened version of a layered file so that it can be opened in programs that don't support layers. The LZW Compression choice will apply lossless compression in an attempt to reduce the file size. This is mainly useful when you have large areas of solid color (text and graphics instead of photographs), and it is not as useful with complex photographic images.

Preferences

The settings in this area are optional. If you use actions, this is where you can direct the Image Processor to run your action, or if you work with ICC profiles, this is where you can indicate whether you want to embed a profile in your processed images.

To load the actions you'd like to use in the Image Processor, choose Load from the side menu of the Actions palette.

Run Action

The Run Action choice allows you to access and apply any of the actions that are currently loaded into Photoshop's Actions palette. If you don't find the action you're looking for, then click the Cancel button to return to Photoshop and either create or load the action into the Actions palette. Using actions is how you can add features to this dialog box. I most commonly use an action when I need to sharpen a large number of images. The action will be applied to the images after they are scaled to the size specified in the File Type area of the dialog box.

Copyright Info

Whatever info you type into the Copyright Info field will be attached to the image as part of its metadata. This will also cause the Copyright Status field in the File Info dialog (**File>File Info** in Photoshop) to be set to Copyrighted, which will also cause a © symbol to appear at the top of the image when it's opened in Photoshop. I use this for all of the photos that I send to friends and clients so I can make sure the copyright ownership on the image is clear.

Entering information into the Copyright Info field will cause a copyright symbol to appear at the top of each image in Photoshop.

Include ICC Profile

An ICC Profile describes the exact colors of red, green and blue that make up your image. Turning on this checkbox will include that color information with each image so that programs designed to accurately reproduce photographs can correctly display the image. (If you're not familiar with profiles, then I suggest you download my free *Color Management for Mere Mortals* handbook at www.digitalmastery.com/color.) The only time I turn off this checkbox is when I know the images will only be viewed in a web browser or a pro-

gram that doesn't accurately reproduce colors. In that case, I use the JPG file format and turn on the Convert Profile to sRGB choice.

After you've applied the Image Processor to a series of images, you'll see that a folder (with a name that reflects your chosen file format) has been created in the location you specified. Inside that folder are all of your processed images.

Load & Save Buttons

If you find that you use the same settings over and over again in the Image Processor, then consider clicking the Save button to save the settings you've specified so that they can be quickly loaded at a later time. A good place to store the settings is the **Photoshop CS2/Presets** folder.

Improved 16-bit Support

16-bit images can contain up to 32,769 brightness levels instead of the standard 256 that come along with the 8-bit images that most people use. You can see how many bits an image has by opening it in Photoshop and seeing what is checked under the **Image>Mode** menu. Support for 16-bit images has been an evolutionary thing where each new version of Photoshop expands the range of tools and features available. In Photoshop CS2, Adobe has added support for the following features:

Additional filters have been made to work in 16-bit mode, along with many of the filters that are new to Photoshop CS2 (see table).

Enabled Compression when saving in Photoshop file format with the Maximum Compatibility option turned off. This is a mixed blessing because turning the checkbox off will produce a smaller file size, but will also cause Bridge to have to read all the 16-bit layers in order to produce thumbnail and preview images.

The other problem is that these less compatible files cannot be opened in earlier versions of Photoshop. This is unfortunate, but for some people the savings in file size will be worth the incon-

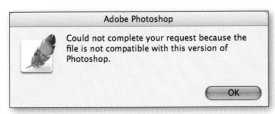

Saving a 16-bit image in .PSD format with Maximum Compatibility turned off will cause an error message to appear when you attempt to open the image in earlier versions of Photoshop.

16-BIT COMPATIBLE FILTERS
Menu Path to Filter (bold indicates new support)
Filter>Liquify
Filter>Vanishing Point
Filter>Blur>Average
Filter>Blur>Blur
Filter>Blur>Blur More
Filter>Blur>Gaussian Blur
Filter>Blur>Lens Blur
Filter>Blur>Motion Blur
Filter>Blur>Radial Blur
Filter>Blur>Shape Blur
Filter>Blur>Surface Blur
Filter>Distort>Lens Correction
Filter>Noise>Add Noise
Filter>Noise>Despeckle
Filter>Noise>Dust & Scratches
Filter>Noise>Median
Filter>Noise>Reduce Noise
Filter>Render>Fibers
Filter>Render>Lens Flare
Filter>Sharpen>Sharpen
Filter>Sharpen>Sharpen Edges
Filter>Sharpen>Sharpen More
Filter>Sharpen>Smart Sharpen
Filter>Sharpen>Unsharp Mask
Filter>Stylize>Emboss
Filter>Stylize>Find Edges
Filter>Stylize>Solarize
Filter>Video>De-Interlace
Filter>Video>NTSC Colors
Filter>Other>Custom
Filter>Other>High Pass
Filter>Other>Maximum
Filter>Other>Minimum
Filter>Other>Offset

Turning off the Maximize Compatibility checkbox will allow Photoshop to apply lossless compression to layered 16-bit images saved in the Photoshop file format.

venience. For instance, a four-layered 4096x2048 16-bit RGB image produced a 65.5MB file with Maximum Compatibility turned on (the same size as saving from Photoshop CS regardless of which compatibility setting was used), while the same image produced a 18.3MB file in Photoshop CS2 with the compatibility checkbox turned off.

Web Photo Gallery

For those of you who like to build your web photo galleries in Photoshop, you'll be pleased to see that Adobe has added nine new style templates, a couple of which are Flash-based. (The Flash - Gallery 1 template is especially cool because the thumbnails magnify when you run your mouse over them.) You can customize most of these styles in custom color combinations and choose which size thumbnails and large preview images you'd like to display. I'm not going to go over all the settings here because I'd just be repeating myself and most of those settings are not new to this version of Photoshop. But let's look at the templates in the order they appear in **Web Photo Gallery's Style** pop-up menu.

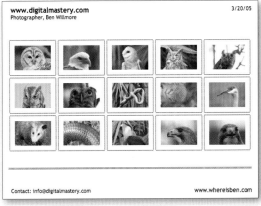

Dotted Border - Black on White

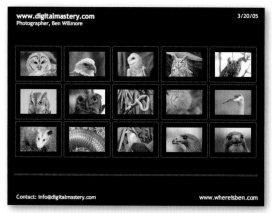

Dotted Border - White on Black

Flash - Gallery 2

Flash - Gallery 1

Gray Thumbnails

When you're done perusing the new gallery styles, you will get to a new feature, the online photo sharing/printing service offered by Adobe and Ofoto. You can also build a web photo gallery using this new service, but there are major differences between the two features. With Photoshop's Web Photo Gallery styles, you are basically creating mini web site that you would upload to your own web server (or if you're doing work for hire, to someone else's server). You have complete control over how the web site looks and how it presents your images. In fact, you can even edit the templates that Photoshop provides for its Web Photo Gallery styles (which I'll not go into here, because that capability is not

Simple - Horizontal Thumbnails

Simple - Thumbnail Table

Simple - Vertical Thumbnails

Table - Minimal

new). But the bottom line is that you or your client must host a web site to do this. The Ofoto service, on the other hand, hosts the web page for you, and while incredibly convenient, it does come with limitations. Your photo gallery is not accessible to the public (unless you specifically invite them), you must be willing to live with Ofoto's boilerplate layout, and know that not only can prints be ordered, but your photos can be modified somewhat by your invited viewers. In my estimation Ofoto is ideal for sharing with family and friends, but not the best for professional use.

Adobe On-line

Adobe On-line allows you to quickly upload and share or print multiple images. This service is the result of a partnership between Adobe and Ofoto.com (an offspring of Kodak). Let's start by looking at the photo sharing capabilities since they're free, then we'll move on to ordering prints.

Photo Sharing

The photo sharing service is rather simple. You start in Bridge and select the images you want to share (the service currently only supports JPG file format), then choose **Tools>Photoshop Services>Photo Sharing**.

Create Account

That will cause a new window to appear that asks you to create a new account with Ofoto. Let's look at the process of sharing a photo step-by-step.

The Ofoto welcome screen allows you to sign in or create a new account.

Address Book

After signing in, you'll be prompted for the names of the people with whom you'd like to share your photos. When you add new people to your address book, you're only required to provide a first name and e-mail address. The address and phone

The second screen allows you to choose the people with whom you'd like to share your photos.

number fields are optional, but required if you want to order prints to be sent to the person. This is also where you can specify a custom notification message that will be sent to announce your newly posted images.

Upload Photos

As soon as you click the Next button, the images that are selected in Bridge will begin to upload. There's not much you have to do here other than wait and look for error messages. The main message you'll get is if one of the images is not in JPG file format.

/Users/ben/Desktop/test.jpg

0 / 1

Cancel

A progress dialog box will appear while your photos are uploading.

Confirmation

Once the images have been successfully uploaded, all your work is done! An e-mail is automatically sent to the people you chose to share the photos with and a link to www.adobe.ofoto.com appears allowing you to view your photos.

When recipients receive their e-mail, they will be presented with a link to view your shared photos. Clicking the link launches a web browser

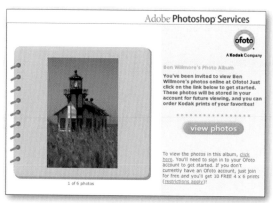

An invitation e-mail will be sent to the people with whom you chose to share your photos.

and takes them to a page that shows the images you've chosen to share. Each time you upload a series of images, they will be grouped into an album. Clicking on one of the albums will display thumbnail versions of each image. Clicking the thumbnail will display a larger version and offer choices for editing the photo (red eye removal, cropping, etc.) and ordering prints. This is also where titles can be added to images and decorative frames can be applied. There's all sorts of cheesy looking frames to choose from. Heck, your invited viewers can even click on the Ofoto store link and order everything from mouse pads to aprons printed with any of your shared photos.

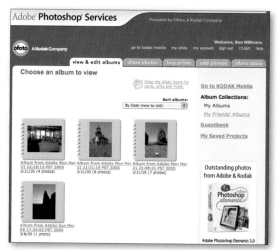

When someone visits the shared photo web site, they will be presented with a list of photo albums.

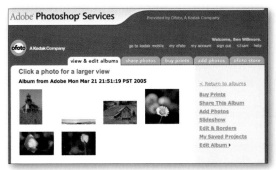

Clicking on an album will display thumbnail versions of the shared photos.

Clicking on a thumbnail image will allow the viewer to see a larger version of the image and to order prints.

Online Photo Printing

Having prints delivered is only a little more involved than sharing your images, although it can be as simple as clicking the Buy Prints link while you're viewing your images in Ofoto's web site. Let's look at what's involved in ordering prints directly from Photoshop or Bridge.

Start in Bridge and select the JPG images you'd like to have printed. Then choose **Tools>Photoshop Services>Photo Prints** (or open a photo in Photoshop and choose **File>Print Online**). As with the photo sharing service, the first step is to create an account or log into a pre-existing account.

Select Prints to Order

The next screen will display a huge preview of your image with options for ordering different quantities of prints. You might need to scroll around to the edges of the preview to be able to see all the options available.

⊖	4 x 6"	$0.25	1	$0.25
⊖	5 x 7"	$0.99	0	$0.00
⊕	Wallets (4)	$1.79	0	$0.00
⊖	8 x 10"	$3.99	0	$0.00
⊖	16 x 20"	$17.99	0	$0.00
⊖	20 x 30"	$22.99	0	$0.00

The print quantities are listed on the far right of each preview image.

Choose Recipients

Once you've specified the number of prints you desire, you'll be asked to pick people from your on-line address book (just as when sharing photos, but these contacts must include mailing addresses and phone numbers).

Select an address where you want to send the prints.

Shipping Options

The next screen allows you to choose which type of shipping you'd like to use and gives you a summary of your order.

Choose the type of shipping you'd like to use.

Provide the billing information for your order.

MINIMUM PHOTO RESOLUTIONS	
Print Size	Minimum Resolution
Wallet-size	320 x 240 pixels
4 x 6"	640 x 480 pixels
5 x 7"	1024 x 768 pixels
8 x 10"	1536 x 1024 pixels
16 x 20"	1600 x 1200 pixels
20 x 30"	1600 x 1200 pixels

As you can see, Adobe is making advances both large and small with each new release of Photoshop. I hope you'll spend the time needed to get used to these features and integrate them into your workflow.

Billing Options

After choosing your shipping options, you'll be prompted for your credit card information and billing address. These details should be familiar to anyone who has ordered a product on-line.

Upload & Confirmation

At this point your images are uploaded to the service and a confirmation message presents you with an order number and other details. Once you've made it to this point, you're done!

Tips & Tricks

Here are a few tips that can make things a little easier or produce the highest quality results.

Since both of the sharing and printing services are limited to working with JPG images, consider using the new Image Processor to quickly convert your images to JPG's. The service also assumes all your images are in the sRGB working space, so be sure to use that checkbox within the Image Processor or use **Edit>Convert to Profile** to convert your images to sRGB before uploading them. Also consider cropping each image to the proper proportions before uploading so the Zoom and Trim feature does not surprise you.

Index

Numbers

A

B

Like this book?

Get more

enlightenment

from Ben and become

a Photoshop master

Ben's trademark style of intuitive, indepth, crystal-clear

explanations can be found in all of his Photoshop training products.

Just ask Jim Workman, publisher of *Photoshop User* magazine, who

said that Ben's best-seller, *Adobe Photoshop Studio Techniques*,

is "Arguably, one of the best Photoshop books ever written."

Whether it's award-winning books, best-selling DVDs, sellout

seminars, or customized on-site training, Ben has a solution that

will take you from blindly following step-by-step instructions to

"Aha! I finally GET Photoshop!"

digitalmastery.com

images ©2005 iStockPhoto.com

free!

Check out Ben's Freebies

Don't stop now. Keep the answers coming with Ben on-line.

Over 40,000 users from all over the world take regular

doses of Ben's tips, fixes, explanations and insights. It

doesn't cost a dime, so take the plunge . . .

digitalmastery.com/freebies

Join the crowd on Ben's Blog!

www.WhereIsBen.com

W9-DAZ-277

STAR WARS
INFINITIES
A NEW HOPE

STAR WARS®

INFINITIES

A NEW HOPE

DARK HORSE BOOKS™

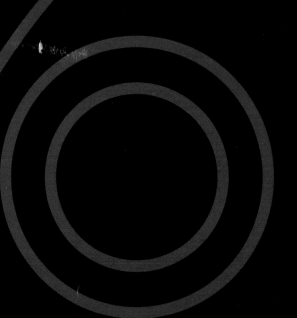

script **CHRIS WARNER**

pencils **DREW JOHNSON** & **AL RIO**

inks **RAY SNYDER** & **NEIL NELSON**

colors **DAVE McCAIG** & **HELEN BACH**

letters **STEVE DUTRO**

cover artist **TONY HARRIS**

cover colors **CHRIS BLYTHE**

publisher MIKE RICHARDSON

editor DAVE LAND

assistant editor PHILIP SIMON

collection designer KEITH WOOD

SPECIAL THANKS TO

LUCY AUTREY WILSON & CHRIS CERASI

at Lucas Licensing

Star Wars®: Infinities — A NEW HOPE

Star Wars © 2001, 2002 by Lucasfilm, Ltd. and TM. All rights reserved. Used under authorization. Text and Illustrations © 2001, 2002 by Lucasfilm, Ltd. All other material © 2002 by Dark Horse Comics, Inc. All rights reserved. No portion of this publication may be reproduced, in any form or by any means, without the express written permission of the copyright holders. Names, characters, places, and incidents featured in this publication are either the product of the author's imagination or are used fictitiously. Any resemblance to actual persons (living or dead), events, institutions, or locales, without satiric intent, is coincidental. Dark Horse Books™ is a trademark of Dark Horse Comics, Inc. Dark Horse Comics® and the Dark Horse logo are trademarks of Dark Horse Comics, Inc., registered in various categories and countries. All rights reserved.

This book collects issues one through four of the Dark Horse comic-book series *Star Wars®: Infinities – A New Hope*.

Dark Horse Books
A division of Dark Horse Comics, Inc.
10956 SE Main Street
Milwaukie OR 97222

darkhorse.com
starwars.com

To find a comics shop in your area, call the Comic Shop
 Locator Service toll-free at 1-888-266-4226

First edition: February 2002
ISBN: 1-56971-648-X

10 9 8 7 6 5

Printed in China

A LONG TIME AGO, IN A GALAXY FAR, FAR AWAY...

...A WAR RAGED BETWEEN OPPRESSED AND OPPRESSOR. BETWEEN REBEL AND EMPIRE.

BETWEEN THE GUARDIANS OF PEACE AND JUSTICE AND THE SERVANTS OF DARKNESS.

A PROUD AND NOBLE TRADITION WAS PASSED INTO THE CHARGE OF A NEW GENERATION.

STEADFAST ALLIANCES WERE FORMED IN THE CRUCIBLE OF WAR.

EVENTS INEXORABLY DRAWN TO A LINCHPIN IN TIME.

TO A TEMPORAL FULCRUM ON WHICH A SPECIFIC FUTURE RISES.

A FUTURE BIRTHED IN ONE WHITE-HOT, BLINDING MOMENT.

A FUTURE MADE, EVENT BY EVENT, LINK BY LINK, A LIVING CHAIN OF ACTION, REACTION... AND CHANGE.

ALTER ONE EVENT, AND A NEW FUTURE COMES TO BE.

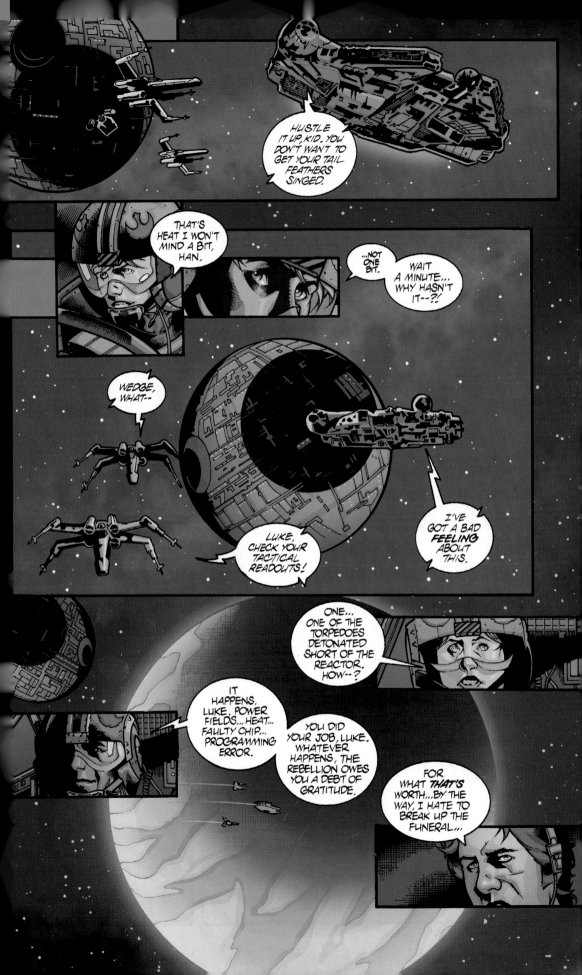

...BUT WE GOT COMPANY.

EVASIVE ACTION!

THERE'S TOO MANY OF 'EM!

GET HIM **OFF** ME!

WHAT DO WE DO?

GENERAL, I DON'T UNDERSTAND. THE TORPEDOES DETONATED--

PREMATURELY, YOUR HIGHNESS.

I ONLY HOPE ENOUGH **DAMAGE** WAS DONE TO BUY US SOME TIME.

PRINCESS, YOU MUST GET TO A TRANSPORT **IMMEDIATELY!**

THE FUTURE OF THE **REBELLION** DEPENDS ON YOUR SAFETY!

FUTURE?

I'VE **SEEN** WHAT THAT BATTLE STATION CAN DO, GENERAL.

THE REBELLION HAS NO FUTURE.

WE'RE-- WE'RE *ALIVE!*

IT'S... NOT POSSIBLE.

CAN YOU RAISE THE ATTACK FLEET?

NO, YOUR HIGHNESS.

THE RESIDUAL EFFECTS OF THE BLAST HAVE COMPLETELY DISRUPTED COMMUNICATIONS.

WE STILL MAY HAVE TIME TO EVACUATE, PRINCESS.

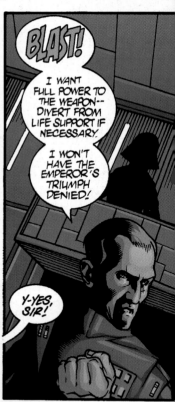

BLAST!

I WANT FULL POWER TO THE WEAPON-- DIVERT FROM LIFE SUPPORT IF NECESSARY.

I WON'T HAVE THE EMPEROR'S TRIUMPH DENIED!

Y-YES, SIR!

AND RELEASE EVERY RESERVE FIGHTER TO INTERCEPT ANY REBEL SHIPS THAT MAY GET OFF THAT MOON. I WANT *LORD VADER* TO LEAD THE OPERATION PERSONALLY.

I DON'T INTEND TO LET *ANYTHING...* SLIP THROUGH MY FINGERS.

WE CAN'T SHAKE THEM!

THEY'RE HEMMING US IN! WE HAVE TO BREAK THE PLANET'S GRAVITATIONAL FIELD BEFORE WE CAN GO TO LIGHT-SPEED.

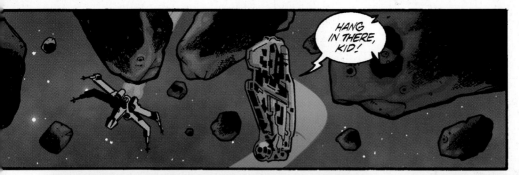

DAGOBAH?

CORUSCANT--A PLANET-WIDE METROPOLIS, ONCE THE CROWN JEWEL OF FREEDOM AND DEMOCRACY BUT NOW THE MILITARY NERVE CENTER OF THE **GALACTIC EMPIRE.**

A NOW **INVINCIBLE** EMPIRE, ITS LAST OPPOSITION, **THE REBEL ALLIANCE**--CRUSHED BY ITS ULTIMATE WEAPON, **THE DEATH STAR**, AT THE BATTLE OF YAVIN.

ORBITING TRIUMPHANTLY ABOVE CORUSCANT, THE IMMENSE BATTLE STATION TRUMPETS ITS VICTORY ALONGSIDE THE BULK OF THE TERRIBLE IMPERIAL FLEET.

AND PREPARES TO DELIVER A PROPER TRIBUTE TO ITS **EMPEROR.**

SHUTTLE **TARQUINAS**, YOUR CODE TRANSMISSION IS CONFIRMED AND YOU ARE CLEARED FOR LANDING.

MRRAN ROWAAN!

I *KNOW* WE NEED A NEW PRESSURE STABILIZER. I KNEW THAT TWO MONTHS AGO WHEN WE LANDED ON THIS MUDBALL. THAT'S WHY WE NEED TO *LEAVE* TO GO FIND A *NEW* ONE.

NEED A *PUSH!*

WORTH A TRY. WE NEED TO *TALK*, PAL.

ARE YOU *SURE* THIS RUST BUCKET'S SPACEWORTHY?

ARE YOU KIDDING? THESE ARE THE HANDS OF A SURGEON!

LOOK, KID--WE MAKE A PRETTY GOOD TEAM. YOU DON'T HAVE TO STAY HERE. COME *WITH US.*

YOUR DESTINY IS *HERE,* APPRENTICE. *GROWN* HAS YOUR POWER, BUT AT PEACE YOU ARE NOT.

LISTEN TO YODA, LUKE.

I HAVE MUCH TO ATTEND TO, LORD VADER. WE WILL SPEAK AGAIN OF THIS. COME, THREEPIO.

HER AMBITION MAKES HER POWERFUL. I AM PLEASED.

I SENSE... A DISTURBANCE IN THE FORCE, MY MASTER.

WHAT YOU SENSE IS THE DESTINY I HAVE PUT IN MOTION.

YOU, HOWEVER, SEEM CONFLICTED, APPRENTICE.

" THE EXTINGUISHING OF THE JEDI FLAME."

GETTING READY TO ENTER THE CORUSCANT SYSTEM. WE CAN LEAVE ANY TIME YOU WANT.

NOT JUST YET, HAN.

INDEED.

LOOKING FORWARD TO THE EMPEROR'S CELEBRATION I AM.

STAR WARS INFINITIES
A NEW HOPE

Cover Gallery

art by **TONY HARRIS**

with colors by **CHRIS BLYTHE**